THE
FREEDOM
LINE

wm

WILLIAM MORROW

An Imprint of HarperCollins*Publishers*

THE

FREEDOM
LINE

The Brave Men and Women Who Rescued Allied
Airmen from the Nazis During World War II

PETER EISNER

HarperCollins books may be purchased for educational, business, or sales promotional use. For information please write: Special Markets Department, HarperCollins Publishers Inc., 10 East 53rd Street, New York, NY 10022.

FIRST EDITION

Designed by Paula Russell Szafranski

Printed on acid-free paper

Library of Congress Cataloging-in-Publication Data

Eisner, Peter.
    The freedom line : the brave men and women who rescued Allied airmen from the Nazis during World War II / Peter Eisner.
        p. cm.
    Includes bibliographical references.
    ISBN 0-06-009663-2
    1. World War, 1939–1945—Underground movements—France.   2. World War, 1939–1945—Underground movements—Belgium.   3. World War, 1939–1945—Underground movements—Spain.   4. World War, 1939–1945—Spain.   5. France—History—German occupation, 1940–1945.   6. Belgium—History—German occupation, 1940–1945. 7. Escapes—France—History—20th century.   8. Air pilots, Military—United States.   9. Air pilots, Military—Great Britain.   I. Title.

    D802.F8E48 2004
    940.53'37—dc22

                                                                2003055847

04 05 06 07 08 WBC/RRD 10 9 8 7 6 5 4 3 2 1

For Musha

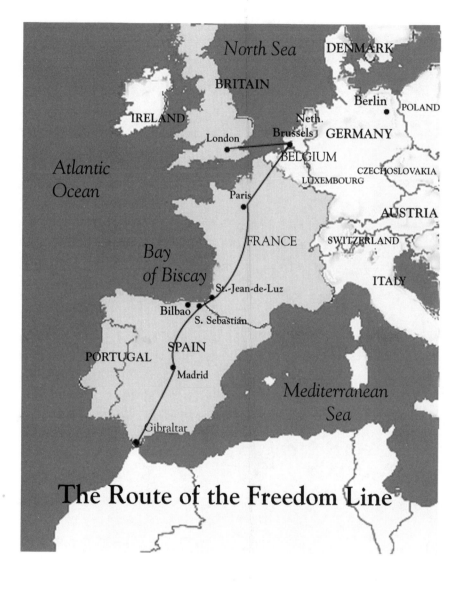

The Route of the Freedom Line

Contents

CONTENTS

PART ONE

January 1943

CHAPTER ONE

Stopped at the Border

Dédée. Urrugne, France. January 14, 1943.

Freezing rain crackled on the tile roof of the farmhouse in the French-Basque village, just a few miles from the Spanish border. There were six of them: three disoriented British airmen; Dédée, the Belgian woman who led the Comet escape line; Florentino, their Basque guide; and Frantxia, who owned the little whitewashed homestead some yards from the dirt road. They had been waiting all afternoon for the weather to improve, but night descended; and the rain kept coming down. The wind rattled the windowpanes, and the gray fog was dissolving into night.

Dédée had led the airmen on the express train down from Paris to Saint-Jean-de-Luz, a Basque fishing village. They'd walked two hours to Frantxia's house in a heavy rainstorm. It had not stopped raining. The airmen were depending on Dédée as their lifeline to get back to England. She was small and slender, and very attractive. She marched with a determined gait as she coaxed them along the sodden paths, and she was also the only one of their guides who spoke English. Dédée looked at them with a penetrating, piercing gaze.

You must be ready to move quickly at any time, without question.
We will tell you when it is safe to go.

Almost always, the escape plan was to follow the hilly goat trails that led through the mountains to the Bidassoa River, the dividing line between France and Spain, not four miles away. These were the old byways known only to the Basque shepherds and the smugglers who packed all forms of contraband over the Pyrenees back and forth across the border. The men coming across told them the Bidassoa River was a flooded torrent. It was too dangerous to cross the river, which meant that the only way to Spain involved a five-hour detour and a risky crossing on a low suspension bridge. That road would be illuminated and was watched by German and Spanish patrols.

Dédée tried to hide her distress, but her furrowed brow was bathed in the flickering light. She'd decided to leave her father at another safe house back along the seacoast and now she feared for his life. The plan had been to bring him here and then cross over to Spain. But he was fifty-eight years old and she didn't think he'd be able to manage under these conditions. She'd kissed him good-bye, promising to come back and fetch him when the weather opened up.

Dédée had misgivings and was feeling more responsibilities than ever. She had finally convinced her father that he could no longer stay in Paris, because the Nazis were on his trail; it was time for him to escape to England. There had been two close calls in the last year, and many of their friends were arrested. It was only a matter of time before the Gestapo would track him down. Reluctantly, he'd agreed to go with her on the next mission south to Spain, as they smuggled another group of airmen to safety.

Florentino, a huge, chisel-faced sort from the mountains, glowered and said nothing, pacing the length of the floor. He knew the mountains; he warned Dédée against chancing the trip when it was raining and the river was high. When the relentless winter rain muddied the dirt paths, the passage was perilous even for him. They would have to crawl in the muck over rocks and boulders, hugging the paths that wound up the hills with barely enough room for a man to avoid sliding off the edge of a cliff. There might even be ice in the higher elevations. The rocks were slippery enough even without ice; legs would be broken, and he was the one who would end up carrying out the injured person on his back. Last year, one of the women guides did break her leg when she slipped and fell in weather not even as bad as this. Florentino carried her for a while, and then fetched a mule and took her to a safe house, where a doctor set the fracture. They were lucky that night to have been on the Spanish side: the Gestapo didn't cross the border on patrol, although the Spanish guards were almost as dangerous.

There were sudden gusts and the raindrops slashed at the windows. The wind had blown the door open a while earlier and gave them a fright. Now, one of the dogs was barking.

Donato is here, said one of Frantxia's three little boys, running in from the storm.

Donato was a farmhand who once worked at this house and was now with a neighbor down the road. He came to the door, peering inside at Florentino and the pilots. Several months ago, Donato had come along with them as a guide over the mountains, but Dédée hadn't trusted him and never asked him along after that. Donato was speaking with Frantxia, in Euskera, the Basque language. Dédée didn't understand a word, but she saw greed in his smile and betrayal in his darting eyes. Perhaps he held a grudge because she'd chosen Florentino and not him as their guide. Donato left and the dog quieted down.

In the dark, everything was uncertain. It was too risky to move the pilots back to town. They could speak neither French nor Euskera nor Spanish. Even disguised in local dress, they would be found out. They were trapped.

I will stay here with them, she told Florentino. *You can wait for us at Kattalin's house.*

Kattalin, the widow, lived in the village by the sea where Dédée and her group hid Allied airmen after guiding them south. She had a little house on a cobblestone street that dipped down toward the bay. It was just off the main highway, a few miles north of Spain. But the highway was not an option for them because it was far too busy with Nazi checkpoints and patrols. The escape to Spain took a circuitous course across the road and up along the farm paths, stopping at Frantxia's, the final safe house before the overnight walk to freedom.

Dédée and Florentino may in fact have dozed. But they were alert to the sounds in the night. Before dawn, Florentino bundled up against the weather and walked out down the path to the sea. The rain had stopped, but the river was likely to remain flooded for several days as flowing streams merged into torrents that rushed from the mountains. Frantxia sent her three children off to school.

The British pilots stayed in the bedroom upstairs, talking quietly and waiting for the word from Dédée to move on. Frantxia brought them coffee. Later, there was hot milk and broth, cheese and black bread. They were in good spirits, because they expected to be going home soon. They were huddled in the soft smell of wood and musty heat, telling stories and sharing half a cigarette when they heard a noise. One of them jumped up and yelled in mock rage, "Here comes the Gestapo!" and the others laughed. But Dédée had already looked out the window and saw the soldiers in their gray uniforms.

Ten German troops barged in, came up the stairs and, using their rifles, pushed the three fliers out into the shiveringly cold yard. The soldiers pinned the three men against the wall and searched them for weapons.

Saboteurs! one of the Germans said harshly. *Saboteurs are to be killed.*

Wait, said a pilot, showing the Germans his dog tags, *we're in the RAF—we're in the RAF.*

The Germans eased off and the Brits showed a bit of bravado.

They weren't going to kill us, I think it was a bluff to frighten us, said one of the Brits.

The others weren't so sure.

The soldiers were equally harsh with Dédée and Frantxia, forcing them to stand in the cold as they checked the stables and all around the house. Three escaping airmen along with two women accomplices was a good catch, but the Germans were not satisfied. The soldiers scoured the house and the hedges and the stables until their commander strode before his prisoners.

Where is the other one? the Nazi demanded, menacing as he looked at each of them. *You will talk, my friends. You will talk.* Dédée realized they were expecting to find Florentino as well. She'd been right about Donato. Only Donato knew how many people were in the house.

The patrol marched Dédée, Frantxia and the three airmen for two hours, hands over their heads, down the farm road back down toward the town. The rain picked up again and dissolved the translucent layer of early morning frost. Dédée was still dressed for the mountains in a pair of loose blue slacks and light shoes, now covered with congealed mud; her hair was soaked with rain. The soldiers led them up to the main highway, away from the Spanish border. They continued single file in a sad procession, passing cottages along the way where their friends could be hiding but were unlikely to peer out at a Gestapo patrol. They approached the little bridge across the inlet that led into Saint-Jean-de-Luz. Dédée, looking for any means of escape, considered hurling herself off the bridge where she might swim and possibly jump to shore before the Germans had a clear shot at her. Any thought of that was lost when she looked down; the rocks were showing at low tide.

Few people were out in the early morning. An occasional horse cart trudged along carrying food or farm goods. Here and there a car swept by, probably confiscated and being used by the Germans. Trucks were grinding their gears up the hill as they rounded the curve in view of the seacoast, and then up to Saint-Jean-de-Luz. The trucks were returning from Spain with food and war imports purchased for the Reich. People from the village pedaled their bikes in the rain, having no other choice but to go to work or to do their shopping in the cold and damp. Few eyes lingered on the patrol leading their prisoners.

It was still morning when Dédée, Frantxia and the three pilots were shoved into the gendarmerie in Saint-Jean-de-Luz. Dédée realized that her father and friends would soon find out about her capture. She hoped her father would not turn himself in.

The Germans conducted a perfunctory interrogation at the little jailhouse. They separated the women from the men, and there was no rough treatment, at least not yet.

Name? a policeman asked.

She gave a false name.

Nationality?

French.

Dédée admitted nothing, showing forged papers that identified her as a local French girl.

She assumed that these were just low-ranking officials and that the Gestapo interrogators would be summoning her soon. Dédée would analyze the situation and figure out what she could best do to save her father and the others. After that, she'd worry about herself. Perhaps the Germans would not kill them.

By the time of her arrest by the Germans on January 15, 1943, Dédée de Jongh had been running the Comet Line for about a year and a half. She'd first shown up on the doorstep of the British consulate in the Spanish-Basque city of Bilbao in August 1941, leading with her the first two men she'd guided across the Pyrenees to safety. They were British Army privates from the Glasgow Highlanders, Bobby Conville and Allan Cowan, happy to have been plucked to safety from otherwise certain capture by the Germans.

The reception at the British consulate was cool at best. Beyond the obvious concern that the Germans might be sending a shill to set them up, Arthur Dean, the British vice consul, was having trouble believing the twenty-five-year-old woman before him had just traveled 500 miles across France, and trekked all night across the mountains into Spain, evading the Germans. Some members of the British legation were ready to dismiss her plan to save Allied pilots out of hand. British bureaucrats were used to dealing with men. Plus Dédée was too pretty.

"But you are a young girl," the vice consul said. "You are not going to cross the Pyrenees again?"

Dédée was fit and strong and not willing to listen to anything that was patronizing or that would dissuade her. She kept her anger in check.

"But yes. I'm as strong as a man. Girls attract less attention in the frontier zone than men."

Dédée had been a volunteer with the Belgian Red Cross, tending to the wounded British and Belgian soldiers at Bruges after the disaster at Dunkirk when the Germans overran Belgian defenses in 1940. When she returned home to Brussels, a passion had been awakened in her.

She and her father, Frédéric, a schoolmaster, agreed that something had to be done. Belgians could not just watch the Germans take over their country. Dédée's eyes burned as she watched the Wehrmacht tanks roll through the streets of Brussels that May. Belgians met the Nazi occupiers with silence. Beneath the surface, though, underground newspapers began operating, and networks of friends joined to give sanctuary to soldiers who were unable to escape Europe on the flotilla of boats that had crossed the Channel back to England.

Dédée could have chosen an easier life, working anonymously as a nurse in a hospital in Brussels. But she was far too determined to defy Hitler's Anschluss. As British and then American air sorties stepped up over Europe, Allied planes were being shot down and some aircrews were parachuting to relative safety in the countryside. Those who were not captured often received aid and comfort from townspeople who encountered them, despite how enormously risky it was for them to resist the German onslaught. The problem was that no immediate way was available to help the aircrews other than to feed them, tend to their wounds and send them out to fend for themselves.

At first, the escape routes took them the direct way, by boat across the English Channel. Some airmen did get out across the Channel and Dédée was organizing escapes to the coast. But by 1942, the Germans consolidated control of their occupied territory and Dédée realized the short route across the Channel was too dangerous to organize a regular itinerary. The alternative was to set up an underground railroad moving Allied soldiers across France and into Spain. It would take a large network of friends and confidants, farmers in the countryside, hiding places in the cities. They would help the fliers blend into Europe by creating false identities and shepherding them slowly toward nominally neutral Spain and onward to the British bastion of Gibraltar on the Mediterranean.

To do this, Dédée needed three centers of organization: Brussels, Paris and the French-Spanish border. When it became clear that Brussels was too dangerous for Dédée and her father, the leader became Jean Greindl, alias Nemo, the director of the Swedish Canteen, a relief organization set up by the Red Cross to give aid to the poor and displaced in occupied Belgium. Nemo was ten years older than the others and used his front at the relief organization to gather up equipment for escaping pilots.

Dédée's father took charge of the Paris operation, working from a series of safe houses. It was not easy; it took money and organization to establish safe houses, transportation links and support services. They needed versatility, discipline and commitment usually attributed to trained intelligence agents. "My father and I have agreed that we shall concentrate on bringing through as many trained fighting men as we can," she told the British vice consul. "All we need is the money to pay our guides and for feeding and housing the men on the long route from Brussels to Bilbao."

The British were noncommittal; they would discuss the matter.

Come back in two weeks, the vice consul told her. He would check with his colleagues in Madrid. Dédée agreed, bade good-bye to Cowan and Conville, her first two clients, then headed back for the mountains.

Dédée went back to organizing operations on the French side of the border. She'd already made contact with a fellow Belgian named Elvire de Greef—code-named Auntie Go—who with her husband, Frédéric— "the Uncle"—fled to southern France when the Germans invaded Belgium. They'd taken up residence outside Bayonne—the northernmost city in the Basque country—and were already establishing their own clandestine network.

The Uncle became a translator for the German army, giving him perfect access to spy on the Nazis from within. Together, Auntie Go and the Uncle became adept at manipulating the black market in food and contraband, even obtaining information about German officers for blackmail if it ever became necessary.

They agreed to coordinate the southern sector. Dédée also had met the widow Kattalin. Kattalin was a woman of the Basque country. She was already in her forties—Florentino's age—and she had a fourteen-year-old daughter, Fifine. Kattalin's husband, Pierre, had died twelve years earlier, suffering for years from the effects of gas attacks when he was a soldier in the French army fighting the Germans in World War I.

Together, Auntie Go and Kattalin prepared the details for the escape operation. They needed forgers and drivers, cooks and people with bicycles and guides to lead the airmen across the mountains. By the time Dédée crossed the mountains to meet the British once more, the network was taking shape.

The British argued a great deal about what to do after Dédée's visit; some said it was unbecoming for diplomats to engage in clandestine activity. Others still questioned whether Dédée was a German agent and, in any case, whether she could deliver pilots as promised. Michael Creswell, a young political secretary at the British embassy in Madrid, had no patience for such nonsense. Creswell didn't like the stuffy bureaucracy of the British embassy. This was not a time for diplomacy, caution or half-measures. It was a war, and he intended to participate. Instinctively, he thought the description of the young woman and her plan sounded right. So he drove up to the Bilbao consulate from Madrid to see for himself.

Creswell was waiting for Dédée when she returned to the consulate. Dédée told him that she wanted independence from government interference and he could relate to that. She sought logistical support and protection from Spanish authorities who routinely imprisoned escapees and their helpers once captured crossing the frontier. Her organization did not expect to be paid, but it did need money for supplies, clothing and food; to organize production of false documents; to pay for bribes, railroad tickets and expenses for the contraband artists who would carry the escapees on the shortest and most demanding part of the passage.

After an extensive interview, it was obvious to Creswell that Dédée was a legitimate, albeit unlikely operative. Her manner was direct and her dark, oval eyes portrayed strength and resolve. "It was a compelling, feminine face, with her hair brushed back over the forehead. She had fine eyes and a determined mouth."

With Creswell's patronage and eventual support of MI9, the military intelligence escape branch in London, Dédée and her newfound friends were moving airmen across the border at a regular pace by the end of 1941. Their tenacity enabled the airmen to return to the field of battle, and the escape lines also provided a source of human intelligence and a mail route for all sorts of Allied intelligence material. By the time of her arrest, she'd crossed the Pyrenees twenty-four times herself, leading at least 118 aviators to safety without losing one.

It was risky business, the work of finding trusted coworkers to shelter fliers and other refugees sought by the Nazis, hide them and organize an inconspicuous way of transporting them out of the country. If caught, the flight crews supposedly would be sent to relatively comfortable POW camps (in fact, many were beaten and forced into work gangs, while some were murdered). But their resistance helpers and anyone related to them faced probable death sentences, or at the very least deportation to concentration camps, where most of them would be killed. Even when they managed to reach Spain, the danger did not pass. The Gestapo had trained Franco's Guardia Civil, and they were inclined to turn the pilots in to the Nazis.

Dédée brought good news back to her friends in France. The British would help and that would guarantee they could safeguard escaping aircrews once they got to Spain. But once most of the network was in place, they required a special person to complete the missing link in the journey, a tireless and fearless guide who could lead them reliably to Spain. It would have to be a man of the mountains who knew every treacherous path and possible route of escape—and someone who shared their passion to oppose the Nazis. Kattalin, the widow, said she knew such a man.

Florentino. Saint-Jean-de-Luz, France. January 15, 1943.

Florentino Goikoetxea's network of friends brought the news to Kattalin's house that the Nazis had captured Dédée. With all his strength, all his energy, there was simply nothing Florentino could do to save her. If he had self-recriminations about allowing Dédée to stay behind, he never told anyone. But he was devastated by her loss.

When Dédée asked for a mountain guide, Florentino was the one Kattalin had introduced her to—the toughest, bravest, most reliable guide in the Basque country. He was proud of the honor and he had come to respect Dédée's role in the organization.

Florentino seemed to have tender feelings for Dédée. The other guides and members of Comet noticed how his gruffness softened when she was around. Of all the people that followed him through the mountains, the little woman was the only one who could keep up with him.

But he was not to be deterred by her capture or because the Nazis were after him. In the spirit of their friendship, Florentino and everyone else in the Comet Line focused more than ever on the work at hand. First they had to notify Dédée's father five miles up the road, and then Florentino had to cross over to Spain to bring word of Dédée's capture to their British allies. Then it was back to work: more pilots were coming down the line.

Florentino had been hiding from the police for years on both sides of the French-Spanish border and even mocked them, using his guile to come down from the mountains to visit friends in town from time to time. He defied authority because he considered it his birthright to go wherever he pleased. An oversize dark beret sat flat like a pancake atop his head, and a stray black cowlick protruded from the center of the cap, plastered in an irregular line to his forehead. He dressed in peasant's clothes: a gray sweater, an old black sailor coat of wool and coarse work pants ending high over his shoes. He stood with his left arm akimbo, at once diffident and rebellious, the hint of an inscrutable smile beneath a deep-set brow and a prodigious Basque nose.

Florentino came from a family of farmers on the Spanish side of the Basque country. He was born in 1898, the same year of the war in Cuba. He grew up with stories of veterans fighting the Americans in Cuba, about relatives who decided to stay in that infernal jungle and about others who'd died there.

He and his younger brother, Pedro, were raised in the mountains;

but it was Florentino who grew to prodigious size, with the back of an ox and hands that were big fat paws. As a teenager he worked digging sand along the Bay of Biscay. It was backbreaking even for a man like him and he got away from the river as soon as he could.

Florentino could pass as a shadow through the city and go up occasionally to his ancestral home, the Caserio Altzueta in Hernani, in the hills above the Bay of Biscay. But the points of reference describe another part of the known world, as if a sea voyage, rather than a hike and a trolley ride, should be needed to span the gap. The language patterns are even different—there are dozens of regional variations in word usage and accent; matching speech with village is a job worthy of a linguist. It means there are no strangers here, only recognizable clan members versus outsiders—those who do not speak Basque. And what outsiders hear is really a mélange of fourteen dialects. So anyone trying to interpret the language of these mountains is outmatched. The regionalisms mirror the sense of distance.

The Basques have lived for thousands of years in the hills, valleys and seacoast coves in the area of the western Pyrenees Mountains. The earliest Basque tribes lived there thousands of years ago, hunters and gatherers whose ancestors mingled with other early Europeans. Basques have been shepherds and hunters and seafarers beyond recorded history.

They were among the earliest mariners of Europe and are said to have traveled to North America with their fishing fleets at least 400 years before Columbus sailed from southern Spain for Ferdinand and Isabella. They maintained their independence throughout a series of invasions of the Iberian Peninsula. Two thousand years ago, the Romans made deals with them for safe passage en route to France rather than fighting for control of their rugged land; the Moors never conquered the northern climes of the Basque country during their 800-year occupation of Spain.

Florentino and his people were late converts to Catholicism; the Basques maintained a great tradition of finding divinity among the elements. Mari, for example, is a goddess who lives deep in a cave, protected by the Beigorri, a wild-eyed beast that roams the mountains.

Renowned both as expert seamen and mountain climbers—reflecting the diversity of their homeland—they adapted their farming and animal husbandry skills to the special terrain of the Pyrenees.

Basques were comfortable on both sides of the Spanish-French border—they had lived in the region before the countries existed. The frontiers created in the Middle Ages never divided the long-settled Basques from one another. Some held French citizenship and others lived in Spain. All considered themselves Basque nationals foremost. From Bayonne to Navarra, they spoke their unique language, Euskera, which is as impenetrable to outsiders as the Pyrenees themselves. The language is not of the Indo-European group and has unknown origins, though it borrows elements from Latin and Spanish when convenient.

Basque nationalists fought fiercely against Francisco Franco's Fascist conquest of Spain from 1936 to 1939 and were singled out for harsh reprisals. Thousands were killed or jailed; they were under siege from all directions by his army and his secret police. Franco had taken on the titles of Generalísimo (the general above generals) and Caudillo (the leader). But the Basques knew him as a harsh and repressive dictator who banned their language and suppressed their customs.

Basque independence played a key role in the development of the Comet Line. Dédée realized the final few miles of the escape could not follow highways or railroads. They would need trustworthy, knowledgeable mountaineers who knew how to cross between France and Spain. Florentino was the unanimous choice. He had fled to France during the Spanish civil war. He appeared to be a rough sort with little in common with his fellow members of the resistance organization. He was twice their age and could hardly speak French or Spanish. Even in his own language, Euskera, conversation was short and to the point. But he shared with Dédée a hatred of fascism and occupation. Florentino was proud to help free the Allied pilots.

After leaving the sand-digging work he became a smuggler, and in the Basque country this had no bad connotations—anyone who lived on the border dealt in contraband or received it as a matter of survival. In the period of hunger after the Spanish civil war, he could deliver anything: coffee, tobacco, beans, beef, lace underwear, even a plump sheep or calf. Florentino could walk all night, propelled by his love of the mountains, fortified with jugs of cognac stashed along the way. His great advantage was his intimate knowledge of the mountains: he knew every possible fork of the trail. As much as he drank, he never faltered, even as his charges slipped and fell back behind him.

He'd always remained more than a step ahead of his pursuers on both sides of the border. He was already legendary for his prowess in the Basque country, and such a reputation among a people known for such traits was no small matter.

He also brought along a reputation among the airmen he'd led across the river. If an exhausted airman collapsed in the rushing river while crossing over to Spain, Florentino would carry the man across, his legs braving a current that would sweep others off their feet.

Herbert J. Spiller of the Royal Air Force was one of the airmen whom Florentino helped cross the Pyrenees to escape the Nazis. "His long craggy face, weather-beaten and walnut-colored, had a kind of rugged nobility and was topped with a flat black beret," Spiller wrote, remembering his encounter with Florentino. "The more we came to know him we marveled at his strength, his ability to sense danger and his instinctive feel for the mountains which enabled him to cover ground in the night-time at a tremendous pace avoiding obstacles and finding safe places to rest. We had cause to be thankful for his kindness and patience as he shepherded us into safety."

Back in England, there were more and more accounts of escapes across the mountains. When Spiller and other airmen got home, they testified to the brave and selfless people who rescued them from the Nazis. Their reports brought hope and relief to the growing number of airmen preparing to fly into enemy territory. If and when they got shot down, the crews knew there was a growing chance that they might get back home. Florentino's strength and Dédée's beauty and prowess were becoming mythic among the airmen stationed at the dozens of fields dotting the English countryside.

Once Florentino delivered his airmen to safety, he never tarried long in Spain. He was a man on the run, sought by the Guardia Civil for his smuggling activities. During the civil war, he'd been ordered to present himself at Guardia Civil headquarters and he did so, riding up on his bicycle. The officer in charge, figuring Florentino wouldn't understand him if he spoke in Spanish, said: *All right, we're taking this guy to Ondarreta Prison.* Florentino looked at them blankly and said to the interpreter, *Damn, if this is going to take a while, let me take my bicycle back to my brother. He needs it to get to work.* Since he'd come in voluntarily, the police figured he wasn't going to be a problem. Fine, they said, take him the bicycle and then come back. Florentino knew what was going on, though. He left with the bicycle and the Guardia Civil never caught up with him again.

Dédée. Bayonne, France. Villa Chagrin Prison. January 20, 1943.

Are you ready for the torture to begin?
  I'm ready.
  You will end up talking, you know.
  And I repeat that I will do everything I can so as not to speak.
  Then let us begin.
  Yes, let us begin.
  Are you sure you are ready?
  Yes, I am ready.

This was a strange charade. Dédée did not know where she found the steel to stop her teeth from chattering, her entire being from trembling in terror.

The Gestapo officer before her—who followed many others who had pressured her to talk—was truly intimidating. She could see that he was smart. And that was the most terrifying thing.

And yet, her outward demeanor did not waver. Her nerves did not show, and she seemed to convince the man that she would not break, that the threat of torture was not enough. Whether for her audacity, the fact that she was a woman, or something else, the Gestapo officer blinked first. He looked up from the desk, closed the dossier and left the room.

Even to be conducting a "civilized" conversation with this man, using her own humanity to control the flow of the questioning, was something that she observed in herself with detached wonder. Perhaps this German officer was considering her youth or figured that she had no useful information to provide, but whatever the reason, there had been no torture. She could take little comfort from that. These winter days—chilly in a damp cell, barely enough food, little water—had brought upon her a torpor, a resignation that she was nevertheless able to shake away when the endless examinations and questioning began. The threats were constant, implicit and not, of what these beasts could do. Still, she stood up to them, and her dignity somehow prevailed. They wanted information, and she gave them the minimum possible, spiced always with lies.

At times, she was in a holding cell by herself. Other times there were prisoners with her, some arrested without even knowing why. There were women recently apprehended, women who had been there for weeks with hacking coughs, all pressed against one another in sweat and sickness. Once she found herself next to a tubercular woman who could hardly move. The place was not fit for pigs, let alone humanity, a word that could hardly be uttered or understood here.

And yet she carried herself in a way that appeared to apply limits on her captors. She did not analyze why. For endless hours, consecutive days, weeks—she could not tell the time—the questions continued, punishing in their detail and in the demands on her clarity and attention. The polished officer spoke to her with a startling subtlety, a diabolical series of nuanced questions that made her lies all the more difficult. Her job was to deflect all inquiries away from her father and her friends. The Nazis presumed that her father was the mastermind behind the Comet organization. Then Dédée confused matters by admitting that she, not her father, was the true leader and founder of the Comet Line. But by then, the Germans could no longer tell her lies from the truth. She told the truth, and they didn't believe her.

Dédée could not be the leader of Comet, the Nazis reasoned; she was a woman. She was too young to have created such a sophisticated organization, one that stretched from Belgium to Spain. Had they believed her, she would have been shot or guillotined.

By now, Florentino had brought the news of Dédée's capture to the British consulate in Bilbao, and Michael Creswell forwarded a rueful cable to MI9 headquarters in London: "Deeply regret Florentino reports Dédée arrested with three pilots at Urrugne. Imprisoned Villa Chagrin at Bayonne. Attempts being organized for her escape."

Frédéric de Jongh, Dédée's father, frantically alerted the other members of the Comet Line that she had been captured. The first man to come to his aid was Jean-François Nothomb, a young Belgian army veteran who was taking an increasingly important role in the escape operations. Jean-François took the train south from Paris and joined up with Dédée's old friend Auntie Go and the rest. They devised what even they would admit was a daredevil and reckless plan to break

Dédée out of jail before she was moved to Paris and further into the clutches of the Gestapo.

The Comet members had no counterinsurgency training and few resources. Besides their boundless daring, their greatest asset was their broad network of contacts; opposition to the Nazi occupation was rife throughout the Basque country. That made logistics easier. Dédée first was jailed at the French-administered Château-Neuf prison in Bayonne, ten miles north of Saint-Jean-de-Luz. By luck, two of the Comet Line's best contacts owned a popular watering hole called Bar Gachy just across the street from the jail. A guard supervisor from the jail was a regular at the bar, and he complained all the time about the Germans. The supervisor was willing to spring Dédée in a general prison break. In return, he wanted to flee the country and get away from the occupation. But before the plan could go very far, Dédée was transferred across town to Villa Chagrin, a castlelike fortress that presented a more formidable challenge. The prison was under German control and was surrounded by a seemingly impenetrable stone barricade that was at least fifteen feet high. That meant there were two options: walking right through the gate or climbing over the wall.

Quick action was required. The arrest of Dédée and the pilots threatened to expose safe houses and operatives throughout the Basque country. One of the airmen had been seen driving around Bayonne with Gestapo agents, and he had presumably already provided information on the resistance operations. In addition, someone at the British embassy in Madrid made a foolish mistake. Without Creswell's authorization or knowledge, a member of the MI9 staff sent an easily decipherable warning to Comet members on BBC World Service: "Attention, Nemo, Dédée [has] caught the plague." Nemo was Jean Greindl, Dédée's friend, the Comet Line leader in Brussels. The Nazis monitored such radio traffic; that could lead them to recognize Dédée's importance to the escape organization.

There were a number of key trusted contacts with access to Villa Chagrin. One was a Red Cross worker—code-named Madame X—who brought messages back and forth. They also had a friend whose job as a plumber gave him constant access to the prison.

The report on Dédée was not good. Her spirits were high, but she was held at times unfed in solitary confinement for days when she refused to answer questions. Other times, she was in a cell so cramped that she could not lie down to sleep. Thanks to a detailed description, they were able to put together a map of the prison and the location of Dédée's cell, which was close to the outer prison wall.

Madame X was able to bring news from the outside and told Dédée that her friends were organizing an escape. Dédée questioned whether they could carry out such an operation without endangering many of the others. She wanted no one else captured; as for herself, Dédée remained resigned to her fate. Her urgent repeated warnings were about the probability of more arrests, and she sent word of a security problem: not everyone had been spared the torture sessions.

Tell them, she told Madame X.

"Les enfants ont parlé et dit tout ce qu'ils savent." *The boys have told everything they know.*

At least one of the captured pilots, subjected to beatings, was talking—there was great danger that everyone the Allied airmen had met in the Basque country could be compromised.

The Comet team held a quick strategy session. Dédée's father was willing to do anything, bribe anyone—even, as Dédée feared, surrender to the Germans—in return for her release. Eventually, the others dissuaded him and the decision was made to sneak into the prison and get Dédée. They would scale the fortress walls and break her out of her cell.

Jean-François and the others jury-rigged an iron grappling hook to a homemade rope ladder. They gathered up cutting tools. On January 20, the team left Auntie Go's house. There were four of them: Auntie Go,

Jean-François and two other operatives, Albert Johnson and Jean Dassié. They set up operations at the Bar Gachy and waited until nightfall. The full moon was obscured by occasional clouds and cast long shadows as they crossed the river and headed for the fortress prison of Villa Chagrin, walking along the outer perimeter of the wall, trying to appear as inconspicuous as they could to anyone out walking the streets. Had they been accosted, they could not have explained the grappling hook, rope ladder and hacksaws they concealed under their overcoats.

Bathed in moonlight, one of them tossed the hook over the top of the stone fortifications. Jean-François was the designated climber. Tying off the hacksaws under his coat so that he could slice through the cell bars, Jean-François scaled the wall using the rope ladder hand over hand, moving slowly to avoid noise. Johnson and Dassié held the rope ladder at the bottom while Jean-François climbed and Auntie Go stood lookout.

Partway up, there was a sound. Everyone froze as two German soldiers approached on patrol. The moon was casting intermittent light. Johnson stood against the wall, holding the rope tight for Jean-François, who was hidden by the branches of a tree. Dassié, wearing a large cape, thought quickly and pressed Auntie Go against the wall just at the place where the end of the ladder emerged behind the tree. When the Germans walked by, they saw a couple in an amorous embrace and didn't see Johnson crouching in the shadows nor Jean-François halfway up the side of the wall. The German soldiers turned away in embarrassment and kept walking.

As soon as the soldiers rounded the next corner, Jean-François resumed climbing. At the top, he was just in sight of Dédée's cell when their moment of triumph collapsed. Unseen from any other vantage point, the prison had an inner nine-foot-tall containment barrier, set so that it was impossible to climb down from the higher wall and scale the lower one. Dédée's cell was beyond reach. Dejected at the prospect of having made it so far in a plan that was now hopeless, Jean-François climbed back down. The operatives went back to the bar and then retreated to Auntie Go's house to figure out another way to get Dédée out of prison.

Jean-François shook with a combination of outrage and fear. "I wasn't paying enough attention to the risk that we were running—me more than anyone—and if I had been thinking clearly, I would never have risked climbing," he told his friends. "It wasn't a brave thing to do—it was idiocy."

He was being too hard on himself. It was Jean-François's loyalty to Dédée that forced such extreme action by an otherwise cautious, meditative individual. Dédée recruited Jean-François in mid-1942 by putting out the word that she wanted someone "young, and someone who has no family depending on him. It was required that he be athletic and that he have the look of being Basque as much as possible; and that he learn Spanish quickly; and that he know English as well."

Jean-François was a short, wiry twenty-year-old with an unruly shock of curly black hair and a pleasant, understated manner that sometimes masked his determination. His sun-browned complexion gave him the look of a southern European, but he didn't speak Spanish, as required. He could get by in English. He'd quit school in 1937 at the age of eighteen to join the Belgian army; he was serving when Belgium was overrun by the advancing Nazi blitzkrieg. The Germans imprisoned him. He broke out once from a POW camp near Nuremberg but was captured after three days on the run. He escaped a second time and was successful. He crossed from Germany into Luxembourg, taking advantage of lax security and smuggling contacts. Returning to now occupied Belgium in October 1941, he planned to flee toward England and depart from there to ride out the war in Africa. But he met Dédée and found a new sense of mission. He agreed with her straightforward judgment. We Belgians, she told him, have a duty to fight the Nazi oppressors, no matter what the consequences.

A few days later, they hatched another escape plan, this one more improbable than the first. Auntie Go's contacts around Bayonne were clerks, workmen, even Frenchmen infiltrated among the prison guards who would help them. Comet could use these sources to smuggle messages to and from Dédée. They would lure several of the prison guards on duty to their friends' bar and get them drunk. Jean-François and Johnson, wearing stolen German uniforms, then would walk right through the front gate. In advance, the plumber would open the ventilation duct near Dédée's cell and get her out to the yard. Plan B involved smuggling her out in a wooden barrel. None of this scheming ever came to anything, because Dédée was moved to another prison before details on either variation could be implemented.

The new prison was called the White House and was located in another part of the city. They thought about further escape options, but these also were thrown off balance when they received a new warning from Dédée. The Germans were making headway in their interrogation of the pilots. Something bad was going to happen. One of the British fliers was beaten into telling the Gestapo that he recognized the safe house where they'd been sheltered before joining Dédée in the mountains. It was the home of Jean Dassié, who had saved them by embracing Auntie Go during their attempt to spring Dédée at the wall of Villa Chagrin. Dassié, who had lost an arm in World War I, was a supervisor at the telephone exchange and could monitor German communications all over southwestern France. But he was caught by surprise when the Gestapo swooped down on his house and seized him and his wife.

Auntie Go hopped on her bicycle, warning the rest of the network to lie low and avoid other safe houses that might have been compromised. Dédée was dismayed to see Dassié and his wife standing before her at one interrogation session, but she learned that none of the others in Bayonne were caught.

By now, Dédée's organization had become an important focus for MI9 escape headquarters, Room 900 at the War Office in London.

The MI9 operatives had become emotionally involved in the exploits of this young woman and her friends. Comet Line had been assigned to Major Airey Neave, a former prisoner of war himself. He almost cried as he read the cable from Creswell about Dédée, saying, "the worst thing of all was to be chairborn in London and unable to do anything but wait for news."

Dédée's father was imploring the British for help. MI9, in turn, used its International Red Cross contacts to argue that Dédée was nothing more than a nurse wrongly imprisoned. British intelligence was cautious, however, knowing they ran the risk of calling attention to her if they expressed too much interest in her case.

Pained by Dédée's capture and the feeling of powerlessness, Airey Neave decided to send reenforcements from London—including a Belgian radio operator who had been receiving insurgency training. The hope was that the young operative would give the Comet Line direct contact with London for the first time. Neave would be able to relay messages from operatives in Spain, send supplies and rotate out some of the more threatened agents for rest and insurgency training. And officials in London would also be able to confirm that new people offering their services and the pilots showing up on their doorstep were legitimate and not double agents planted by the Nazis.

Neave drove the Belgian recruit with all his communications gear down to the RAF Tempsford airfield, fifty miles north of London, between Northampton and Cambridge. Neave was more nervous about the mission than the Belgian was. He felt personally responsible for everyone in the group; if this man arrived safely, perhaps Dédée's friends would finally be able to take advantage of more logistical help.

Neave drank coffee with the radioman and they did a final check of the paraphernalia and gear: parachute harness, revolver, fake ID cards and occupation money. They walked to the tarmac; Neave saluted as the four-engine Halifax aircraft rolled down the runway. The radio-man jumped into the Belgian countryside and was never heard from again.

German agents, monitoring the operations of the Comet Line, tracked him down and killed him soon after he landed.

CHAPTER TWO

Restoring the Line

British Embassy. Madrid, Spain. February 1943.

M ichael Creswell, Dédée's first champion among the British, had been working virtually full-time since early 1943 on coordinating the escapes from occupied France. Each time Florentino came down across the mountains, he would contact embassy operatives and Creswell would smooth the way for the Allied flight crews. Dédée hadn't gone along on every trip herself, but when she did, Creswell prearranged a meeting in San Sebastián, the closest Spanish city to the French occupied territory. It was a beach resort, a pleasant place for a meeting. They'd deal with organization and expenses, and discuss tactics and schedules. Dédée was tireless, and Creswell was primed to provide any possible support. He'd been waiting for her on January 16 and was worried when she didn't show up. Predictably, he was distraught when Florentino contacted him several days later with the news of her arrest. But operations could not wait.

Like Florentino, Jean-François and the rest, he reacted to Dédée's capture by working harder than before. Creswell argued with London for more support to nourish and protect the Comet Line. He could see that it was becoming an increasingly valuable cog in the war effort. They had moved more than 100 pilots so far, and the air war was just now starting to pick up speed.

The unassuming thirty-three-year-old diplomat was shuttling often to His Majesty's consulate in Bilbao, a sooty port and industrial city fifty miles from France, or the much more attractive option of San Sebastián, farther up the road. Creswell was quite unlike the stereotype of a British diplomat: he was unpretentious, plain-speaking and focused on avoiding all bureaucracy and red tape to get things done. He'd come to Spain following his first overseas posting in Berlin from 1935 to 1938, where he witnessed firsthand the rise of Nazism and was disturbed by the appeasement policies of the prewar prime minister, Neville Chamberlain.

Creswell, unknown to most, had been a member of a secret underground network within the British government that funneled intelligence to Winston Churchill when he was out of power and was watching Chamberlain's fruitless and naive attempts to forge peace with Hitler. Churchill used Creswell's reports to organize his policies toward dealing with Hitler and preparing for the coming war. When Germany invaded Poland, Chamberlain resigned in disgrace on May 10, 1940, and Winston Churchill replaced him. So when Creswell, still a junior diplomat, came to Spain, he had a direct channel to the prime minister.

The British ambassador, Sir Samuel Hoare, on the other hand, had been a member of Chamberlain's cabinet and defended the indefensible policies of appeasement. Sir Samuel realized that his assignment to Madrid was virtual exile by Churchill, who wanted no appeasers anywhere close by.

The situation was unusual. The stuffy, conservative ambassador was out of favor with Winston Churchill. In Spain, he practiced his own variety of appeasement with Franco and wanted nothing to do with clandestine operations and spying, which he feared would offend his fascist host. That attitude and mind-set permeated the British diplomatic representation in Spain.

Hoare described selfless men such as Florentino as mercenaries who rescued the pilots only because they were being paid—just as they would be paid for any other merchandise they smuggled across the border. The British ambassador shared his disinterest in the escape lines with Carlton Joseph Huntley Hayes, the U.S. ambassador in Spain. Hayes thought that Spain was actively helping the escapees, a notion that could easily be disputed by anyone who'd ever dodged the Guardia Civil's patrols on the frontier.

Both men were far from the field of battle and were dead wrong about Franco's government. Dédée, Jean-François, Florentino and their colleagues were under constant threat of arrest by the Guardia Civil. The Spanish government acted favorably only in response to pressure from the Allies or the Germans about the status of escapees. Members of the Comet Line had been captured and imprisoned in Spain for helping airmen. Even the Allied airmen were imprisoned in Spain, released only when Creswell intervened.

The activities of Dédée, Jean-François and the Comet Line fell under the aegis of MI9, rather than mainstream British intelligence or the Office of Strategic Services. The organizations sometimes overlapped, though. Both countries used the Comet Line as couriers for their information networks. The Americans in Madrid were hardly involved at all with the escape operations, even though most of the escapees were U.S. airmen.

Creswell knew it was best to steer clear of his own ambassador and the one from the United States, who forbade his staff from getting involved in dealings that could harm relations with Franco.

After the failed rescue of Dédée, Jean-François came down to Madrid to meet with Creswell so that they could talk about how to prevent further disasters. During their meeting, they decided to open a new route.

The problem was always the river; the smugglers' road was the most direct route through the mountains from Saint-Jean-de-Luz, but not always the safest. Dédée would not have been captured at Frantxia's house on January 15 if the weather had allowed them to move more quickly the night that the river was flooding. So Jean-François agreed to try out an eastern route across the Pyrenees, near the Spanish village of Elizondo, thirty miles southeast of Irún on the Pamplona road, where the Bidassoa River already has veered north and disappeared into the mountains.

In late February, Jean-François went back to France. He gathered up three airmen in Paris—two Britons and a Canadian—and brought them down the line to Bayonne. Instead of continuing west to the sea on the old escape route, they made their way southeast toward Saint-Jean-Pied-de-Port. They hiked all night in the mountains and emerged in a rolling field before dawn, walking along relatively flat and open paths. The frontier was unmarked farmland and suddenly they were in Spain. They found a place to hide at the first farm on the Spanish side and Jean-François had the airmen wait there while he walked into the center of town, about two miles away. Elizondo was a quiet Basque village in the province of Navarra, a traditional mix of farmhouses, modest shops, a manor house, an old town square, and a parish church. At dawn, no one was about. The area was lightly patrolled.

Jean-François found a telephone and called his contact, Bernardo Aracama, a Basque auto repairman and chauffeur for the British consulate. Aracama, who had been waiting in San Sebastián, sent out a trusted taxi driver to pick them up on the Irún-Pamplona highway.

About an hour later, Jean-François flagged down the taxi and the four men crowded inside. They thought they were home free, until Jean-François saw the silhouettes of two Guardia Civil soldiers on a bridge just outside Elizondo. As Jean-François prepared for the worst, the guards motioned them to stop.

Identity papers! they demanded, brandishing their rifles, after flagging them down.

No tenemos. We don't have any, Jean-François answered.

Jean-François's first problem was that he was carrying forged Spanish identification. His second was that Creswell had given him four different forged ID cards with four different names, and he was carrying all of them. If the guards searched him, he'd obviously be in trouble. Meanwhile, how could he explain that while the three airmen were dressed in shabby clothes, he was wearing a new jacket and pants that he'd bought in Spain. He needed to have a story, and there weren't many options.

I am a pilot, he said, in Spanish with a heavy French accent. *We are in the Royal Air Force.*

He didn't seem British and even a fool could see how he stumbled and struggled to explain what was happening to his English-speaking charges.

You speak French?

That's because I am a French-Canadian pilot, Jean-François said when they asked him about the obvious communication problem. *That's why I speak French.*

The Spanish police were not convinced and decided to take the four men to their headquarters in Pamplona, thirty miles to the west.

The jail in Pamplona was a nightmare. A prison intended for five hundred men probably had five thousand inmates packed into a small central courtyard. Most of the detainees were Frenchmen who'd been fleeing south to try to escape mandatory Nazi work details. Jean-François was not aware that this was high season for Frenchmen escaping the Nazis. And unless he could come up with a plan, he was in trouble. Captured Frenchmen were being sent back across the border to occupied France.

Jean-François and the three airmen were herded into the throng of men milling about the prison. In the course of the day, they were summoned one by one for interrogation. In the meantime, Jean-François had managed to destroy and dump his fake IDs.

When it was his turn, he was taken to a barren office for a session with an interrogator who spoke Spanish and nothing else.

Okay, then, you say you're Canadian. Where in Canada are you from? the officer asked.

Jean-François paused, and then named the first place that came to mind.

Québec, he answered, not remembering whether Québec was a city or a province or both.

What's your address?

Deep into it now, he blurted out the first English address that came to mind.

Number Ten Downing Street.

What difference did it make? Perhaps these local police wouldn't even notice.

The Spanish official, it seemed, knew less about the New World than Jean-François did. Somehow, the police believed him.

While all this was going on, the British consulate in San Sebastián already had word of trouble. When the taxi didn't return to San Sebastián, Aracama called the British consulate. The next morning, the taxi driver was set free and provided details about the capture.

Creswell back in Madrid was notified of the arrest and told that Jean-François and the airmen were in jail but they were safe. Now all they had to do was get them released.

William Goodman, the British consul in San Sebastián, was chosen to be the lead negotiator. Creswell remained in the background. They contacted police officials in Pamplona, who confirmed that they had four RAF fliers in custody, two British and two Canadian. That was also good news. It meant that Jean-François was passing himself off as one of the escapees. Efforts to get them out of jail involved diplomatic notes, bureaucracy and paperwork that would take a while. In the meantime, Goodman asked for permission to meet with the imprisoned men.

Several days into the routine, Jean-François and company were summoned to the visitors' area. Goodman was there, making it clear with a wink that Jean-François should pretend they didn't know one another.

We'll be getting you out of here, men, just a question of paperwork. Wait a bit more, and you'll be going home, Goodman said in crisp English. *No need to escape*. Goodman raised an eyebrow toward Jean-François, who didn't understand all the words but got the idea.

Once the British identified their interest in the captured airmen, conditions in Pamplona were less threatening. Jean-François was certain that the Spanish figured he was some sort of spy, but they didn't single him out for bad treatment. He was just another prisoner, forced to mill about in the crowded prison courtyard.

Worse than everything was the prison food. It was a gruelish broth with fava beans and something else. Closer inspection revealed a science experiment of worms and vermin swimming around for space alongside the legumes. Food then was difficult. So was the tedium.

Goodman dealt with that problem by paying someone to have special meals brought in. But it was only fair to share those meals with the other men in their cell even if there wasn't enough to go around.

The prisoners were segregated by religion. The guards figured that anyone from France or Spain was Catholic and that Americans, Britons and Canadians had to be Protestant. Jean-François and the real airmen were placed in a small cell for non-Papists only. Jean-François, a devout Catholic, didn't like that but said nothing.

In the prison yard, Jean-François was popular with the other inmates. They craved word about the outside world and asked him all sorts of questions. It didn't take long to figure out that some of the questions were much too persistent.

How's the war going? one inmate asked.

Very well.

Are the British fighting hard? What about the Americans? Where are they bombing?

Very well, the tide is turning and we will win the war, he answered.

Jean-François improvised until he started hearing questions that sounded suspiciously technical. One of the prisoners had heard about a new British fighter plane.

Have you seen the new plane? What kind of engines does it have? Can it fly faster than the German fighter planes?

Jean-François looked around at the men waiting for his answers. Of course, he knew nothing about British planes and had scant news about the war. But if he evidently was to be taken for a British spy, he figured he would play the part. He looked at them slyly and spoke in conspiratorial tones.

These questions are matters on which I'm sworn to operational secrecy.

The following day, no one came near him. Apparently, the informants who questioned him had been put off by his refusal to provide information. Better for him this way, even if they did figure he was a spy.

After two weeks Jean-François and the three airmen were summoned once more and an oversize British diplomatic car was waiting for them. Creswell and Goodman had succeeded in having them released. Several Free French officers also being sent back to England came along for the eight-hour ride to Madrid, which was a raucous exercise in misunderstanding. The embassy driver assumed that Jean-François was Canadian and therefore capable of translating from English to French. The French officers figured the same. Since Jean-

François couldn't trust anyone's identity, he was not about to admit the truth: that he spoke miserable English and understood less.

But the British driver spoke nonstop, pausing only for him to translate for the Frenchmen. The Frenchmen in turn spoke to the driver and the airmen and asked Jean-François to translate back to English. Jean-François kept talking for the entire 350 miles to Madrid—and made up the entire conversation, since he understood not a word the Englishmen were telling him. He had no voice left and fairly collapsed from exhaustion when Creswell met the car in Madrid. The airmen and the French officers were sent off to Gibraltar and Creswell took Jean-François to his own residence, warning him against speaking in the presence of the servants and helpers, which was no problem after the car ride. Creswell said some of the workers at the embassy residence were undoubtedly spies capable of turning him in as a resistance operative.

Creswell argued that it was too dangerous to go back to France.

After the Pamplona jail, your photograph will be made available to the Gestapo. You're a marked man.

I have to go back.

They even carry around little boutonnière cameras to take your picture. The Gestapo knows you, Creswell said.

I don't believe all that.

Wait for a while in Spain, Creswell insisted. *Don't let them see you back in France.*

No, said Jean-François. *I want to go back right away.*

Creswell gave up. *Well then,* he said, *always dress like a Basque, keep a beret on your head and don't speak to people you don't know.*

Creswell, ever the den mother, begged him to take care of himself, avoid risks and eat well; the young resistance leader received an allotment of expense money, threw some bartering goods in a suitcase and was ready to head back north to France. After three days of rest, Creswell sent him in a diplomatic car back to San Sebastián; the

Guardia Civil saluted when the car went by. Ironic, Jean-François thought. *The same men who arrested me now treat me like an important diplomat. If only they knew.*

Rather than wait for Florentino, Jean-François decided he would undertake the return trip to France on his own. He felt exhilarated with the freedom of knowing the route all by himself, of gliding like a knowing spirit into the darkness of the mountains. He rode the tram beyond the northern outskirts of San Sebastián. The street wound along hills that hugged the port district, where orange-rust-tinged hulks of freighters from Spain and any country he could think of were tied down at a succession of docks. Iron cranes swung loads of materials from ship to shore and back, foodstuffs and war materials—coal and oil and sardines and iron and oranges and olives—bound to and from both the Nazis and the Allies, since Spain was trading with both sides. Jean-François could see the shipping traffic at the end of the tram line. He walked across town until the roads turn into the hills toward Oyarzun, where he crossed down into the center of the village, and then up the winding road into the hills again, where they had a safe house at a farm called Sarobe. After a rest, he continued climbing the smugglers' road toward the French border.

It was a much faster journey without the responsibility of leading airmen all in a row. Once in a while, he passed one of the Basque smugglers, all friends of Florentino. He found his way down the mountain easily and made it to the Bidassoa River before dawn. He crossed the highway silently in the dark to avoid the Guardia Civil patrols, then jumped the railroad tracks and hopped down the embankment to the river. He crossed quickly in water just above his ankles. Strange this river, sometimes an innocent spit of a current, other times a dangerous torrent. You never knew what you'd find.

Jean-François stopped off briefly with Kattalin. She gave him the bad news about the arrest of Jean Dassié and his wife. She also told him there had been a lull in the arrival of pilots. Everyone thought there were problems in the north. He felt even more pressure to find out what was going on.

On the morning of March 25, he headed directly for the Bayonne train station, where he would take the daily express to Paris. Jean-François had his own perfect alibi for riding the rails. As always, he carried well-forged papers that identified him as Jean Noto, a student at the Sorbonne. In this role, he was able to travel around France and south to the Basque country. His identity card and internal papers also allowed him to travel along the French coast. Students were expected to be moving around the country, whether visiting family members or taking a holiday from their studies.

So he was confident as he waited for the train, knowing that his documents would protect him, not fearing the presence of the Nazi soldiers nearby. He was so immersed in thoughts about reviving the escape line that he didn't notice the gathering commotion: vehicles pulled up outside the station, cars, the sound of orders called out in German.

Along the platform, people dug their hands into their pockets and moved aside. Perhaps it was the clock tower's bells striking the hour that caught his attention. He looked up and a phalanx of German guards, bayonets drawn, was moving briskly in his direction.

And then, there she was. They were moving Dédée north to Paris. By coincidence and fate, Jean-François and Dédée were taking the same train.

Jean-François had wrenching, conflicting feelings: immediate joy that she was alive, horror that she was being marched away, a reminder of their failure to rescue her. He wanted to run, to blow up the train; but he could do nothing. Everything centered on Dédée, who walked at the middle of a German patrol, followed by Jean Dassié, his wife, and the three captured British airmen.

Dédée, pale but standing tall, saw him there and went through the same range of shocked sensations. The man she would embrace as her friend, and freedom, were close at hand, and yet they were trapped, not even making the slightest move of recognition.

Jean-François acted as if he were reading the newspaper or thinking about anything else; if the Nazis spotted Dédée looking his way, it would be a disaster for both of them. Slowly, very deliberately, he circled around to a spot on the platform where they could observe each other from a distance.

She saw him, but they could hardly risk raising their heads, and talking was out of the question. When the train pulled in, Dédée and the other captives boarded a specially fitted wagon with iron bars on the windows and helmeted guards posted at each entrance. Jean-François boarded the next wagon and saw that men with jackboots blocked a view forward to the prisoners.

All other thoughts were gone now. He strained to think of a plan. But what could it be? Unable even to speak with her, he was in a way as much of a prisoner as she was. Jean-François considered creating a diversion; he thought about train wrecks, about jumping from the train to pull the soldiers his way, anything so she could escape. And Dédée was worried that Jean-François would be caught trying to help her. But there was no logical way to do it. The train stopped at Bordeaux, a short distance after leaving Bayonne. Jean-François walked on the platform and saw her face through the bars. They exchanged a furtive glance, imperceptible to anyone else. That was all they could do.

On the train once more, it was a torture for Jean-François to be held suspended on a journey with Dédée so near. Every hour was far worse than the uncertainty of being held in prison himself or the perils of dodging Nazi patrols crossing the mountains. In those cases, he was in command of his decisions and could decide when to act. This was a time horribly spent, praying for her safety, for her health, that somehow she would be free. He'd forced from his mind the frustration of

the failed escape attempt in Bayonne, where he'd been so close to success. All the way to Paris, five hours of thinking about Dédée
intensely, he searched for the key to her rescue, but there simply was
none. He endured the ride in a state of absolute powerlessness and
desperation. When they finally arrived at the Austerlitz station in
Paris, he loitered about so he could see her fleetingly one final time
before the soldiers and the Gestapo bundled her into a car. Then she
was gone.

Dédée's presence and his inability to act made him feel almost
physically sick. It was wrong to castigate himself for not rescuing her.
Even if there had been advanced warning, any attempt on the train
would have been suicidal. She would not have wanted him to be reckless. It was part of their pact—don't be foolish, make sure that our rescue line survives.

Dédée was transferred from Paris to St. Gilles Prison in Brussels,
where she was held for the spring and part of the summer. Belgian
friends were able to track her whereabouts as long as she was there.
She withstood interrogation sessions, but the Germans grew disinter-
ested in her after a while. She was sent before a Belgian occupation
court and in a kangaroo trial was condemned to death for subversion.

Eventually, there was word that the St. Gilles prisoners were to be
moved to German jails and concentration camps. Not long before the
transfer, she was in the prison yard where she had a somber encounter
that was as much a blessing and a curse as it had been to see Jean-
François on the train. Although prisoners could not congregate, sometimes they milled about in the yard and could approach one another
for a fleeting moment. The jail was filled with Belgian opponents of
the Nazi occupation—hapless, beaten patriots; the old and the young,
men and women. Out of the crowd one day, she saw the steely, intense
gaze of a man standing apart from the rest. It was Nemo, her friend
and leader of the line from Brussels. She hadn't even known he was
arrested and didn't want to believe it was him. Instinctively, in the

way that prisoners learn to avoid attracting the attention of their keepers, Dédée and Nemo affected uninterest and slowly circled toward each other.

In January, just days before her fateful last trip south, Dédée had warned Nemo that he was in danger. Friends had been questioned; they were all being followed, and they had become aware that the Nazis were developing agents to track them in Brussels and Paris. That was why Monsieur de Jongh had to flee Paris. And it was just as important for Nemo to leave Brussels. But Nemo refused.

Creswell had passed along information from Neave and the others at MI9 headquarters in London that the Nazis were likely to step up their efforts to shut down Comet. Spy reports said that Hermann Göring, who was in charge of the Luftwaffe, had come to realize that airmen were being rescued in Brussels. To counter this, the Nazis were recruiting agents to track and infiltrate Dédée and her friends. They were finding out about helpers and safe houses, and people were being arrested.

"You know that there's a nine-in-ten chance that you'll never come out of this alive," she had told him.

Nemo just smiled. Then, on February 6, Nemo was also arrested at his headquarters at the Swedish Canteen. It was almost an act of resignation. He'd known of Dédée's capture. There also had been earlier seizures in Brussels, including Dédée's sister, Suzanne, and her young friend, Andrée Dumont, code-named Nadine. He was dedicated to the fight and he would not run.

Ironically, Dédée was arrested three weeks before Nemo was, but this was no time for recriminations. The meeting was bittersweet. Nemo had been beaten down physically, but his demeanor was strong. They could hardly speak.

I am condemned to death, he told Dédée.

As am I.

It was a chance contact; words were not adequate to express their emotions. They knew they likely would never see each other again.

They kept their talk brief, lest the guards become interested and use one to extract information from the other. Dédée, rueful that Nemo also had been captured, was at the same time grateful for the moment. It was all fate, she thought. They could only be proud of what they had done and accomplished.

Dédée was shipped with thousands of other political prisoners to Germany; she saw a series of prisons and eventually was sent to the Ravensbrück women's concentration camp. Nemo was imprisoned in Etterbeek. For the remainder of the war, they were to be lost behind the curtain known as *Nacht und Nebel,* "night and fog," a tactic the Nazis used to make underground and resistance agents disappear. Heinrich Himmler, Hitler's deputy, described the strategy in a decree: "The Führer is of the opinion that in such cases penal servitude or even a hard labor sentence for life will be regarded as a sign of weakness. An effective and lasting deterrent can be achieved only by the death penalty or by taking measures, which will leave the family and the population uncertain as to the fate of the offender. Deportation to Germany serves this purpose." The decree blocked information from being provided to the International Red Cross or anyone else. Dédée, Nemo and all the others disappeared, and their fate was unknown until the war was over.

Less than a week after Jean-François left Madrid, Michael Creswell faced a serious threat to escape operations through Spain. The Nazis were increasingly aware of the resistance workers' success at moving Allied airmen, and they increased their pressure on the Spanish government to stop the clandestine activity. Unfortunately, this seemed to have an effect. Francisco Franco's government threatened to close the border and said it would start shipping American and British pilots back to Nazi-occupied France. All along the border Spanish police were threatening to turn back anyone who was escaping from occupied territory.

The Spanish government in the border zone issued orders on March 30, 1943, demanding that all local officials report anyone helping people escape from Nazi territory. The order said officials should "report on transients from . . . our neighboring country occupied by Germany . . . who by having no known means of support or by conducting a noticeable lifestyle beyond their known and legal means, or by dedicating their activities to activities contrary to public order, may be elements who aid, guide and protect evaders."

And that wasn't all. The Spanish foreign ministry, in a fraternal gesture, sent to Berlin a list of "Red refugees who in accord with [the German] government should be removed from the border."

In this case, Ambassador Hoare was forced to support Creswell and the escapees. The lives of Jean-François, his Comet colleagues and scores of airmen were at stake. On March 29, Hoare protested vehemently. "For nearly three years the Spanish Government has, in accordance with the recognized interpretation of the Hague Convention, allowed escaped prisoners of war who arrive in Spain to be repatriated," he told the Spanish foreign ministry. "How can it be claimed that there is any impartiality in action that is nothing less than active cooperation [with Nazi Germany]? . . . Is not this instruction contrary to all the dictates of humanity?"

Franco and his government responded typically by trying to placate the Germans while at the same time not jeopardizing the economic support they were receiving from the United States and Britain. Spain simply made no further pronouncements about sending escaped pilots back to France—or not. They tacitly suspended the order to halt the escapes, but Creswell had to become more personally involved in protecting airmen and helpers. As often as he could, he traveled to San Sebastián, implicitly challenging the Spanish military to cause a diplomatic incident by mistreating the escapees.

The British ambassador had little else to say about the escape operations. Sir Samuel's main priority was to run his embassy and protect the image of Spain among the upper crust. His class-consciousness and sense of fair play did not allow for what he considered to be the seamy side of life.

Jean-François. Paris, France.
June 7, 1943.

It took two months for Comet to reorganize after Dédée's capture, and when it was done, Jean-François was their new leader. After he arrived in Paris that day in late March on the same train with the captive Dédée, Jean-François could see that Paris was changing. The Gestapo and German air force intelligence were circulating, well aware of the escape operations. The Germans seemed to see 1943 as a year to crack down on resistance forces. A number of Dédée's friends were arrested, both in Brussels and Paris. Jean-François did not consider the possibility that these arrests had been coordinated, that there could be a security breach inside the Comet organization.

He left the Paris organization to Monsieur de Jongh and resumed the passages south to Saint-Jean-de-Luz. He did change the route, no longer riding the nonstop express from Paris but choosing local trains and a series of connections that included walking, bicycling and hiding overnight in additional safe houses. The Germans were getting smarter. Throughout France and Belgium, riding the rails meant the constant risk of document checks. Whenever Jean-François arrived at the home of the widow Kattalin, Florentino was waiting for him, ready to head to the mountains once more.

And Dédée had been accurate in assessing the danger to her father. Monsieur de Jongh was a wonderful man, Jean-François said, but he was too trusting, a bit naive, and not a very good judge of character. All through the spring of 1943, the Gestapo had relentlessly pursued the clandestine resistance organization. Their break had come when Monsieur de Jongh unknowingly opened the door to a traitor.

Perhaps as a result of the pain of Dédée's capture, Monsieur de Jongh had abandoned thoughts of his own safety. Perhaps it was carelessness. He devoted himself to the escape line and immersed himself in reestablishing safe houses and transit for escaping airmen. He may have sacrificed caution.

Camille Spiquel, a trusted operative for the Brandy organization, another group of rescuers, approached Monsieur de Jongh and introduced him to a new Belgian who was facilitating the transfer of pilots from Brussels to Paris. His name was Jean Masson, and he came well recommended. He was a very talented fellow; he had friends in the Belgian and French customs services. Would Comet be interested in working with him? Monsieur de Jongh was enthusiastic. Under constant attack, Comet had lost its connections from Belgium. Camille set up a meeting and Masson offered his full efforts to the Comet Line.

I can transfer twelve airmen a month, said Masson.

Masson was a fair-haired little chap around twenty-two years old. He had an appearance that some would have called shifty and devious. He was carrying blank identity cards and showed them to Monsieur de Jongh. He said he never had any problem with these documents. The authorities in Lille always accepted them.

When can you start?

Whenever you're ready.

Masson made several trips in April and May and managed forged transit papers and identity documents for the airmen that seemed good enough to be the genuine item. He had a knack for staying cool under pressure and was remarkable in his ability to deliver pilots on schedule.

But to Camille's lasting shame, no one had checked out Masson. The line had people in Belgium who could have reported on his background—and if they had, they would have discovered that police on the Belgian border were looking for him. He was a petty thief and had been in jail. Unfortunately, they weren't asked; by the time Camille tried to warn her friends in Paris, it was too late.

Jean Masson was one of the most successful and diabolical Nazi double agents in occupied Europe. He managed to immobilize Camille Spiquel's Brandy Line and then infiltrated Comet with ease. Masson, a Belgian traitor whose real name was Jacques Desoubrie, had led a procession of operatives and pilots to the Gestapo before engineering the arrest of Monsieur de Jongh himself.

Masson brought through a succession of escapees in April and May. Never had so many airmen been transferred in such a short period. Fortunately for those airmen, Masson was letting them pass through the line to build up intelligence on the organization and spring the trap on Monsieur de Jongh and the others. He planned to decapitate the organization in one sweeping blow.

In early June, Masson visited Monsieur de Jongh at the Comet safe house on the rue Vaneau, saying that he planned to escort five more Allied airmen and would arrive at the Gare du Nord on June 7 at 4:30 P.M.

Be ready. I have a large party from Brussels.

You will need all your helpers to take them over on arrival in Paris.

It was strange to move so many airmen at the same time, but Monsieur de Jongh apparently was not suspicious. He called on Robert Aylé and his wife, who lived on the rue Babylone.

We have a number of pilots. Jean Masson will bring them tonight.

Monsieur de Jongh and the others arrived at the Gare du Nord according to plan.

They saw Masson approaching them, waving and walking briskly, trailed on the platform by five airmen. He smiled broadly, but there was something odd in his behavior. He was too conspicuous, considering the nature of their clandestine operation. Masson was ebullient, as if he were greeting friends on a stroll.

He greeted Monsieur de Jongh and the others heartily, shaking hands, smiling broadly.

Hello, Masson said. *We've had a great trip.*

Within seconds, a dozen German soldiers surrounded them. They were taken at rifle point to the railroad station's police office, handcuffed and then transferred by car to Gestapo headquarters in central Paris. Monsieur de Jongh and the Aylés rode separately from Jean Masson and the airmen. When they arrived at the imposing Gestapo building on the rue des Saussaies, Monsieur de Jongh and the Aylés were led to a holding room. As they waited to be interrogated, a door opened and Jean Masson stood there smiling once more. He was not under guard, and he was no longer handcuffed.

He strode into the room and spat on the floor in front of them.

"Well, you fools," he sneered.

Aylé rushed forward and punched Masson in the mouth before being beaten and dragged away. It was only a trifle. Masson calmly rearranged himself and left the room.

The traitor was not going to let the attack by Aylé spoil the glory of his achievement that night. Masson was slight, short of stature—about five feet five—with chalky, pale white skin and dirty blond hair with a scar at the hairline. Someone recalled that he had fat earlobes. He spoke French with a distinct Flemish accent. A resistance fighter who confronted Masson for the first time at Gestapo headquarters said, "He had the look of the liar, of a miserable person."

There were humanists and psychologists who might analyze where Masson went wrong. They discussed his past, how he was trained as an electrician while still living with his family in Tourcoing. He had a loving grandmother back home. There were attempts at a psychological profile: he was born out of wedlock, the union of Raymond Desoubrie, a Belgian doctor, and a girl, Zoë Note, who'd abandoned him at an early age. The doctor had taken responsibility and legitimized him, but the poor boy was scarred for life. What could one expect from such beginnings? He'd had an unhappy childhood. And then there were those who knew this story but didn't care for psychology. They preferred to give things their proper name and said it simply: He was a dirty bastard.

There were a number of other arrests that evening as a result of Masson's cunning. The June 7 operation completed Jean Masson's near clean sweep. Masson had captured the heart of the Comet operation—Monsieur de Jongh, Nemo and the people around them. The Comet Line was decimated in France, and there had been many arrests in Brussels. Those who were not executed would disappear, serving as a warning to other collaborators. But still, Masson's work was not done, and he was not satisfied.

There was one more Belgian, a man code-named Franco, whom he'd failed to capture. This Franco was said to be the leader of the organization. Masson was hoping he'd have been caught with the others at the railway station.

But these enemies of the Reich were persistent fools: Jean-François would undoubtedly return to Paris and attempt to reorganize their operation. Masson would give it time. He would patrol the railway stations, looking for subversives. It was easy to capture them, but Masson wanted to walk among them, earn their confidence and help them with their plans. In that way he learned about their membership and their methods. And then he would strike at the center of the operations and destroy them. It would take time, but Masson was winning praise for his latest victories. He would go slowly, and when the moment came he would destroy them all.

While Masson was still searching for Jean-François—the man he knew only by the code name Franco—none of Jean-François's friends could warn him. Neither Jean-François nor any of their other comrades knew that Masson was the traitor or had any idea about the trap that Masson had sprung that night. For reasons of operational security, Jean-François had never even met Masson.

The night of the arrest, Jean-François was several hundred miles away in the Basque country, waiting at the train station in Dax, west of Bayonne, for the arrival of the pilots Monsieur de Jongh had promised were on their way. When the airmen and their handlers failed to arrive, Jean-François took the train north to Paris to find out what was wrong, heading directly to look for Monsieur de Jongh at the safe house on rue Vaneau.

Jean-François didn't spot anything wrong in the flat and assumed Monsieur de Jongh would soon return. He changed his clothes, noting in passing that he couldn't find his favorite necktie. Still not suspecting a problem, he went to the kitchen to prepare some coffee. He opened a pot on the stove and found a layer of mold on a week-old meal that had never been touched. The atmosphere suddenly felt charged with danger. He gathered up some papers and clothes and left the building hurriedly.

He went quickly to the house of his friend Max Roger, whose apartment was on rue Pigalle across the Seine, about two miles away.

Max, where is Monsieur de Jongh? Jean-François asked. *The apartment at rue Vaneau is empty.*

I don't know.

The two young men waited for the night, then quietly returned to the rue Vaneau safe house. There was no sign of anyone outside the building, so they entered, opened the elevator and pressed the button for the fifth floor. The apartment was on the fourth but whether for some engineering reason or to save electricity, the elevator only stopped at every other floor.

The gate on the old lift clattered shut. As they started up, Jean-François heard sudden commotion, voices, laughing and footsteps echoing in the halls. By the time they reached the fifth floor, he could discern the unmistakable voices of men speaking in German.

A door slammed and Jean-François caught his breath. Peering through the wire mesh of the partially enclosed elevator, he saw several men wearing hats and long black overcoats at the stairwell. It was the Gestapo. Neither Jean-François nor Max moved or made a sound. If the Nazis decided to walk up one flight to the elevator, they would be caught.

They heard the sound of a key in a lock, more echoing voices and then the report of shoe leather on the stairs. The Germans were walking down. The sounds trailed away; Jean-François and Max slowly opened the elevator door and watched through a hall window as the Germans left the front entrance, entered a waiting car and drove away. The young men delayed some minutes more, quietly walked down the stairs and left through the rear entrance.

From there, Jean-François and Max went several blocks to Robert Aylé's flat at 37, rue de Babylone. The Gestapo had left a stamped seal on the door. They left in the shadows.

They had other helpers on rue Oudinot, just around the corner. They approached carefully, but the concierge heard them and motioned them closer.

You must leave, he said. *La Gestapo est déjà venue*—*the Gestapo has already been here.*

All their friends were gone.

PART TWO

October 1943

CHAPTER THREE

The American

Soignies, Belgium. October 20, 1943.

S*omewhere in the distance, Bob Grimes heard the dogs barking.*
The twenty-year-old American pilot had been drifting in and out of consciousness, lying in a hedgerow in farm country north of Brussels. Branches and brambles poked and scratched at him. He was disoriented and felt stiff in his flight suit and heavy boots. He shifted a bit and looked around; the sun was going down. He looked at his watch, but it wasn't working. He had to wait for it to get dark.

He had been dreaming of home, driving along in the black Chevy coupe he'd picked up for three hundred and fifty dollars. Turning off Portsmouth Boulevard onto George Washington Highway, he drove around to his family's house on Alywin Road. If he turned onto Belle-haven Road instead, he'd end up at the back of the Cradock High School football field. He could recall every hillock and divot, and he remembered smacking into a lineman in a football game and the free-dom of extending his legs on the stretch to win a track race. He imag-ined himself playing basketball again. He was captain of the team.

Bob was proud to live in Cradock. There were sidewalks and real sewers and running water—not everyone in Virginia could say that. The town was planned on an anchor-shaped grid that was appropriate for a place that catered to the navy. He had friendly neighbors, kids to play with, and now some of those friends were shipping out just like he had two months before. But very few of them were going to be officers in the Army Air Corps.

His family had a nice house and hadn't suffered much during the Depression. Grimes had three sisters and three brothers, so it was a big family, but they always had food and clothing, because his father had a good job as a carpenter at the Norfolk Naval Air Station. To one degree or another, most of his family—his three older sisters, his older brother and his father—were all doing something with the navy. His two little brothers were still in school.

Didn't he still owe something to Rella, the sister he was closest to in age and temperament? This was her car really, because he was too young to sign the papers. He was always paying her back, even if it was the fifty cents he needed to take his girlfriend to the movies.

Bob felt good about the decisions he'd made in life. Everything worked out. He'd left college for a while but intended to go back. He just didn't think it was right to spend all that money without having a direction. Bob didn't want to waste time. First he took the civil service exam, scoring the second highest out of about 500 applicants. Soon he was working in the Newport News shipyard, as a helper on the aircraft carrier USS *Hornet,* which was so big that it had seven boiler rooms. He was learning a lot at the shipyard, but the trip there from Cradock was long and difficult. He had to walk to the streetcar, ride to the ferry, take the ferry across the bay and catch another ride from there. It took about three hours each way. So eventually he had to board in Newport News and saw his family only on the weekends when he came home.

After six months, he got a chance to transfer to the navy in the aircraft instruments shop at Norfolk. Anything to do with planes was for him: he caught the bug reading about Charles Lindbergh's flight across the Atlantic and the barnstorming pilots of the 1920s. As a kid, he used to make balsa models of old biplanes and learned about rudimentary aerodynamics. This new job was more interesting. The closer he was to airplanes, the more he wanted to learn how to fly. He applied for flight training, but the navy recruiters turned him down, saying he needed to get two years of college.

Then somebody told him it was easier to become an air cadet in the army, because they had no college requirement as long as you could pass the exam. It was an IQ test, and Bob scored 144—top of the heap. Before long, he got the call from the army recruiters in Richmond and was inducted as a private at twenty-one dollars a month while waiting to be called as an aviation cadet.

When he told the navy lieutenant in charge of personnel at Norfolk that he was leaving, the guy chewed him out good. He was insulted that somebody working for him would consider bolting to the army. And he apparently thought he could convince Bob that he was breaking the law by being in the navy and the army at the same time, figuring that Bob might get scared and stick with the navy job—good workers were hard to find.

What the hell do you think you're doing? said the lieutenant. *You can't hold down two government jobs. You should be in the penitentiary. We're going to throw you in jail.*

Bob knew that he wasn't doing anything wrong. He hadn't joined the navy. He played innocent. He laughed all the way home. He was going to be a pilot.

Flight training went fast: there were ten-week courses in Alabama, Tennessee, Mississippi and Arkansas. He remembered his first flight, a PT-17 biplane with just a stick and almost no flight instruments; later, he almost washed out with the twin-engine trainer because he had trouble making a three-point landing. The B-17 training came after receiving his wings and being commissioned as a second lieutenant in the Army Air Force. He soon received orders and transferred to a combat training unit in Washington State. Before long, he picked up nine crew members and it was his job to make an integrated combat unit out of them.

They shipped out to England in the summer of 1943. The crew picked up a brand-new B-17 and flew east from Spokane, hopping across the Atlantic from Gander, Newfoundland, to Prestwick, Scotland. After training in England for a few weeks, they were assigned to Snetterton Heath Airfield. And now, just a couple of months later, he found himself lying in a bramble bush in occupied Belgium. It was bad luck, followed by good luck. He was still alive.

The sound of the dogs was closer now.

Lieutenant Robert Grimes had been on his fifth combat flight over occupied Europe. He had arrived in England on August 7 and was assigned to Snetterton Heath, the Eighth Air Force, 96th Bomb Group, 339th squadron, based in East Anglia, 100 miles northeast of London, between Cambridge and Norwich.

The first few weeks of the assignment in England had been easy enough. They did all sorts of training, the same type of thing they'd done at Moses Lake, Washington, and Pendelton, Oregon, back in June and July. That was when they flew out over the Pacific Ocean and practiced navigating and submarine search missions. On the way home, they would select towns for simulated bombing runs. Now in England, the men knew one another well enough, but flying over England was different and the training was closer to combat conditions.

Daytime, if the sun was out, the navigator could use landmarks to navigate. That wasn't so bad. Still, they would practice triangulating—say, flying thirty minutes in one direction; 120-degree turn, thirty more minutes; 120-degree turn, 30 more minutes. With luck that brought you back home.

At night or in bad weather, it was different. Bob took off and flew by dead reckoning. Sometimes, the idea was to meet up with another plane at a predetermined point. Only there was no radar, and he wasn't supposed to depend on the radio unless it was an emergency. It was daredevil stuff that they hardly gave a second thought. Bob was supposed to take this big hunk of metal up into the air, figure out how to find a target by calculating heading and speed, join up with other airplanes and fly wingtip-to-wingtip for hours, then return home, rain or shine, night or day.

The plane was hurtling through the air at around 160 miles per hour, and Bob knew that there were dozens of other planes in the sky doing the same thing. Sometimes, when they were forming up before dawn or in the early-morning fog, Bob would have Kellers, the flight engineer, toss out a flare to illuminate the sky for a second and signal their position to other planes.

"Darkie, darkie, darkie," Bob would say into his radio at one of those rare times he used the radio during night training sessions. The network of low-power darkie radio stations around England could guide aircraft when necessary. He'd give his code, ask for a heading and then keep flying. Bob always found his way back to the airstrip. He had no radar—he had no visibility at all. It was like flying with his eyes closed.

After all the training missions, the first combat flight was scheduled on September 27. The American Army Air Forces were flying daytime missions and the British Royal Air Force flew its sorties at night. Bob knew nothing of high-level debates about whether the daytime flying should be continued, but he knew that with his nighttime training, he was ready to fly whenever the call came.

The training made flying in any conditions routine, and the command wanted Bob and his crew to believe that their first combat mission was just one more routine airplane ride. Nobody believed that.

On the morning of September 27, Bob and his other three officers—Pickett, the copilot, McElroy, the navigator, and Carlson, the bombardier—woke up in their Quonset hut before dawn. They dressed and went over to the mess hall. Bob ate what they called GI bread, a hard chunk of black bread that sat well in the stomach. He slathered some apple jam and peanut butter on it and it kept his stomach full and settled. It suited him more than powdered eggs and greasy bacon.

Then he and the rest of the crew piled onto the back of a two-ton truck that drove them from the living area to the airfield. The crew separated for individual briefings—the gunners, the navigators, the bombardiers and the pilots and copilots each had specialized rundowns of what to expect. The briefers described the mission, the assembly point for establishing their formation in the air, what to look for during the flight, and details about the target. The first mission was an industrial complex at Emden, Germany, southeast of Wolfsburg.

Dawn was just breaking when Bob rolled down the runway, about forty seconds behind the previous B-17. Twenty-one airplanes flew for two hours to Emden, dropped their bombs, turned around and went home—flying in formation, wingtips just a few feet apart. Bob noticed some ground fire, but it wasn't too bad. If he didn't concentrate on where he actually was, the flight wasn't so different from a training mission. Bob felt isolated from the war in the cockpit of his B-17. From 26,000 feet, he didn't hear the bomb explosions or the antiaircraft fire. For those five hours, Bob spent all of his energy keeping the airplane in formation, adjusting the controls to keep close but not too close to the wingtips of the plane next to him. It was a draining job.

They were back at Snetterton in the early afternoon. After landing, Bob walked around the plane and saw a few pockmarks from antiaircraft fire but no real damage. Then he and the rest of the crew had separate debriefing sessions, in which intelligence officers asked details about each step of the mission. By late afternoon, they could go back to their bunks, relax and grab something to eat.

The second combat mission was over Frankfurt on October 4, a week after the first. They flew some training missions in between, but the weather was so bad that combat missions were being scrubbed all the time. More than once they thought they would be heading out on a combat mission, but the weather closed in after they took off and they were called back to base. This time, the mission went forward. Same routine: take off at dawn, make formation and fly to the target. Frankfurt was no problem. Bob did notice more ground fire and fighters, but he flew without incident.

The third mission came only four days later, on October 8. It was a bombing run on the port city of Bremen. This time, German ground-based antiaircraft fire saturated the sky. Bob could see that there was a method to the ground fire. The ground forces apparently calculated the altitude and position most likely in the flight path of the bombers and then concentrated a wall of fire in that area. The flak looked like it was sitting in a translucent cube drawn in the sky. There was nothing to do but fly right into it. In addition, the German navy had ships in Bremerhaven. Bob could distinguish between ground fire and naval antiaircraft guns—the German navy seemed to lay down much more precise ordinance. He could tell the difference when the navy was down there firing. The black puffs of smoke were inching closer; and he prayed they would stop. The plane wasn't seriously damaged, even though the flak was heavier on that third mission. They dropped their bombs on the target and went home.

It was a rare occurrence to have good weather on two consecutive days, but October 9 was forecast to be clear, and the Eighth Air Force command took advantage. Bob's fourth mission that day was a long-range flight to Gdynia, Poland.

The flight plan was a long triangle at almost the outer limit of the B-17's range. They flew up the North Sea, around the German coast, and turned east until they came to Gdynia, a port on the Polish-German border. When they got there, the Germans had obscured the target by blanketing the port, shipyard and adjacent buildings with smoke bombs. So they flew over the city once, and their fearless leader swung around in a big 180-degree turn to take them in for a second pass. Bob and the other planes dropped their bombs on the return run, but this gave the antiaircraft guns another chance: more than a dozen B-17s were shot down. Because of fuel limitations, they couldn't double back over the North Sea. The direct and only route was a straight shot at 28,000 feet over Germany. So they swung another wide arc and turned for home. Bob looked down as they crossed near Berlin. At that height, there was smooth flying, above the worst antiaircraft fire. They didn't encounter any serious problems until 300 miles to the west, near Essen, more than an hour later. Suddenly, shards of metal from ground shells were exploding all around them. Bob flew right into it because there was no choice—the flak covered the sky. The idea was to keep flying and hope for the best. Passing by at 160 miles per hour, the razor shards of metal looked like a black cloud flecked with dust. When the shrapnel hit the plane, it sounded like rocks and baseballs thrown against the side of a house. Everyone was scared, but they controlled the feeling, pushing it away and acting brave for one another.

The plane shuddered and quaked. Bob steered through the sleet of metal as best he could, pieces of steel nicking and popping on the fuselage. The plane's thin skin was little protection from the projectiles. Bob was worried about something coming through the windshield. Some of the guys were sitting on their parachute packs, because they thought the extra protection would save their butts if metal pierced the plane beneath them. That was questionable.

Bob just made sure the navigator had them on the closest line to the open water of the Channel. And he kept in formation. So he hardly noticed a thing when, as they were flying along through the flak and the smoke, the plane buffeted slightly. One of the men in the back fired up the intercom.

We've got damage.

A shell had burst right in front of Jerry Nawracaj, the waist gunner, who was at the right-side window about midway between the wings and the tail, from which he pivoted and fired his .50-caliber machine gun. The plane jerked and jumped, and suddenly the wind was blowing into the plane. Jerry had been thrown back onto the deck, and the machine gun was sitting on his lap.

What happened? Bob called back on the intercom.

Jerry's side window got blown in. He's on the floor, but he's okay, one of the men said. Through some miracle, the gunner was hardly nicked, and Bob was still flying. In minutes, they were over the Channel and the ground fire trailed off. A thousand things could have gone wrong. There must have been shrapnel damage, but Bob could fly the airplane, which meant the hydraulics were fine, the engines were untouched and the fuel tanks were intact.

It was still nearly an hour back to Snetterton, and all he had to worry about was Nazi fighter planes. The best German fighter in October 1943 was the Focke-Wulf Fw 190. It could fly more than 100 miles an hour faster than the B-17. Its 20-millimeter cannons had more range than the B-17's guns. Sometimes, the Fw 190 pilots would actually fly in the wake of a bomber returning home at night after a mission, waiting for it to turn on its landing lights, then blast it and take off. It was one more thing a pilot could worry about, if he wanted, although worrying didn't help if you couldn't do anything about it. The tail gunner and belly gunner kept a lookout for planes, although in the clouds and fog, they might not catch the reflection of a plane on their ass.

Nothing happened; there was no plane back there in the daytime, and Bob made it back to base. He came in for a smooth, uneventful landing and taxied to a stop. A truck came around, everyone piled on their gear and then hopped onboard for the ride back to the debriefing room at base operations.

Bob held back for a minute and walked around the airplane. The B-17 was a wreck. There was a gaping hole where the gunner's window used to be, and the rest of the fuselage was shot up like Swiss cheese—Jerry the waist gunner was living a charmed life. Bob knew it was just blind luck that the wiring and engines and fuel lines were intact.

Lots of holes was all he said when he hopped on the truck with the rest of the crew for the ride in from the runway. He had a sick feeling about all the damage.

None of the crew—nor any of the other crews—spoke about the fear they'd felt in the pit of their stomachs that this mission—any mission—could have killed them. After debriefing, Bob went to look for the chaplain, just to talk, even though he didn't know what he wanted to say. The chaplain wasn't around, though. He was out at the officers' club getting drunk.

On Wednesday, October 13, Bob hitched a ride from Snetterton to Norwich and took a train to London on a three-day pass. The train arrived at the Liverpool Street station. He took a cab to Piccadilly for a shilling or two and checked in at the officers' hotel to drop off his things. He checked in as he always did at the USO desk for play tickets. There was a comedy parodying Americans at one theater and he was thinking about going to see *Blithe Spirit* by Noël Coward, which had been running for more than two years at the Piccadilly. Perhaps he'd go to the movies instead, although that was somewhat unnerving. London audiences often defied air raids and stayed in their seats. Next, he went over to his girlfriend's house. She wasn't really a serious girlfriend—at least not on his part; she was good company when he was in town. They had lunch, and he left a carton of cigarettes for her father. The army handed out cigarettes, but Bob didn't smoke. It was a luxury for the Brits in wartime.

Life was easy for the Americans in London, especially because everybody loved them. There were girls everywhere, souvenirs to shop for, big black taxis to ride, people all out on the streets. It was a great city! The American soldiers had missed the worst of the Blitz, which had receded by the time they began arriving. Thousands of people had died and fires had burned for days in the rubble, but now some of the evacuees were coming back to the city. London was determined to carry on. Even at night, with the air raids and with the streets blacked out, it was the same. The smells were of diesel and smoke and you barely could see the red buses coming around the rotaries with their headlights blotted out. At night there were prostitutes waiting at darkened corners, and there were men strangely and openly hawking illicit wares with an accent that sounded so out of place for what they were saying. No matter what the Brits said, they sounded as if they were selling tickets to the opera at Covent Garden.

Bob was still in London on leave on Friday night, October 15, when five Luftwaffe Junkers 188s left Chièvres, Belgium, to attack London. They followed an indirect course so they could hit London at just the right angle to evade the British night fighters. The Junkers 188 was a two-engine bomber, a relatively new plane in the German arsenal, with a range of about 1,200 miles. The planes took an evasive course, flying north from Belgium and coming ashore abeam of Ipswich before heading south. Happily for the Home Guard—civil defense—spotters, the Luftwaffe had had the bright idea of painting the underbellies of these planes a shade of baby blue. That made it easy for the Home Guard to spot them using searchlights and field glasses, and to give warning soon after the planes crossed the English coast at 20,000 feet near Harwich, about 80 miles northeast of London.

Sirens blared and searchlights crisscrossed the sky; they cast a familiar glow and created wispy patterns on the clouds. Bobbies and air raid wardens started corralling unenthusiastic passersby into shelters, mostly into the network of underground stations, the tube, where people had taken to sleeping with their entire families. "In you go, then," the wardens called out. "Off the street, please."

Bob took the stairway down. The dank passage smelled of grease and mold. When he reached the bottom he saw hundreds, maybe thousands, of people sleeping on wooden bunks, built three levels high, lined up all along the passageways and tunnels, even as the tube trains rumbled by not far from their heads. Whole families had set up little homes or just slept on pillows and blankets, oblivious to the noise and the lack of privacy. The underground smelled of humanity and grease and ozone, and the echo of voices wafted from the great entryways that led far beneath the city. There were old folks, mothers and babies; some people were well dressed, others were in rags. There was orderliness to it, something that testified to the will of these Londoners to put up with anything and survive.

The five German planes reached London and attacked about fifteen minutes after the sirens sounded, each adding three more tons to the hundreds of thousands of pounds of TNT that already had fallen on London. The five planes then continued south, running for the Channel.

Deep under London, Bob did not hear the low rumble of the explosions, nor did he see the lightning in the distance and the searchlights seeking the invaders. British Mosquito fighters scrambled from a base outside London and chased the bombers. They intercepted the 188s and shot down three of them as they fled back toward the coast amid flak and cannon fire. One of the pilots was Flight Lieutenant Karl Geyr, whose fuel tank caught fire. He parachuted out before his plane crashed and burned near Birchington, in Kent, seventy miles southeast of the city, just a few miles from the Channel. Geyr was captured and sent to a prisoner of war camp.

When the all clear sounded, Bob climbed the stairs back up to the darkened street. He knew nothing about Karl Geyr, but when he looked up at the searchlights over the Thames, he did know that up there somewhere were German bomber pilots who flew missions for a cause, dropped bombs on anonymous targets and then headed for home.

An air raid was not going to spoil anyone's fun. Londoners didn't mind the air raid sirens, and neither did Bob. People used to say that the whirring sound of the buzz bombs was a good thing—it was only when they stopped making noise that you had to worry. That meant their engines had cut off and they were about to explode somewhere nearby. That was when it was time to duck for cover.

The street soon was bustling again, with people scurrying everywhere in the dark. It was impossible to see where you were going. Love affairs could start on the street just by walking into some girl whom a soldier didn't see until she smacked into him, about chest high. Things could get amorous quickly. Bob, unfortunately, only remembered bumping into the nose of a lady wearing a hat. She was too old. She just smiled, said, "Pardon me," and kept walking. Strange how people got used to life under these conditions.

Bob set off to his first nightclub of the night. The clubs were underground in fortified basements around the city, in places like Camden Town and Belsize Park. They were dank, smoky nightclubs that were comfortable hangouts for soldiers. At the first one, he got a beer, cultivated his new taste for Scotch whisky and shot the breeze with other soldiers and the cute English girls.

He got bored after a while and headed for the next place, where he stayed a while longer because they were staging a comedy review. The Brits dressed up like American soldiers and imitated the way they talked and the way they were always trying to pick up the girls. The Brits were always playing around with the Americans. It was all good fun, meant to take everyone's mind off what was going on. It never really worked, but everyone pretended that it did.

At the next table, there was a bunch of fighter pilots. You could tell the fighter pilots by the red background they wore under the silver wings emblazoned on their pockets. The bomber pilots wore a blue patch under their wings.

The bomber pilots started teasing the fighter pilots about how worthless they were, how they always disappeared before the fighting started. The fighter pilots made fun of the bomber pilots for how slow they were and how badly they flew. It started out with jokes, but then somebody got drunk and there was a fight. That was Bob's signal to head for the door and find the next club.

When he finished hitting the clubs, Bob hailed another cab. He'd lost track of where he was, which was easy, since he didn't know London in the daytime, let alone at night under a blackout. He couldn't figure out how the taxi driver could see where to take him. But for a few shillings, the driver deposited him back at his quarters off Piccadilly within minutes. Bob was tired enough and had drunk enough so that he collapsed into bed. If there were any more bombings or flashes on the horizon or rattling windows that night, Bob wouldn't have known. His friends always teased him about being able to sleep through anything.

The next morning leave was over, and Bob took the train from London back to Norfolk. He hitched a ride to Snetterton and made it on time to the Quonset hut he shared with the other officers of his crew, Pickett, McElroy and Carlson; the enlisted men lived separately. There was talk about a bombing run two days earlier on October 14 on a ball bearing factory in Schweinfurt in northern Bavaria. They were calling it Black Thursday. Sixty B-17s flying out of England were lost, with 600 men missing—so many losses that the Allied command was considering the elimination of daytime bombing. By chance, Bob and his crew were on leave that day.

Air command never said anything about losses. First there were rumors and scuttlebutt, and then command sent somebody from the adjutant's office to pack up the gear from a bunk that hadn't been slept in for a few days. That's how the men knew a guy wasn't coming back. There was no way of knowing if the missing man was lost, captured or dead. Fliers didn't talk about any of that. But one thing Bob noticed was that not too many people came back—very few of them, in fact. All a flier had to do was fly twenty-five missions, and then he could go home. The problem was that Bob didn't know anybody with even half that many.

Art Pickett, Bob's copilot, had also been on leave that weekend in London. They had gone their separate ways. Bob always thought Art was a lot wilder and more adventurous—or at least Art talked it up a bit more. Art was always bragging about his time on leave. He was funny, talking about all of his girlfriends. "This gal that I am going with in London is really on the neat side," Art said. "She's a real gal and not any of the usual English cheap stuff. You ain't never seen a real jit'-buggin' till you see these English gals. There are no cars to go park in and nothing to do but dance so I reckon that's one reason they are so much better dancers."

Pickett was sitting on his bunk, writing home on letter paper with his gold-tipped fountain pen. It was the closest anyone in the crew came to talking about what it was like getting shot at. He acted like he was too tough to worry, but you could see how he felt.

"They come straight at you with their wings a mass of fire from their cannon," he wrote. "Boy it all makes for a hell of a good show. One good show and most of the boys would almost as soon be in the States and back to Mama. I said *almost*. Some of the cannon shells are timed to burst without striking anything and there are white bursts everywhere. You can look way back and see the 88's sitting there spittin' away while the 190's come in from the side or front. Any bastard that tells you the jerry ships aren't good; tell him to go to hell for me, will you."

Monday morning, October 18, there were more training runs.

When they got off duty after a full day riding the plane, Bob and Art went out to fool around. They'd scavenged an old motorcycle in some abandoned garage—an ancient piece of junk, but they got it working. They made a deal with a private down at the motor pool to get a gallon of gas when they needed it, and sneaked off base to race the thing. Art drove and Bob hung on for dear life on the back. They had a swell time racing around the countryside on the motorcycle; the object was to go as fast as you could, anywhere you could. There was no particular destination; life at Snetterton was either going out on a bombing mission or waiting for the next one. They had no place else to go.

The weather cleared up on October 19, and the operations officer said they'd have a mission the next morning. But nothing was definite these days; after the recent losses, maybe it would be a night mission. That wasn't so worrisome, because Bob was well trained in night flying. Besides that, missions were being canceled every day because of bad weather; October had been very rainy. A couple of times when they took off, it was so foggy they couldn't even find the other planes to get into formation. It was amazing they weren't crashing into one another and falling out of the sky.

Bob got a good night's sleep; wake-up call on the morning of October 20, 1943, was a flashlight in his face. The weather was good, and the mission was going as scheduled. Bob rolled out of his bunk and got suited up just after daybreak. He went over to the mess, had his breakfast of GI bread and jam and went to the flight briefing.

There was a map on the board at the front of the room. They were headed for a target in Aachen, right on the Belgian-German border, about 300 miles due east of Snetterton. The briefers said this was supposed to be a milk run, a couple of hours' flight, easy in, drop your bombs, a couple of hours back and it's beer time. They were told to expect a little bit of flak action in antiaircraft range, maybe some German fighters, but not much to worry about if they stayed in formation.

Don't let them pull you out of formation, the briefer said. *This is what they want. Resist the temptation to evade. You are safer flying in formation.*

Bob and Pickett and the other eight crew members rode the truck from the staging area out to the field and were dropped off in front of their aircraft for the day. Because of the damage from the fourth mission to Poland, their last plane was in maintenance. This was a replacement aircraft with the nickname *Shack Rabbit II.* Bob walked around the airplane and looked it over. He couldn't tell the difference. It was one of 3,400 identical B-17 F series bombers built by Boeing. They called the B-17 the Flying Fortress and it was the workhorse of the air war over Europe. It had four Wright R-1820-97 Cyclone 9 cylinder radial air-cooled engines, rated at 1,200 horsepower each. That translated to a cruising speed of around 165 miles per hour and a maximum airspeed of 287 miles per hour. Its range was 3,400 miles—good for a round-trip deep into Eastern Europe to drop a payload of up to 8 tons of bombs.

It sounded easy, but Bob didn't feel that way. He just knew how to do his job. It took concentration and guts to fly in close formation—constant action and reaction to maintain distance and speed and to keep an eye out for anything that could go wrong, knowing all the while that a big fat Flying Fortress in the sky could be a sitting duck for enemy fire.

Out on the tarmac, maintenance men had towed out a dozen B-17s. Maintenance crews were making adjustments, gasoline trucks were topping off tanks, and mechanics were crawling around the machines doing their checks. Bob climbed up the forward ladder, shimmied up to the flight desk through the passageway in the middle deck and arranged himself in the left seat. Pickett was already there in the co-pilot's seat, adjusting his Mae West, the appropriately named bulky flight vest, checking the gear in his jumpsuit, arranging his mask and radio headset.

There was no joking around or bravado about the weekend in London. This was far too serious business; the men were left to their own thoughts. There was a lot of waiting before takeoff. Bob looked over his shoulder and did a radio check with the rest of the crew. McElroy, the navigator, and Carlson, the bombardier, crawled forward and slightly underneath to their positions in the nose.

Midway between Bob and Art was the engineer, Kellers, who could stand up in the bubble at the top of the aircraft and spin around firing his .50-caliber gun. The position gave him a 360-degree view at the top of the aircraft. One could walk to the rear of the plane on a narrow beam gangway through the bomb bay and into the radio compartment and then on into the rear section of the fuselage. The tail gunner, two waist gunners, and the ball turret gunner were back there checking their gear and preparing their guns, each of which was slotted and could arch around a fitting in one of the side or tail glass windows so they could search for enemy targets in a wide range. Bob saw Nawracaj, his waist gunner, who might have looked up, smiling sheepishly, remembering how the flak and machine gun had blown in on him the week before.

Metlen, the ball turret gunner, probably had the most precarious position on the plane. A switch rolled the ball turret gunner down into a glass sheath that was suspended beneath the aircraft. Like the enclosure for the engineer up above, this gave him the ability to pivot in all directions to hit targets at a low angle below the plane. It also left him exposed to fire and flak from all directions. It was laborious to get out of the ball turret in case of emergency. More than one turret had failed to operate quickly enough, and men had died inside, unable to swing out to get back into the plane and jump.

Bob was pretty satisfied with the crew; they knew their jobs, and he understood their personalities. They'd drilled on day bombing and night bombing as well as hitting targets and emergency exits from the plane. He'd gotten them down to less than two minutes once the bailout signal was given. A pilot needed to know that his men could move quickly if the plane was disabled. They understood the basics of fighting as a unit, of maintaining radio silence, of obeying commands. Bob had realized during the training phase of becoming a pilot that there was more to this than just keeping the plane flying. He'd become a twenty-year-old psychologist and, for the time he was in the air, a father figure to the nine men who depended on him for a safe round-trip home.

The preflight checklist gave Bob and Art enough to do before the flight leader rolled his own plane into position and each of the other Flying Fortresses followed one by one.

Gear switch, Bob read from the checklist.

Neutral, check, said Art.

Cowl flaps. Open right. Open left. Locked.

Parking brakes. Hydraulic check. On. Checked.

Booster pumps pressure. On and checked.

Bob and Art went through the list, and the pressures, hydraulics, fuel and oil levels on all four engines looked fine. Bob ran up all four engines and they sounded right, the manifold pressure was good. He waited for the next plane to move.

It was late morning when Bob taxied the plane to the end of the strip, watching the one in front of him start rolling down the runway. There was no talking. Bob adjusted his oxygen mask, moved his hands to the controls, steadied his feet on the rudders, took a look at the pressure gauges and double-checked the fuel readings. He confirmed that the brakes were locked, set the trim tabs and made sure the tail wheel was locked. He pushed forward on the throttle. All four engines were whining. He made sure the gyro was set and watched the revs and the pressures on each engine. Everything checked out. There was a deep growl as the plane creaked forward until he let out the brakes; then *Shack Rabbit II* lumbered down the runway at full throttle. It took every bit of the strip to lift the twenty-six tons of metal off the ground at about 110 miles per hour, practically skimming the treetops in its slow climb.

The plane gained altitude painfully; Bob eased back on the power, brought up the wheels, adjusted the cowl flaps and banked south. The climb was slow and the plane seemed for a while almost to scrape the rooftops of East Anglia, which were intermittently hidden by light scattered clouds. As usual, there was silence on the radio waves, because the Germans were good at listening in and providing a welcome party.

Bob made a looping slow climb into the sky over England, some lazy turns in the vicinity of Ipswich, and then flew down past the mouth of the Thames along the southeastern English shoreline. The planes started making formation about 1,000 feet over a beacon located just off the coast. They drew together one by one, creating a six- or seven-plane group, then two more at different altitudes, forming a formidable twenty-one-plane wing, each aircraft taking a position as they moved up behind the leader. About half an hour into the mission, Bob eased the plane to the right flank, second position to the squadron leader, and they continued their steady climb, wingtip-to-wingtip, as close as ten feet apart. Once arriving at that position, he was constantly allowing for turbulence and prop wash from the other planes, adjusting the speed, trimming the tail and leveling the wings.

At the same time, a squadron of fighter planes flew in to escort them across the Channel. These were the rival pilots with the red border behind their flight wings, and they could do loops around the slow-moving Flying Fortresses. Sure, the bomber pilots always called them chicken for peeling off before they got to enemy territory. But they didn't realize that Allied fighter planes did not have enough fuel capacity to give them the cruising range to provide protection for the bomber wings as their Delta formations—three levels of up to twenty-one planes—advanced over Nazi territory. The fighters had the range to stick with them until they reached the coast of Europe and then went back home. The slower speed of the B-17s would be counteracted by the fact that any approaching German fighter would find a closed rank of sixty-three planes. Each plane had at least eight machine gunners—the formation could blanket the sky with gunfire in all directions if enemy fighters approached.

Bob kept the climb steady over the Channel, put on his gloves as the temperature went down and zipped up his jacket against the cold. It got well below zero at high altitudes and every bit of skin needed to be covered.

In fifteen minutes or so, Bob saw the European coast in the distance. And just about then, he had trouble. The supercharger on engine number four, outboard right, was malfunctioning. At 12,000 feet it wasn't so bad, but the higher the squadron went, the lower the air pressure and the manifold pressure in the engine dropped. As the engine lost power it overheated, and the propeller turned more slowly, acting as an airbrake that slowed them down even more. The rest of the pack was still climbing, but Bob started falling back because of the drag. Someone else moved into his position on the right flank. Finally, realizing the supercharger was not going to fix itself, Bob cut power on that engine, feathered and turned off the faulty turbo supercharger and turned off its fuel supply. That reduced the drag, and he pushed the throttle forward on the remaining three engines.

He could compensate by increasing power on three engines and reach the group when they leveled off at 22,000 feet, knowing that the extra fuel consumption on a relatively short trip to the Belgian-German border wouldn't be a problem. He fought his way back to the formation and took a place at the end of the line to the spot they called "tail end Charlie," bottom and back of the delta. At that point, everything looked okay. But as they crossed the Belgian coast, the group saw a wall of bad weather and the leader lifted his nose to climb again up over the top of the clouds.

Bob's plane couldn't climb any higher and he had some instant decisions to make. There was little time for debate.

Go back, he told himself.

I can't go back. We have to drop the bombs, the mission is the mission.

Go back, you won't make it. Catch up to the others, your three engines won't let you go higher.

He was stuck down below, a straggler that was the easy prey that German fighter pilots like to dine on. *I can make it, just stay close.*

The intercom came alive all at once.

Bandit, said Kellers from the upper turret.

Bandit, said Nawracaj from the waist.

Bandit, bandit, twelve o'clock high, they said from the nose.

Incoming bandits, nine o'clock.

At least six German Fw 190s were coming at *Shack Rabbit II* from all directions. Head-on, a fighter was visible at the windshield, its guns looking like flashing semaphore as it fired directly at him.

Metlen, the ball turret gunner, pivoted around, trying to lead the planes with a spray of fire from his .50-caliber guns.

Bandit, bandit, called Metlen from the ball turret.

Bob dipped one wing and looked for clouds to hide in.

Guns were spinning in their cradles as the German fighters looped in and out at them.

Incoming, incoming, bandit, bandit, the men were calling on each run of the fighters that appeared, fired their guns and sped out of sight.

The machine guns were blazing and the plane buffeted and jolted as Bob aimed for a low patch of clouds.

It was all in a matter of minutes from when he lost the rest of the formation.

Bob saw one fighter diving right at him, heard gunfire spattering against the fuselage and kept the plane weaving in evasive action as he banked toward the clouds.

Bandit, they kept calling, eight sets of machine guns spinning and trying to catch the much faster planes.

The plodding B-17 could not outmaneuver the firepower of planes flying twice as fast. Seconds more and there was a jolt, rocks at the window, rattling, then a clanking noise like a rattling sardine can.

A 13-millimeter German machine-gun bullet had hit the inside cowling of the number two engine next to the pilot seat, had broken in half and ricocheted end over end through the fuselage, cut through Bob's flight suit, sliced into his quadriceps muscle, penetrated the soft tissue, and lodged along the upper quadrant of his femur. It felt like someone had hit him in the leg with a hammer.

Bandit, bandit.

As he pulled back on the wheel to keep the nose up, Bob shook his head clear and saw another engine was going, smoking, definitely hit by the sparking flashes from the Fw 190 cannons. Bob felt more shudders on the stick, and then the plane was not responding to the rudder. It was as if his feet were set free and the controls weren't doing anything. He pulled back on the stick to keep the plane up, and he saw the fighters spinning figure eights around the plane, and he feathered that smoking engine and cut the fuel so it wouldn't burn.

The plane can fly on two engines.

But Bob could hardly keep the plane flying straight, the two remaining engines were pulling and yanking the right wing down. He could only fly straight by pulling as hard as he could. And still, there were bumps and the splattering noise of hot metal on the fuselage. It wasn't going to work.

Silence was starting to envelop him now, rushing air that was overwhelming the creaks and bumps of the cockpit, the sound of wind current on his ears that was overtaking the violence of the firefight.

Pull, pull the plane back.

It was going into a steep diving turn. *Pull it, pull it up.* The rudder and elevators were not responding. The plane was not going to make it.

Bandits, came the call on the intercom, followed by Bob's voice for the first time.

Crew, abandon ship. Get out! Get out! he called, hitting the microphone switch along with the emergency bailout alarm, just as they had drilled.

One, two, three. . . . He started counting slowly to 120, the number of seconds it should take the nine men under his command to strap on their chutes and jump from the airplane.

The absence of control grew, and Bob felt he was imprisoned in a capsule of air; he heard nothing else on the intercom and moved mechanically now, instinctively doing what he had been trained to do.

Eight, nine, ten, eleven. . . .

Pickett was already on his feet. The copilot stripped off his mask, reached for the parachute under the seat and clipped it to his front harness. He went down through the hatch in the floor to the middle deck and jumped from the side door. Bob was busy trying to pull the plane level, playing for time. He focused on counting the two minutes they'd rehearsed for everyone to get out. The plane was pulling back against him, forcing an inevitable left turn that would broaden into a steeper and steeper angle and finally a death spiral toward the ground.

Thirty-four, thirty-five, thirty-six.

How much time? Was two minutes enough for Metlen, the ball turret gunner?

The ball turret was usually the last out of the back of the plane.

Forty, forty-one. He tried to steer by gunning the throttle and pulling hard against the stick.

He had drilled and drilled them. McElroy, the navigator, and Carlson, the bombardier, were up front. They definitely had time. Then there were the five men in the back; not like there was time to go back there and check. McManus, the radio operator; Nawracaj and Sheets, the waist gunners; and Jansen, the tail gunner. He was most worried about Metlen in the belly. Did the ball turret work and was he able to squeeze out and jump with the rest of them? He had to figure they'd bail if they could.

Sixty, sixty-one, sixty-two, sixty-three. . . .

Bob couldn't hold it steady. He looked up at Ted Kellers, who was operating the machine gun in the turret above him. Everyone else should be bailing out, but Kellers was still up there. It was typical of Kellers—he wanted to keep fighting.

Get the hell down, get out of here. Get out, get out.

Seventy-three, seventy-four. . . .

Was he calling to Kellers, or was that Kellers calling him? They both had to jump now. Bob motioned with both arms to his engineer. They didn't have much time. Finally, Kellers came down from the turret, squeezing through to the midsection exit door.

Eighty-seven, eighty-eight, eighty-nine. . . .

Could he even make it to 120? The plane was going into a long spin. Bob started loosening his seat belt and just as he was about to leave the pilot's position, something caught his eye: damn but if it wasn't a German plane pulling up on the port side, flying in formation to have a look. It had to be a single-engine Fw 190, but was he seeing double? He thought he saw two engines.

Bob and the German pilot couldn't see each other's faces, what with the oxygen masks. But the German was looking right at him. This must have been the pilot who made the kill. There was something about the way they looked at each other, as if the German were asking Bob a simple question:

Why are you still in the plane? You're going nowhere.

Another thing: the German wasn't shooting. He'd done his job. Pilot to pilot, it was a signal: it was time to bail.

It might have been five seconds or more after that. Bob had lost the count. He told himself that it was enough, that two minutes had passed, time for the rest of the crew. Bob yanked his mask, stripped off his gloves, pulled up his parachute pack from under the seat, hooked it on his harness, and eased out of his seat toward the exit hatch.

Time, how much time? He knew he was losing the plane.

Bob remembered isolated images after that, but nothing coherent. He had no sensation of the cold, the wind or any sound. He didn't remember squeezing down off the flight deck; he didn't remember the wind blowing through the hatch in the fuselage.

He saw Kellers thrown against the floor, fumbling to get his parachute clipped on right and then jumping into the sun.

Bob didn't remember jumping. At one instant, he could see the controls, along with the sound of metal popping, like somebody throwing pebbles at a window. He heard the engines and the sounds of fighting. And then time contracted toward the moment that he was sucked into the sky and there was a torrent against his face and the rushing of air in his ears that hurtled him end over end.

And then, it was calm and quiet, and he was plunging through the air, mouthing words that were taken by the wind.

Heaven, this must be heaven.

There was a problem, though. He hadn't double-checked his parachute harness. Maybe that was a good thing, because here was something to keep awake by: he didn't have the harness rigged correctly and one leg strap was loose. When the chute opened, all the power of the wind filling the parachute pulled the strap into the center of his crotch, which made it feel like his balls were being forced somewhere right up in the vicinity of his mouth. His eyes were wide open.

He forgot about steering and looking below. He saw the clouds and the dome of the sky. There was silence—no more splatter of metal and the ringing from the engines; his nose was clear from the burn of his oxygen mask. Any reveries were interrupted as he pulled down on one side of the chute to take the pain and pressure off his crotch. All he could do was look down helplessly and see the field, a road and two figures, maybe animals moving along, stopping. Then he saw people and bicycles. Time sped up for him; he tumbled to the ground and crawled on all fours to gather and unhook his chute.

The parachute brought him down near a road, and the man and the boy came running.

He heard the barking dogs again, closer perhaps. It was a wrench in his stomach. Dogs hunting for him.

Deutscher, *Deutscher,* the old man had said. Where was he? At first he thought the plane must have been over Germany when he jumped out. But the man and the boy sounded like they were speaking French. Bob pulled the silk map from the escape kit in his flight suit. The old man plopped his finger down on it, indicating they were in Belgium.

The old man hid his parachute in a culvert under the road, and the little boy led him across the tree-dotted pastureland to a hedgerow far from sight. Hopefully, by the time the patrol passed by, they would keep to the road, finding no sign of his parachute nor any indication that he had come down there.

Now hidden in the bramble hollow of the bushes, Bob realized the boy and the old man were warning him about German patrols. They definitely would have seen the plane come down and they probably saw the parachutes. They were out searching the woods, looking for Bob and his crew. He must have passed out—how much time had gone by? Bob looked down at the torn left leg of his flight suit and saw that it was wet with blood. He took note of it while also noting that he didn't feel any real pain. He was not cold, and it never occurred to him to eat or drink anything; he hadn't gone through the other items in his escape kit. There were Horlicks malted milk tablets, cigarettes, Benzedrine, water purification powder, money in different currencies, a compass, and passport photos for false ID cards. He'd forgotten that it was there.

He fiddled with his watch. It had stopped at 3:15. The stem must have popped out when he jumped. He pushed it back in. He didn't know how much time he'd lost—a couple of hours probably, but he could at least measure the hours from this point forward.

His thoughts were like the tattered fragments of his flight suit, disconnected from the rest of him. Pure will to survive brought him to assess where he was and what had happened: this surely was not heaven, more like somewhere in between. The boy said he'd come back after dark. Bob would have to sit tight and wait. He had trouble making it this far to these hedges over the rolling grassy field, half crawling. His leg was stiff. He was certain that by daylight he would be captured.

The barking echoed around him. The sound brought his mind back to his surroundings. It was a tether to the world, almost a comfort, reminding him that he was awake. There was reason to be worried. The Germans were looking for anybody who bailed out of the plane.

It was not a single strand but a series of conflicting thoughts: going over the mission, thinking about home, wondering what would happen next. None of these thoughts did any good, but he couldn't help it. Every so often a sound would startle him.

He reran every detail of his contact with the boy and the old man. They had dropped their bicycles and come running. The old man had taken the chute and the harness and went back to the road, stuffing the gear in a drainage ditch. He went away after that. The boy motioned for Bob to follow him across the open field. Bob moved with difficulty, and the boy motioned him to stay low, which meant he was half crawling, half dragging himself to the hedges, where the boy made a staying motion with the palms of his hands.

How did he know that the boy would come back? In sign language, he had said he would. The boy spoke French, so how was Bob going to understand what the boy meant? Two years of high school French back in Cradock didn't help at all. How old was the boy? Maybe ten years old, or twelve. How did Bob know that the boy and the man weren't bringing the Germans? Anyway, there was nothing he could do about that now; he was surrounded by blackness. He was lying in a small thicket of trees that gave him shelter, but which also cushioned him from a stark problem: He could not remember any contour or detail of the land and had no idea of his bearings. Where was the road? Where were the trees? Where was anything? He was beyond being lost. He was utterly without orientation.

Night came down upon him and with it the sensation of absolute isolation. He couldn't see his watch, or even an inch in front of him. What time was it? At least the regular pacing of the dogs' barking had ceased to be a threat. Instead there was only silence, other than the sound of his own breathing. He was awake. His feet and hands were cold. Grass and mud stained his elbows. He stripped bitter leaves from a branch with his fingers and put them to his lips. He was hungry. Alone. And in a panicked realization, he suddenly understood the obvious. He spoke to break the hissing emptiness in his ears.

The kid isn't coming back.

He was on his own. He had to move. But where?

CHAPTER FOUR

Crossing the Border

Along the French-Spanish Border. October 20, 1943.

The sun was setting. It was cold in October at the foot of the Pyrenees on the French border with Spain. Jean-François didn't make every trip across the mountains, but all summer he had been working mostly between Paris and the border, making sure that all the logistics were in good order. He accompanied the airmen during railroad transfers, bike rides and strolls past German checkpoints. The losses of the winter and spring had been significant, but they were being overcome and pushed aside as the Comet Line carried on.

But now MI9 had summoned Jean-François for a strategy meeting in Gibraltar. He had never been to Gibraltar before and was looking forward to it as a short vacation from the war. Michael Creswell would meet him just beyond the Spanish border, in San Sebastián, and then they'd drive down together across Spain, south to Gibraltar, that impenetrable fortress that was so key to the British defense.

Jean-François had waited for the next evacuation of airmen, and when they got to southern France, he accompanied them on the road with Florentino. They had ridden the train from Paris, and then Jean-François met the men at Saint-Jean-de-Luz. From there, they walked a mile or two to Kattalin's house along the seashore.

He would stay with Florentino and the airmen all across the mountains until they were safely in Spain. Once they got to Sarobe, the safe farmhouse in the mountains on the Spanish side of the border, Jean-François would let his friends take care of the airmen the rest of the way. Creswell would have his aides guide the airmen and would wait for Jean-François in San Sebastián.

Throughout the summer Comet averaged twelve rescues a month, two crossings in July, four in August and six in September. Jean-François had made five crossings since the end of July. He even had a list of the men, which he hid at Kattalin's house. He remembered faces, although after a while they began to blend together. Since much of the trip was in the dark and communication was limited, Jean-François couldn't connect the faces to the names.

Except one, Cole Clifford, who was unusual not only because of his rank—he was a major in the U.S. Army—but also because he thought it would be a good idea to practice his French while riding the trains.

Mais oui, mademoiselle, he said to a woman who asked for a match. *J'ai du feu.*

Jean-François was horrified. *Just what I need*, he thought, *someone who thinks he speaks French. It's worse than not speaking French at all.*

Jean-François ordered him to keep his mouth closed, and Clifford was taken aback.

Do you know who you're talking to? the major asked.

Jean-François told him to shut up, that in this territory he was the commanding officer. Walking through the mountains a few weeks later, Jean-François could think about it and laugh, because they didn't get caught. Clifford would probably not forget. *I think he, and the rest of them, all remember me*, he was thinking, *but I don't remember too many of them.*

———

While Jean-François saw Comet functioning as an efficient machine, the perspective from London was different. For them, disaster was always close by. Military Intelligence was deeply concerned that continued losses would paralyze the Comet escape line. Military planning was gearing up for the heaviest bombing campaign in the war so far: the softening up of German defenses, attacks on strategic installations, and a day and night bombing campaign to disrupt the Nazi machine. The London operatives feared that Jean-François and his friends could be captured just when the need to rescue fliers was greatest. Even with Jean-François's successful reorganization, debates were ongoing in London throughout the summer about how to consolidate operations, especially as the time approached for the massive air assault on Europe, followed by the Allied invasion of the mainland that was sure to come.

That was why MI9 summoned him for the late October meeting in Gibraltar. Jean-François figured the British would make a case for more control; they would argue that he could guard more effectively against future traps set by the Gestapo if London provided more training and expertise. But he was determined to reject the offer, standing by Dédée's oft-stated demand for total independence from Britain. Dédée's position was based in part on the notion that Belgians should be fighting their own battles against the Nazis. But she also thought that working for the British would slow them down, bog down the operation in bureaucracy far from the field and make them more vulnerable to attack by Nazi agents.

Jean-François also supposed that MI9 would ask him again about opening a second route across the border. They wanted more flexibility to move a larger number of pilots. If surveillance increased at one spot along the river, a second route would enable them to keep people moving at another part of the frontier. It was logical enough, but Jean-François didn't like the idea much. The last time he tried it, he was arrested in Elizondo. That was the third time he'd been captured—twice by the Nazis in 1940 when he was in the Belgian army and once by the Spanish. So far he'd been able to escape, but he didn't think his luck would hold out forever.

There were subtle but important changes following the disastrous arrest of Dédée, her father and the others. Safe houses, of course, were changed. An intensive vetting process was introduced for all new members of the line. A questionnaire was administered to all airmen—the Germans were sending in English-speaking double agents.

A year ago, Dédée's style had been to play the elegant lady and travel first-class all the way from Belgium to Saint-Jean-de-Luz, part of the overnight trip. But as the war progressed and the volume of escapees increased, the main rail line to the south was swarming with troop carriages and Gestapo officers, not to mention suspicious customs agents and train conductors. So now the rescuers no longer followed the express line from Paris to the Spanish border, observing that the higher-priced direct trains were frequently subjected to spot searches and interrogation of passengers. In the summer, Jean-François developed a roundabout route, traveling in third-class open coaches on lower-profile, less monitored local train routes and spur lines.

That was his method of travel on October 20, 1943, when he was on his way to meet Michael Creswell and travel to Gibraltar for the planning session. It was the same day Bob Grimes parachuted from his plane over Belgium. Jean-François had not heard yet about Black Thursday, the previous week's bombing raids over Schweinfurt, in which 600 Allied fliers were lost. The quickened pace of bombing runs meant that Comet was to have a growing number of men to rescue from enemy territory.

The local train eventually brought them south, close to Saint-Jean-de-Luz. One by one, the airmen arrived at Kattalin's house, each accompanied by one of the guides. Many of these helpers were young girls who did everything they could to appear like innocent, love-smitten teenagers out with their boyfriends. A Nazi patrol was un-likely to be suspicious seeing a boy and a girl walking down the cob-blestone street to Kattalin's house on the bay. They walked downhill to the two-story house with a balcony, which looked no different than the row of connected buildings hugging the incline that went down to the seashore. Kattalin greeted them with a smile and provided food and drink. The fliers bunched up on the floor and got some rest.

Jean-François looked at the men. They were naturally high-spirited. They were all speaking rapidly in English and joking. Many of them had been isolated in the countryside for weeks. Jean-François reminded them firmly that they had to stay quiet. No one should hear them speaking English; there should be no suspicions.

Florentino arrived late in the afternoon. He looked over the group of airmen and made sure they had proper clothing for the cold night in the mountains. In particular the Basque focused on their feet. Each man traded in his solid laced shoes for *alpargatas*, the Basque country's traditional cloth and rope-woven espadrilles, which tied at the ankles with rope. Lightweight and noiseless against the echoing hills, alpar-gatas drained easily and were perfect for maintaining a pliable footing on mountain trails and in the riverbeds when they waded across to Spain. The espadrilles were easy to replace when they fell apart after a soaked night trudging across the border. The Allied airmen thought they were ridiculous and not a reasonable substitute at all for sturdy shoes built to withstand sharp rocks and muddy trails. But they did as they were told, and in the course of the night they grew to understand their functionality. Florentino treated the alpargatas seriously, period-ically wandering among his team of airmen to make sure they were properly tied. He carried a string of replacement alpargatas around his neck because everyone would need a new pair in the course of the passage through the Pyrenees.

At nightfall, Jean-François mustered the airmen and gave them their marching orders. They would travel all night. They were to remain silent, walk single file and follow instructions without hesitation. Their lives depended on it.

The airmen wore country garb—old rough shirts, baggy trousers and ill-fitting wool jackets that were moth-eaten and crumpled. They placed berets on their heads to blend in as much as possible and listened quietly, still not comprehending what lay ahead.

Braced against the wind, Jean-François and Florentino left Kattalin's house, came to the edge of the village and crossed the main coastal road, hoping to avoid German patrols on this first part of the trip.

They walked along the narrow strip of French seacoast along the Atlantic Ocean known as the Bay of Biscay. Looking inland, there were little farms, cows and stands of corn along sloping hills and rolling forests. Walking along a winding old farm road, suddenly one would enter an ancient village square; there was always a church tower made of stone, the village hall and a monument to the French who died during World War I. By now, the fall of 1943, the Nazi flag flew from every government building; its presence attacked the pastoral beauty like a blight driven on the wind. No one was safe, and people walked with their heads down as the patrols passed. The danger of discovery was constant.

Stretched out behind them was a panoramic view of the rocky, irregular coastline of France. The wind obscured the sound of waves on the beach several hundred yards below them; they could see a line of white foam forming on the craggy shore. Florentino waved them into the woods, which led to the undulating hills at the start of their overnight trek. Quickly now they crossed the road. A Czech-made Skoda automobile, the preferred vehicle of the Gestapo, drove by, but the boys were out of sight. The car continued down the road toward the Spanish border, Nazi flags flapping in the breeze. The airmen still had their false French documents should they meet a German patrol out in the open. But in the forest they'd rely on Florentino's stealth and guidance. There was only one possible explanation if a Nazi patrol caught them skulking through the hills: they were escaping, and they could be shot on sight.

The Basque guide immediately set an unyielding pace. The first part of the crossing was about two hours over rolling farm roads to Urrugne, the neighborhood where Dédée had been captured in January, still the staging point before reaching the Spanish border. Since their narrow escape from the Nazis, they'd changed their destination to another house in the village and rarely stayed longer than necessary to take a short rest. It was a cool evening; fog rose from the Bay of Biscay and settled in the hills, bathing the trees in mystery. Florentino trudged along ahead, rarely allowing the men to rest. It took every effort by the airmen to keep up, and they were soon dog-tired and disoriented. Occasionally, Florentino would hold up a hand, tap his alpargatas on the ground, and then speed up once more as he listened for any signs of pursuers.

There were shepherds along the way, their presence forewarned by the dull sound of tin claxons or perhaps a barking sheep dog. *Tais-toi*, Florentino said in fractured French to the rest of the men. *Be quiet*.

Five hours after leaving Kattalin's house, the trail opened in a sudden clearing on top of the mountain. Jean-François huddled with Florentino and agreed to let the airmen rest for a while. From this point in the mountains, just east of Biriatu, the view extended all the way to the mouth of the Bidassoa River, where the lights of Spain—the resort town of Fuenterrabía—belied the European war. At night one saw the lights along the beach, which formed an arc that ended at the mouth of the river and the Bay of Biscay beyond. It was a narrow piece of land lapping like a tongue of fire at German-controlled Europe, whose lights were blacked out against Allied air attack. Spain may have kept the pretense of neutrality, but its German friends were known to patrol both sides of the river with no argument from Franco's border patrols.

The escape route was a turnabout from the late 1930s, when Spaniards crossed in the opposite direction to escape Francisco Franco's conquering Phalangists. At that time, people were actually wading across the Bidassoa from Spain into France. Now they fled in the opposite direction.

Crossing at that spot would be suicide, even though the fishing boats moored and anchored there seemed to make it possible. Jean-François could imagine what to do. You could sneak down to the port and wait for nightfall. If you were quiet enough, you could tread water and swim between the anchored fishing boats from the French side to the Spanish side. It had never worked, though, because the Germans and the Spanish Guardia Civil patrolled both shores. Approaching the bank with any appearance of escape was a fatal mistake.

From this high vantage point, just beyond the port, Jean-François could trace the Bidassoa River upstream to the railroad and highway bridges that divide Spain and France.

The railway workers were all Basque, and some of them set up a rescue operation in 1942. They smuggled refugees all the way to their machine shop by the tracks right along the river. It worked for a while. But then the Germans got wise, thanks to the Spanish police. French Basque railway employees smuggled a resistance agent named Michel Irribarrain crossed the railway with his wife, Janine. But Spanish police in Irún captured them. Searching Michel's pockets, they found troop estimates and other intelligence information. Spain returned the couple to France and the Germans made a big show. They shot Michel and Janine and announced in the papers that anyone else trying to sneak out of the country also would be executed.

Jean-François looked down at the lights of Spain and thought of freedom. Because of the danger with the rail line, the port and the highway in this populated area, the obvious choice was to operate here, several miles upstream, where the Germans had never been, on the goat paths in the precipitous hills lining either shore. Before Florentino motioned the men to continue down to the river, Jean-François could not help looking to the southern sky. The lights of San Sebastián, the Spanish city that was his destination ten miles away, cast a glow on the horizon. To get there on this circuitous route, it was first downhill to the river. Then another four-hour march to their safe house on the Spanish side. They also would continue to elude the Guardia Civil, who were under orders to arrest escapees from France.

Allez, allez, called Florentino. He was gesturing for everyone to crouch down among the ferns and brush. *Doucement, doucement,* Florentino said suddenly. He motioned the men to crouch low and move toward him.

Jean-François looked up to see Florentino staring back at him. *Quietly, gently,* in French, one of the few words Florentino could speak in anything other than the Basque language.

At certain points, this old smugglers' route cut across farm roads and a highway or two that could be patrolled by the Germans. There was the hum of an engine echoing far below down the hill and the glow of a distant headlight ricocheting off the trees.

The men heard the sound and understood that they should not move. They could hear more sounds, voices in the distance: Germans. Usually they'd not stray far from their vehicles. They had no way of knowing these hidden trails. After a moment they heard more voices, a car door and engines gunning as the patrol continued along the road.

It was always possible that a German patrol could be traversing one of the nearby roads and accidentally spot them from below. Usually the sounds and whistles were accounted for by other Basque climbing parties—smugglers and friends of Florentino who also knew these trails. Satisfied that they were alone, he circulated among his charges and made a routine check of the airmen's alpargatas. They would need to be secure for the river crossing. *Doucement, doucement,* he said, and they started again along the twisting path to freedom beyond the Bidassoa River.

Beyond the leafy vista was a broad expanse of sky that hinted at the cliffs and the drop to the Bay of Biscay off the coast of France. The hills and the countryside were always visible, but the contrast was absolute.

On the way up the hill there were vivid fields of lavender—*izpiliku* in Florentino's language—verbascum and poppies and dandelion threatening to overgrow the mossy steps. Even children learned quickly to step around the poisonous climbing ivies and henbane and cicuta that gathered at the base of ancient, crumbling foundations of forgotten buildings along the road. The route was a stitchwork of intersecting byways up, down and around the forest glens and knolls, where Romans trod but whose sudden steps did not remain. Since the Middle Ages, pilgrims walked here in narrow file on their way to pay religious homage at Santiago de Compostela.

Occasionally over the rise of a knoll there was a faint clanking bell and a gathering commotion, but it was nothing to fear, because it was usually some untended goats or a flock of sheep and a shepherd walking apace. It would not be the police or the Germans, who had a distinctive, plodding way of going through the woods. The contraband traders, shepherds, threshers and harvesters recognized the sound and could signal warning to one another. Everyone here was known; no one carried firearms, and the code of honor among the Basque clans and families precluded theft and mischief. No imported policeman or Gestapo minion out to learn the secrets of the Basque country could penetrate this terrain. The Basque homeland had outlasted eons of hegemony by others, going back to the time of the Vascones, who lived here before recorded history. The people of Euskadi knew, one way or another, they would outlast any pumped-up fascist—Spanish, German or French—in a silly uniform who attempted to manipulate or circumvent *los fueros*—the ancient Basque laws—or curb Basque independence. Florentino was leading them among friends and family.

The hike uphill was a torture for the weary Allied airmen. Tired muscles relaxed when they appeared to reach a peak in the climb, but then the path wound around the mountain and began to ascend once more. Finally, there was a broad muddy expanse at the highest point, where again the lights of Spain contrasted with the bleak occupied shadow to the north.

It was an hour or more to the Bidassoa River, the rock-strewn stream that divides France from Spain at this section of the border. The river starts in the Pyrenees about 100 miles away, gathers force from tributaries running downhill from the mountains, and cascades along boulders and a pebble-and-stone bed about fifty feet wide. Unless it had been raining, the crossing took no more than a minute or two. The water was usually not even waist-high.

The moon appeared intermittently between clouds; Florentino frowned. The river would be illuminated by moonlight. Florentino motioned Jean-François and the three pilots to stay low, but he saw no sign of patrols.

One of the airmen was a Canadian who spoke some French. Jean-François told him to tell the others that they would cross the river.

The Canadian complained about the goat's milk he was offered.

Goat's milk and cognac cocktails.

Drink it, Jean-François said. *It gives you energy.*

The goat's milk stank, and the Canadian had to hold his nose to get the concoction down.

These Basques eat terribly, he said to his companions.

On the train when they were coming down from the Belgian border, somebody had made him drink two raw eggs in a glass of cognac. It was like a lump in his stomach.

Haven't these people ever heard of sandwiches and soda?

Quiet, said Jean-François, and Florentino also turned around with his hands to his lips.

They'd reached the river. A German patrol was crossing the bridge close by, the lights from an accompanying car occasionally illuminating shadows in the trees.

Before crossing, Florentino motioned the airmen to hold back from the shore while he went down to the riverbank. When all was clear, he waved to them to come along. All crouched low in the undergrowth before the open area just below where the hills dropped off to the river. Even though it was bright, no Germans were visible on the French side and the Spaniards on the other bank of the river were probably getting drunk in their guard hut.

On the French side of the frontier, low-ranking German foot soldiers were not as interested in the hunt as the more diligent SS troops and Gestapo might have been. Likewise, the Spanish border guards, who earned all of ten cents a day for their efforts—if they were lucky—preferred to hang about in their crumbling but dry barracks rather than to look for smugglers and spies.

That was fortunate, because the weather was too pleasant for the crossing. Florentino and Jean-François preferred cloudy skies and mist, which camouflaged their movements in the night.

One by one in the darkness, the men stepped into the river, obeying Florentino's command. The river itself was no obstacle; it was only a foot or so deep, not even up to their knees. They only needed to roll their pants up a bit; the current was strong but inconsequential. It took several minutes to wade gingerly to the other shore.

After that they crossed a narrow dry bed on the Spanish side, followed by a steep incline, an old rail line and then the Irún-Pamplona highway, which extends from the Spanish coast to Pamplona and Barcelona. The chances were great that a border guard might notice a silhouette or hear something in the few seconds of running for cover on the opposite shoulder. On clear nights the Guardia Civil usually patrolled frequently. They were known to fire at anything or anyone moving by the river—and if they didn't throw you in jail, they were capable of sending anyone caught in the act of crossing the border right back to France and Nazi custody.

Soon the men were gathered up, shivering and drying their feet on the Spanish shore. Jean-François warned them not to take off their waterlogged alpargatas unless they needed a replacement. "Once you take them off, you'll never get them on again," Jean-François said.

After a rest they started moving again. The first step was to cross a small area of underbrush, then over the railroad tracks, and finally another thirty feet to the steep embankment by the Irún-Pamplona highway. Florentino went first, then Jean-François sent each of them at intervals.

The Canadian was up next; he made it to the railroad tracks but tripped on one of the rails. He fell hard, and the others heard the sound of gravel sliding and a muffled cry. Dogs barked in the distance, and a light came on in the guard post on the road. Florentino, motioning from ahead, again waved them to stay flat against the ground. Fortunately, the dogs stopped barking; the light went out. After ten minutes, they resumed the crossing.

Florentino knelt at the side of the road and looked for any sign of the guards, who could have been sleeping on duty but easily might have been awakened by the dogs.

Allons, allons! he whispered, almost exhausting his French vocabulary, and motioned each of them one by one to a rocky meeting point on the other side of the road. Running low when the moon was hidden, they made it to the brush on the other side of the highway.

After that, there was a sheer cliff to climb and then another series of undulating hills, skirting around the peak called Peña de Aya and past the Castillo Inglés, a building in ruins that was neither English nor a castle but was so dubbed following a local predilection for assigning whimsical names. For one who has never marched this way before, it is an unending punishment of paths that tauntingly head downhill before mounting a steep hairpin incline around an unseen crook in the trail. They reached the crossroads known as Bosbieta—the five paths—then staggered down the hill at dawn to the safe house that everyone called Sarobe.

Sarobe was a small farming homestead with a vegetable garden, some sheep and some cows, a bull, and a stand of apple trees. It was like an apparition in the rising dawn—an enclave surrounded by trees and rolling fields, a chimney signaling that the hearth already awaited them. It was not even seven miles from the river, but it had been an interminable passage through the mountains. The pilots were exhausted. Their replacement alpargatas were wasted, dangling from raw, bleeding feet.

Paco Iriarte-Recalde, the little nephew of the patron of Sarobe, was waiting for the group as Florentino led them down the slick, rockladen path. They emerged near a stand of plane trees that overlooked Sarobe and the valley leading down to Oyarzun below.

Paco looked up to Florentino, and the bristly guide gave him a pat on the head.

Do you remember what we told you? Florentino asked, speaking in Euskera for the first time all evening. *What do you do if the Guardia Civil comes?*

Bai, Florentino, bai, Paco answered proudly in Euskera. *Yes, Florentino. I will never tell them anything.*

Florentino flipped him a ten-peseta coin.

Before reaching the entrance, the guides and the three pilots could see the smoke from the chimney and smell the aroma of food being prepared. The Iriartes—Manuel, Francisco, Regina and Fermina—whose family had owned Sarobe for generations, welcomed the men with their customary bonhomie, even though they had been surprised to see the airmen. They never knew when men were coming.

The scent of sizzling oil and the other smells of breakfast cooking seeped through the door of the farmhouse. For the first time all night, the Basque was trailing behind Jean-François and the pilots, who almost ran through the front door.

In the dim light of the stone-arched foyer, the visitors saw all sorts of traditional farm implements hanging from rough-hewn wooden beams: various types of lanterns; a scythe; an ingenious balance bar to carry pails of milk on the shoulders, with a shorter pivoting plank on top to prevent the liquid from spilling; a wooden device called a *matraca*, which looks like a New Year's party ratchet, and is used instead of bells to call the faithful to church during Holy Week. Herbs were tied in bundles and hung from hooks in the rafters; there was lavender and mint and a garland of garlic, all smells that defied the cold and combined with the musty odors from the rain and the humidity of the drenched clothes.

Sarobe had been a way station in the mountains along the frontier as long as anyone could remember. It was a typical Basque *caserio*. Caserios—best translated as "homesteads"—for centuries have been a focal point of Basque heritage. A caserio is a gathering of extended family under one roof, in a building that has evolved with a distinct architecture. The style in some ways is reminiscent of a Swiss chalet. It at once makes use of the terrain, rich in hardwood and stones quarried from the mountains, and embellishes the natural setting with folkloric design. Sarobe was a good example of the style. A front facing of exposed, squared timber was surrounded by stone and mortar; the whitewashed walls were contrasted by green and red shutters and trim—the colors of the Basque national flag. There was a gate surrounding the house, fencing in the cattle, sheep and goats.

Jean-François came to Sarobe almost every week now, but he never lost the pleasure of arriving at dawn for the breakfast meal. For the average person in France and the rest of Europe under German occupation, food was severely rationed. The normal fare was a bit of potato and a thimbleful of dried meat, which would flavor the broth and vegetables. Even with black market money, one could barely expect to eat a piece of suspect black bread and watered-down ersatz coffee mixed with ground oats. In Spain, the cities faced real hunger in the aftermath of the civil war, and the rationing of meager staples was now getting worse.

In the large country kitchen, Paco's aunt set up pans with warm salt water so the men could soak their blistered feet. Before them was a long table covered with delicacies: there were hearty quantities of cheese, fresh milk, *talua* (a form of corn bread), succulent tender sausage and cured ham, all produced right on the farm, a rare wartime delicacy for the outsiders. First there was hot milk; the family sat before them with evident pleasure, watching them eat.

She motioned the pilots to sit on a bench at the long table as she prepared food. The Canadian, still complaining about the aftertaste of goat's milk and cognac, couldn't wait for a drink of water. But it wasn't water that he was served.

Oh no, he said, smiling, since his hosts wouldn't understand that he was complaining. *More goat's milk.*

There was no water on the table, just the milk, a bottle of wine, warm beer and coffee.

Little Paco came into the kitchen and watched the airmen, smiling and awestruck as they ate and drank without stopping, faces buried in their food.

The other members of the farm also came around to watch the pilots, smiling. Paco's old uncle had an impish smile; he was the host. He spoke the Basque language to his family and to Florentino, who sat with the pilots, laughing and wiping his maw; he drank the wine and cognac as if he hadn't been up all night.

It was a feeling of celebration. The homesteaders at Sarobe knew they were doing their small part to help win the war against fascism, and the product of their labor was happy, well-fed American, Canadian and British airmen, who they referred to collectively as *los pilotos*—the pilots—not knowing or worrying about their nationalities or whether they flew the planes, rode the tail gun or dropped the bombs.

Paco's aunt turned her back long enough to prepare the *tortilla de patatas* that Jean-François especially loved. She diced some onions, told Paco to fetch some eggs from the chicken coop and cut chunks of potatoes. She heated some oil over the fire, then sautéed the onions and softened the potatoes in the mixture, adding some salt. Meanwhile, she was beating the eggs, which were then added and cooked to the consistency of a thick, slightly browned omelet.

She sliced ample portions of the tortilla de patata. They all ate with relish, but Jean-François especially looked forward to breakfast at Sarobe. All the way down the line from Paris, and then hiking through the mountains, he would be anticipating the warm reception at Sarobe. The distinctive aromas of the hearth and the smoking fire at the end of the escape route were a symbol that—at least for a while—he was out of the Nazis' reach, safe and tasting freedom.

Sarobe was memorable for the airmen too. The travelers hadn't seen such abundance since they'd left England. After the meal, sated with food and alcohol, even Florentino was ready to sleep. The family led them to the stairway between the farmhouse entrance and the kitchen, which led to an open second floor, a hayloft, where dry straw was laid out with blankets on the bare planks for the men to sleep.

Jean-François told the boys to catch some rest, but they were always edgy. Some weeks back, there'd been a knock at the door and the airmen jumped from the loft window into the corn tufts, fearing arrest. It had been a man from the village selling insurance.

Through the window the airmen could see a bull at the back of the building, several grazing sheep, rolling cornfields and scattered whitewashed caserios up and down the valley. They slept uneasily.

After their rest, the next link in the chain was down the hill to another safe house and bar owned by the Arbide Garayar family. Their three teenagers, Venancio, Vicente and Luciano, would give the men a ride in a wagon to a meeting point where a driver from the British consulate was waiting. Under Creswell's orders, they would be transferred as quickly as possible to Gibraltar.

While the travelers slept, Paco's aunt was busy checking Florentino's supply of alpargatas. Most were rope-soled. Sometimes a pair was found that had soles made with scarce supplies of old tire treads. She went down into the village markets to buy whatever kind there were but never picked up more than a pair or two at the same place to avoid attracting attention.

British intelligence paid all the expenses: alpargatas, food and equipment, bribes and train tickets—as well as the camouflaged leather *botas* and flasks of cognac that Florentino hid in the hills and valleys. Other than that, Florentino had little use for, or interest in, money. He was supposed to get 1,500 pesetas for each crossing. Jean-François had walked into Florentino's room at Kattalin's house one day and found the payment from many voyages stuffed into a drawer of a dressing table, the coins wrapped in carelessly crumpled banknotes.

After staying with his friends at Sarobe, Florentino would head back across the river to prepare for the arrival of more pilots. But Jean-François didn't sleep. He had an appointment with Creswell down in San Sebastián.

A bientot, adios, agur, mis amigos, Jean-François said in French, Spanish and Basque, to cover everyone.

He walked down the hill to Rentería, where he could catch *El Topo*—"The Mole"—the subway line that ran along the border from Irún to San Sebastián and stopped just north of the city. Then he walked down toward the port. Michael Creswell had driven up from Madrid and was set to pick up Jean-François at one of the British consulate's safe houses. There was no doubt that the survival of the Comet Line escape network—as well as that of the wounded American pilot, Bob Grimes—was at stake.

_____

CHAPTER FIVE

Gaining Strength

Brussels, Belgium. October 1943.

When the sun went down on the evening of October 20, 1943, Bob Grimes started considering his options. There weren't many: he could stay in the bushes and starve or get caught; or he could look for help. If the boy who helped him wasn't coming back, he was going to have to move.

He pulled himself to his feet and noticed that his leg was throbbing. He realized that he was wounded, but he didn't know how bad it was. The thing to do was look for a farmhouse. He chose a direction and headed off across the fields, searching for lights, hoping that even with a blackout, he'd see something. Dragging his left leg, looking all around, he finally spotted a lamp in the distance. He soon entered a barnyard and approached the farmhouse just across the way.

The farmer, Louis Carlier, and his family watched him approaching from the window—a bedraggled young man who looked like he was bringing the war to their doorstep. Their first instinct was to keep the door closed.

Bob knocked and called out to them. *Please, please, American, American.*

Allez, allez, they said. *Go away.*

Finally, the Carliers relented and opened the door.

The young man before them was a mess, covered with dirt and scratches on his face. But he was the handsome image of an American all the same, a blond-haired, thin, fair-skinned fellow with big blue eyes and an honest smile. Whether or not he was a collaborator; whether or not the Germans would swoop down and kill them all, sympathy won out over fear. They knew the Germans were looking for him; patrols had been all over the village. The young man was bleeding and needed help.

Please. My leg. American. Merci, merci.

High school French was little help, but the family at this house was compassionate. They looked into his eyes as he beseeched them, and they finally ushered him into the kitchen.

Madame Carlier placed bread, cheese and beer for him on the table.

Merci, said Bob, which was about as far as his vocabulary would go.

The children came to the kitchen.

Je suis Louis et c'est ma soeur, Yvonne.

The children smiled.

Their mother looked at the wound, brought iodine and poured it right onto Bob's leg through his torn flight suit.

Bob didn't feel a thing. They gave him a blanket and he sprawled on the floor of the kitchen, falling asleep in an instant. Yvonne and Louis peered around the door.

All night, the Germans swarmed through the area of Soignies and Silly, about forty miles southwest of Brussels, conducting house-to-house searches. The Carliers were justifiably frightened that they might be found harboring an Allied pilot, if that's what he was. Maybe he was a German spy. Just in case, old man Carlier, the children's grandfather, kept his blunderbuss trained on the wounded man all night from behind the kitchen door.

In the morning, Louis nudged Bob, who looked up.

Avec moi. Avec moi.

Louis brought him out to the road and a truck came along. Some men came around, hoisted Bob onto the back of the truck and drove him down the road. Bob was on the move for the next three nights. The Belgian farmers were able to alert one another when a German search patrol was approaching so they could hide Bob and shift him under darkness to a house that already had been searched. It appeared to be the only choice for now; at six feet two, he was taller than almost any Belgian, so they worried he would stand out. And even though he couldn't speak to them, he was ingratiating. Diffident, smiling, gently grateful to the people around him, he appeared to be what he said he was: a wounded pilot who needed help. Fortunately, it was not difficult to outsmart the Germans; it was dangerous, but there was a certain pleasure to it.

The arrangement would have been fine except for one thing: Bob had more and more trouble walking. His leg was swollen, and he was becoming feverish, even delirious at times. After a few days he could no longer stand up.

Lily, the Comet liaison in Brussels, received a report about the wounded pilot. A little boy had seen him parachute to the ground and had helped hide him in the hedgerows. The boy's father forbade him to provide any more help to the flier, fearful of reprisals by the Germans. The parachute had been retrieved and seemed authentic. It was already being cut up to make clothing and table linens. The helpers in the countryside needed medical help, and they needed to move the American before the Germans caught them all.

Even without an injured airman, the Comet Line was under considerable pressure and increasing risks, some fatal. The pace of gathering escapees was increasing. Besides this wounded man, a number of other men were waiting to be moved, both in Brussels and in outlying villages.

Just as British military intelligence had predicted, the increased Allied sorties over Europe were causing more casualties, and more men parachuting to the ground. That meant that the Comet Line would need to work fast.

At the same time, the Germans were stepping up their efforts to capture pilots and punish the people who helped them. In the past couple of months the Gestapo and Luftwaffe secret police had sent in English-speaking operatives to pose as Allied fliers. The Germans probably would not go to such lengths of disguise as to seriously injure the infiltrator, but it wasn't worth taking a chance. The resistance knew that German-Americans—some of whom spoke English with no accent—had gone back to Germany when the Nazis took power.

The Nazis were also infiltrating the escape organizations, posing as helpers but delivering members of the resistance and the pilots they were helping to their deaths. Not only was the loss of trusted operatives serious and tragic, but it also created a chilling effect among those who remained, as well as among the loose alliance of Belgians who were brave enough to rescue fliers when they came parachuting down in their fields. The German warning was clear—and had just been reiterated. On October 20, the day that Bob Grimes parachuted into Belgium, word came that eleven Comet resistance helpers had been caught and executed by the Germans in Brussels.

The news was reported in *Le Soir,* the collaborationist newspaper, with the warning that German authorities would deal the same way with anyone who dared to aid and abet escaping pilots.

There might have been a twelfth man executed that day, because these Comet operatives had been arrested in Brussels along with Dédée's old friend Nemo whom she'd seen one last time at the St. Gilles Prison in Brussels. But fate spared Nemo from the firing squad: he had died in an Allied bomb attack at Etterbeek, Belgium, about six weeks earlier, on September 7, 1943.

With this heightened threat, the organization had to be sure that this pilot was not some new low in the deceit of German agents and collaborators. But as they investigated the facts, the young pilot's story seemed to check out. A B-17 crashed near Quevaucamps on October 20. The Luftwaffe base at Chièvres reported that its Fw 190 fighters attacked the B-17 and watched it plummet to earth. Luftwaffe police and their dogs scoured the region and recovered the bodies of four men: one in a parachute that didn't open properly and three others who had been killed by enemy gunfire before the plane crashed—their bodies were found in the wreckage. The parachute of another American brought him down hard against the side of a house in Harchies and he didn't live long.

His tags bore the name Arthur Pickett—Bob's copilot. "He lived only a few minutes," said Madame Franz Lefebre, the president of the local Belgian Red Cross. "Just before he died, our priest put a cross within his hand by the shrine of the Crucified." Before the Gestapo could arrive, Madame Lefebre and her friend Maximilienne Style rescued Arthur Pickett's personal effects, "some letters from his home we found, his pilot's ring and then another ring and a pin, and his gold-capped fountain pen." They sent these items to his mother in Warren, Pennsylvania, along with a letter and something more. "Reverently, dear madame, as though you were standing there, we took from the head of the one you bore three locks of light brown hair."

Another flier, Theodore Kellers, was alive and also was hidden by Comet operatives. Both Kellers and Grimes were submitted to an extensive questionnaire, part of the difficult task of verifying that they were genuine escapees. Anyone failing the test was assumed to be a German plant. This was not a game; he would be taken for a long, one-way walk in the woods.

The list of questions was standard: home base, mission, details about English operations that a German should not know and cross-references with other specific information that they might receive.

When did you leave England?

On October 20, Grimes said.

He did not know that October 20 was the same day that eleven members of the escape line had been executed in Brussels.

Where do you fly from?

Snetterton Heath.

What is the number of your unit?

Eighth Air Force, 96th Bomb Group.

Everything checked out. Kellers and Grimes named each other and Pickett as part of the same flight crew. The existence of two airmen gave the group the chance to match one story against the other. Kellers said he was from Ohio and told them he was the flight engineer on Grimes's plane. He also seemed legitimate, but the final test was to observe the contact between the two.

First, they had to stabilize the wounded pilot. He was running a high fever and drifted in and out of delirium. His leg was now badly swollen; something had to be done. They could not amputate the leg, because that would mean almost certain detection by Nazi sympathizers and agents. Grimes would die before that happened.

Logistics to provide medical attention, however, were difficult and potentially just as deadly. The Germans had collaborators in the countryside capable of detecting any overt medical intervention. Hospitals were closely watched: Nazi bureaucrats monitored types of injuries, charts, medicines and procedures. There could be no surgery without the chance that someone would inform the Germans.

Two doctors came to see the pilot, but they suffered from lack of facilities. The first one poked at the hole in the young man's leg. Bob winced in pain, bit down on his pillow and gripped the bed.

He needs an operation. I can do nothing.

The next night another doctor came and also probed the wound. Bob held on tight and bit his pillow again to brace against the pain. He'd had enough. Neither doctor could find out what was wrong with his leg. It was now infected and swollen, and he was running a fever. The doctor left, promising to send a nurse to take care of him.

The nurse, Rolande Cruseau, brought a stock of sulfa powder and dollar-size pills, and ended up saving the pilot's leg and possibly even his life. She soaked the wound repeatedly and then applied the powder—and luckily, there was an immediate improvement: the swelling decreased, and his fever broke. Bob woke up on his fourth morning in Belgium to see a familiar face: his engineer, Ted Kellers.

Hello, Lieutenant.

Kellers, what about the rest of the crew? Bob asked.

I don't know.

Neither man had heard anything about their eight other mates. Most important for Grimes, Kellers eased his mind about the crash.

Do you know what happened to the plane?

Kellers didn't know where the plane had crashed. After he bailed out, he'd also been rescued by villagers and delivered to Comet. But the engineer was able to ease Bob's swirling worries about the mission.

When the Fw 190s attacked, they shot away most of the tail. It was a goner, Kellers told him.

He had seen the entire rudder break off in a solid piece and watched it flutter away from the plane. Bob was still worried about the rest of the men, but he realized there was no need to second-guess the flight that day. He'd been shot out of the sky.

Well, I did all I could to keep her flying, Bob said.

You can't fly a plane with its tail shot off, said Kellers.

The Comet helpers were satisfied by the conversation: the men were legitimate escapees. Their handlers were too nervous to make this a long visit. Kellers was escorted away. After that, the helpers kept Bob on the move to a series of hiding places. Finally, several mornings later, Bob was awakened in his bed at the home of the local parish priest.

Time to go, the priest said. Bob shifted around to get dressed. They'd given him some ill-fitting clothes, some pants that were short and tight, a torn shirt and some old shoes.

The priest and a young girl from the parish helped him down a flight of stairs. His leg was down to normal size. The sulfa powder and pills had worked, but his leg was still stiff and painful when he flexed it.

A bulbous 1936 Lincoln Zephyr was waiting for him by the church. Two smiling teenage boys were at the car. The priest kissed him on both cheeks.

Good luck. Au revoir.

One of the boys drove; the other helped Bob into the front seat and climbed in with him. Why should the three of them be in the front seat? He looked in the rear and saw slabs of beef sticking out from under a blanket. It was obviously contraband.

No problem, said the boy who was driving. He showed Bob his gun. That was hardly a comfort.

Automobile traffic was strictly watched at the entrances to Brussels. It was obvious that these underground operatives were well connected: they switched to a municipal van when they approached the city.

And when a German sentry stopped them and looked at Bob, they all smiled.

We were playing soccer, he hurt his leg, one of the Belgians said.

The German was not suspicious; his expression did not change as he waved them on.

They drove toward the center of the city, turned onto rue Marie-Christine, right off the streetcar line, and stopped at a row of town houses.

The boys patted Bob on the back and drove away.

An old woman with an angular face framed by short, dark hair answered the door at number 160 and led the pilot slowly up a flight of stairs. There was a foyer, then another door that opened to a two-room apartment.

Hélène Camusel was a middle-aged spinster active in the escape network. She was well prepared for short visits, but this was likely to be a longer stay. There would be a medical procedure, and the pilot would need to get back his strength before making the arduous trip to Spain.

Hello, Robert, said a girl who greeted the pilot after he hobbled up the stairs. She spoke a bit of English. *I am Lily*, she said. *Let us look at your leg.*

Lily was not what she seemed. She was a head and a half shorter than Bob, a pert, tiny, dark-haired girl wearing a blue jumper over a white blouse, white socks and patent leather shoes. She wore her hair short and had a quick smile. Bob had figured her to be twelve or thirteen years old, but he was wrong. She helped him to a chair, and then she helped him off with his trousers so that she could change the dressing on his wound. Despite her little-girl appearance, she was a twenty-two-year-old trained nurse.

Lily—her real name was Micheline Dumont—was already a veteran of the resistance group, even though she'd only been working with them full-time for a year. At the start of the war, her mother and father were doing what they could for the resistance, and her older sister, Nadine, was working with Dédée de Jongh while Lily was off at nursing school. In November 1942, the Germans swooped down on the rest of the Dumont family, dragging them off to St. Gilles Prison. Lily took the characteristically brazen step of going to visit them in jail. A guard told her to go away, saying she could not be a member of the Dumont family, because the whole family was already in jail.

She was distraught but could do nothing to help her parents and sister. She contacted Dédée and offered her services to the Comet Line. Soon she was in charge of logistics in Brussels, organizing safe houses, working with photographers to produce identity cards and, most important, leading airmen on their way from the countryside to the French border. She also continued her nursing duties by visiting the sick and wounded at clinics and hospitals around town.

The work wasn't easy, and there was always the lingering fear that the Nazis could catch her any minute. One day, it almost happened. A friend at one of the clinics alerted her that the Germans had tracked her down and were about to move in. Good fortune saved her that day, because the clinic had an outer fire escape with a crossover to a neighboring social services office, where she knew people she could trust.

Raymond, Raymond, I have to get out! she called to the next building.

Voilà, vite, vite. He rushed her to a side door as the Gestapo ran up the stairs of the adjacent building to arrest her.

After that she'd been underground, living in Hélène Camusel's flat on the rue Marie-Christine under her assumed name, complete with an identity card that said she was a sixteen-year-old student.

Every day she left the apartment in the morning and did her rounds. More airmen needed help all the time. She'd coordinate with the people receiving the pilots in the country, make sure there was transportation to Brussels, work out the schedule for moving the men from one safe house to another, gather up clothing, buy food and visit friends who were hiding other pilots to make sure they were safe. She carried money for expenses to the safe houses and delivered messages from one place to another about when to expect new arrivals of airmen. Lily saw so many pilots, she couldn't remember their names or faces. But Bob was a special case, because he was staying for a while. They became friends.

For operational security, Lily didn't tell Bob or anyone else where she was at any given time.

I don't want you to know anything if they catch you. It is better, she told him in halting English, which was a bit better than him trying to speak in French.

At night, she'd come back to Hélène Camusel's apartment.

How are you feeling? How is your leg? she asked Bob.

Not so bad, he replied. He wasn't one to complain.

Lily became Bob's best entertainment. He'd watch her come bounding up the street when he dared to sneak a peek out the window, risking reprimand for breaking security. Bob looked forward to her returning from work at some medical clinic or wherever it was she went. He had no idea that she was running the Brussels operation. All he knew was that she was with the underground, and she was protecting him. Beyond that, he wasn't supposed to ask questions. She was his only distraction. Bob and Lily would sit up laughing and finding a way around the language barrier to talk to each other long into the night, until Mademoiselle Camusel called Lily from the other room to say it was time for everyone to go to sleep.

Life in Brussels for Bob settled quickly into a routine—do nothing and wait. Hélène Camusel's second-floor apartment was tightly packed; the kitchen, which was also the sitting room, had a sofa-cot set up for Bob. It was just as well, because Bob couldn't move around very well. While his leg no longer was swollen, it was stiff, and he couldn't stand up for very long.

There was a closet filled with men's clothing in the bedroom where Lily and Mademoiselle Camusel slept. Bob found some shirts and a worn blue suit that fit him better than the temporary clothing he'd gotten from the farmers. He was confined to these two rooms and to the toilet, where he would shave his light beard several times a week.

There was a bathtub in a separate room off the outside foyer, but the Belgians considered it a nuisance to haul in hot water for baths. It almost never happened.

He couldn't go outside, couldn't make noise, couldn't go near the window—and couldn't speak French. His communication with Mademoiselle Camusel during the day was mostly hand signals—she spoke less English than his smattering of southern-accented, high school French.

Mademoiselle Camusel decided that French lessons would be a good way to pass the time, so she started with the basics, like: *I am a woman. You are a man. How are you?*

When Bob didn't understand something, she thought the remedy was to say it louder.

Je suis une femme. Vous êtes un homme.

Bob laughed.

Do you have paper and pencil? he asked. *We could make flash cards.*

She understood what he meant, but the answer to that was a firm *non!* It would be suspicious to leave signs that she was teaching him French.

He begged the two women for something to read, and someone gave them an old English magazine. Bob was eager to devour every word and was disappointed to find it was only a tattered old World War I relic with nothing to it. Other than that there were no newspapers— no news at all. The temptation to look out the window was unbearable; Bob had to force himself not to. Once in a while he did it anyway, hobbling around the periphery of the room on his gimpy leg back to the wall so he could peer at the outside world through half-open shades. There wasn't much to see: the kitchen window faced the rear of the town house. He saw the backs of other houses and the occasional person out there hanging clothes to dry. Several times a week, though, he'd recognize the sound of horse hooves on the street below. It was the beer man.

Il y a de la bière; il y a de la bière.

Mademoiselle Camusel trooped down the stairs with empty wire-top flasks, and Bob would sneak a peek past the curtain. The beer wagon was a horse-drawn carriage hauling an enormous, froth-splattered wooden keg. The beer man filled new bottles and snapped on the lids. Bob hopped away from the window and back to his cot before Mademoiselle Camusel came back up with the new supply. Bob developed a taste for Belgian brew; he imagined the beer man was confused by an old lady and a little girl consuming so much of his product.

They would sit in the kitchen when Lily came home, and Bob could polish off a mug. It was a perfect complement to their constant diet of bland boiled potatoes and unsavory hard bread, which was all that ration tickets could buy.

Within days of Bob's arrival in Brussels, Lily went to visit a doctor, Jean Rouffart, whom she'd met during her nursing training. He worked at a private clinic and could be trusted. She explained her problem.

A pilot is staying at the house. He has a wound, he'll never escape the way he is.

While Bob's wound no longer appeared to be infected, she was certain that an operation was needed; there still was the possibility of gangrene. Beyond the terrible prospect of losing the leg, there was a practical matter: an operation like that would be noticed, and they would all be arrested.

Rouffart looked at Lily. He was a sympathetic sort, and she was persuasive. Each man and woman had to make choices during the war. An amputee could not be expected to escape and was likely to be captured by the Germans.

I will see the pilot, Rouffart said. *I will stay for two minutes.* That afternoon, Bob could tell right away that something was up. She hadn't promised him the doctor, but he realized she was coming home with someone else. Either that or it was the Gestapo, because he recognized every sound he heard outside. With so little to do, his senses had become acute. Bob could hear the lock in the door downstairs. He could count the steps on the flight of stairs and noticed every detail of the sound of the inside door opening. He heard an extra set of footsteps and a male voice. In his linguistic isolation, Bob didn't have time to ask questions. He noted only that Mademoiselle Camusel was unperturbed.

The door opened; Lily walked in, smiling. Close behind, a properly dressed man entered the room, reached out, shook his hand and addressed him in English.

I am Rouffart.

Bob hadn't heard proper English spoken since he'd been with Kellers back in the countryside—not that Rouffart was in the mood for a chat.

Bob lay down on his cot and Rouffart examined the leg, explaining in few words his ability to communicate.

I went to school in England.

He palpated the area of the wound, noting it was no longer infected.

I believe I can help you, he said. In all probability a piece of shrapnel was lodged elsewhere in the leg.

The shrapnel has traversed the muscle and it's near the bone, the doctor said. *I can take it out, but I can't hospitalize you.*

There were informers everywhere. Emergency surgery using anesthetic and sutures would be detected. Normally a patient would stay overnight in the hospital, but they could not trust the other doctors, nurses and aides at the clinic. Even if they were not collaborators outright, the prospect of not reporting unusual activity—perhaps a planted test of loyalty by the Germans—created the possibility of informers.

We will say that you have a sore throat. It will have to be fast. And you will have to leave on your own feet.

Rouffart left quickly just as he said he would. He shook Bob's hand, nodded to Lily and was down the stairs.

Two days later, just after dark, Rouffart came back and with Lily helped the pilot down the stairs to his car. They drove across town to the clinic at the Place des Barricades; Bob adjusted a scarf around his neck to feign laryngitis if questions were asked. The clinic was empty, but there was always the chance that another doctor or nurse might stop by unexpectedly.

The doctor was punctilious. He explained everything to Bob while he prepped for the procedure. First, he said, they would use a fluoroscope to locate the shrapnel. *We will find the object and then we will remove it. Please, stand against the screen.*

The fluoroscope cast X-rays from a roentgen lamp against one side of the leg and projected an image on a screen. Because radiation is blocked more effectively by dense material, images projecting bone— and shrapnel—would be clearly visible.

Rouffart saw the distinct shadow of a splayed, capsule-shaped object lodged at the femur. The doctor marked the least invasive point for entering the area, turned off the glowing lamp and led the pilot to his treatment table.

There is only a light dose of chloroform, the doctor said. *And I can put a little ethyl chloride on the skin so it does not feel so bad.*

Rouffart gave him a towel to clamp down on with his teeth as the operation proceeded. But for the rest, the doctor could only promise he'd be as quick and efficient as possible.

Rouffart signaled that he was ready. Bob bit down hard on the towel and tensed his arms, grasping the sides of the examination table, holding on so he wouldn't fall off. He felt like he was in a John Wayne cowboy movie.

The doctor had made a mark on the inside of Bob's left leg, on the opposite side from where the bullet entered. Just as the cutting appeared to be moving toward an unbearable threshold of pain, Rouffart reached with a small set of forceps into the narrow incision he'd made. He plucked out the bullet. It clanked into a nearby pan.

"It feels like part of the engine of the plane just fell out," Bob said, opening his eyes and relaxing his muscles.

Lily thought he'd been brave, but Bob had been expecting something far more painful—this wasn't nearly as bad as when the country doctors stuck their probes into his infected wound.

Rouffart poured Bob a stiff shot of cognac. His own nerves were steady. They placed a sterile bandage over the small incision. In five minutes they helped Bob slide on his pants. Bob hobbled to his feet, supported by the others, but walked under his own power, trying not to wobble from the effects of the cognac and chloroform.

Rouffart drove them back to Mademoiselle Camusel's place, speaking very little.

Rest your leg and come back to visit in a few days.

They said good-bye, and Rouffart drove away.

Bob leaned heavily on Lily as they walked back up to the apartment.

It's not so bad, he said, easing himself back to his daybed in the kitchen. Life was looking up: no more operations.

Bob smelled a potato stew cooking on the stove. He would drink an extra beer with dinner. He drifted into a deep sleep. In his hand he grasped a dull piece of metal that Lily had rinsed off and given him. It was a two-inch fragment of a 13-millimeter shell, crushed and jagged on the broken tip, a smooth shaft and the lip of the bullet head with a patina of gray. He'd abandoned his dog tags, his watch and all his belongings but decided to keep the bullet as a souvenir of these days— so he could tell everyone about the time he eluded the Nazis and escaped with his life.

Anne Brusselmans, who spoke English and worked with Lily on the Brussels operation, said she could get some supplies from the pharmacy.

"I need bandages, iodine, cotton wool, ether and sterilized lint," she told her druggist, hoping he would not betray her. The pharmacist reacted warmly.

"There will be no charge, Madame," he said. "Come back if there is anything else you need."

Lily stopped by to pick up the supplies. She kept changing the bandages on Bob's leg. The new wound was healing well, and there was no fever.

It was early November now. The fall was dull and rainy, but for Bob it was spring, because he was getting the chance to go out of doors for the first time in weeks.

We must walk, Lily told him. *You must be ready to walk.*

Fine with him. Every night, when Lily came home, they'd go out on the street. At first, they walked around the block, and Bob was unable to go farther. But the walks were a bit longer each time, until Lily had made sure he was strong enough to climb mountains. He was thrilled that he no longer would be a prisoner of Mademoiselle Camusel's apartment.

Lily was determined to take every possible measure to protect him.

First, you will need new papers.

Bob showed her that he still had the ID photos that came along in his escape kit.

Not good, said Lily. *Too British.* They threw them away. The rescuers had found that the Germans sometimes tested photo paper to determine its country of origin.

Together, they rode the tram to have a new photo ID produced by a resistance helper in town. Along the way, they stopped at the Hôtel Métropole on the Place de Brouckère. The building was splendid, even in wartime. There were fragrant flowers and a classical décor of columns and balustrades of ornately carved wood. Bob, dressed in his hand-me-down clothes, felt out of place.

Their budget was limited, so while others sipped beer, Bob and Lily sat for a while, drinking lemonades. They sat awkwardly, not daring to risk speaking to each other in public. Bob was mute when Lily asked for the bill.

Soon Bob had a new identity card; he was Robert Louis Van Tighem, a twenty-four-year-old from Roulers.

At home, Lily went through everything in his possession that might be incriminating. They'd found him Belgian undershorts, because she'd heard of Germans stripping open men's shirts or pants on the street to reveal foreign-made undergarments.

Next, keep your hands out of your pockets. They had seen Americans jangling coins as they walked on the street. *No European does that, it is very American. And keep your hat on, it makes you look more Belgian.*

Luckily, Bob didn't smoke. Americans remove their cigarettes with a side-armed motion, which would cause suspicion—Europeans use an underhanded flair to smoke.

It was the same thing with eating in public. She coached him in the use of silverware.

You Americans cross over with your knives and forks when you eat. It's not European. Cut the food and don't switch the knife.

Mademoiselle Camusel woke up first every morning to prepare that awful-tasting ersatz coffee, along with chunks of bread and some oily butter. Lily came out of the bedroom wearing her little-girl clothes. There wasn't much food, and Bob always felt that Lily was leaving most of her portion so he'd have a bit more nourishment. After breakfast, Lily bounced down the stairs and off toward the tram.

The old lady retired to knitting in her easy chair and started repeating words for Bob to follow.

It was mostly a monologue.

Vous êtes un bon élève. You are a good student.

Je suis un bon élève. I am a good student.

Que-ce que c'est?

C'est une fourchette. It's a fork.

She'd be correcting his accent, never stopping talking. Bob wasn't sure if he was learning a thing.

And then Lily came home. Every evening, they'd go farther and farther away from the apartment. Lily would take him to the tram stop. They'd ride the tram to the end of the line and walk back. Or they'd saunter along for a while, and take a different tram line. They varied routes and times, seeking to avoid suspicion. They could be, well, an older brother and a younger sister. She always wore those little-girl clothes.

The trams were unlike American streetcars that Bob had seen. They had open compartments and passengers sat face-to-face. There was an outer platform separated by glass windows and a door on either side of the tram, and passengers could stand out there or hang from the side of the car.

Bob and Lily made an agreement on how to travel about.

We sit separately on the streetcars. You do not know me. It is too dangerous, she told him.

And if I get caught, act like you don't know me. Just keep moving, Bob replied.

Public transport was subject to German identity checks; if the Nazis stopped Bob, he would offer his papers mutely and hope for the best. It would do nothing for either of them to be caught with the other. He would watch for signals from her and get off the streetcar when she did. It sounded logical, except for the human factor. Bob was naturally protective of Lily and wondered if he could just stand there if she were being led away by the Nazis.

Lily faced far greater danger if she was captured helping an American. They both talked about operational security, but they both violated the rules. She stayed close by him, hoping she could intercede to untangle a sudden question in French that he would certainly not be able to answer.

In town, meanwhile, they often walked hand in hand. They avoided talking in public and were especially quiet on the streetcars. They mingled with Nazi officers and enlisted men who hung out the open doors of the always crowded trolleys. As they bumped and bounded down the line, Bob never got used to jostling with the Germans. "What would they think if they knew who it is they're bumping into?" He could hardly have said a word to the Germans, certainly not in German, and in French only at his peril. But the Belgians had adopted a pose of ignoring *les Boches,* as the Belgians and French called the Germans, grunting and speaking only when spoken to directly—and then only in monosyllables. Bob was as able as anyone to appear to be ignoring the Germans, or to answer them with a curt "Oui" or "Non."

Bob and Lily walked along so peacefully that at times they felt immune to the dangers of the war around them. Capture by the Nazis seemed distant. There was a commonplace, monotonous aspect to life in Brussels. The city was a drab, dark brown and lifeless in autumn, the melancholy of occupation accentuated by the falling leaves and the oncoming cold. Many people had abandoned the city for the country-side when the Nazis swept through Belgium in 1940. Those who remained seemed stiff and mechanical as they walked along streets devoid of color.

Lily and Bob rarely discussed family or work. They chatted about food, how the streetcars worked, money, and the details of everyday life in Belgium. Bob asked abundant questions about speaking French, always trying to expand his knowledge. Occasionally, Bob and Lily went out walking during the day. As they walked, they'd hear sometimes the drone of airplanes, American bombers by day and British planes at night. Bob knew by the time of day whether his comrades were heading to or from a mission. This was very distant contact with the war—indeed, almost the only way he knew anything about the world. Unlike London, there were no air raid sirens in Brussels. Only once during his six weeks in the Belgian capital did he hear what appeared to be the sound of explosions. There were factories on the outskirts of town, but he couldn't tell whether the sound was an Allied attack or some other sign of the far-off war.

If there was music on the radio, there was no war news; listening to the real news, BBC in French, let alone English, was a crime. It was too risky to chance that someone might overhear them tuning in to a prohibited station on the wireless.

Several weeks later, Bob let slip out that November 24 was his twenty-first birthday. He had been in Belgium recuperating from his wounds for a little over a month and it was the day before Thanksgiving back in the United States. Not only back home, but also anywhere that Americans were found, turkeys were being prepared. At Snetterton Heath, Bob's old base in England, the chefs also scrambled to offer up turkey or something resembling it, a taste of home in wartime. Someone from the adjutant's office had already been around to the Quonset hut where Bob had bunked, picking up his things. He and his crew were listed as missing in action.

Let's have a party, Lily said.

She contacted her friends, Hermine and Jeanne Biard. The families were close before the war, and now the girls were also helping provide shelter for pilots. After their usual stroll, Lily took Bob far across town. He wasn't exactly sure where they were going and hadn't understood the part about the party.

But after a change of trolleys, Lily led him walking with determination. She always seemed to know where she was going.

Hermine and Jeanne were waiting.

Happy birthday, Bob.

"Imagine this," the Biard girls said. "One would think the sky was falling. We have a man visiting us at our house." And he was a good-looking man at that.

Does the American know how to speak French?

He's getting better at it, said Lily.

They sat down for a drink—some beer and a good bottle of wine.

Bob smiled affably and was surprised at the good food. The girls had a small grocery store, which enabled them to get around rationing restrictions. It also meant they were useful in providing a little extra food for the safe houses. Considering the times, Lily's friends had prepared a feast. Bob still fought his instinct to eat as much as his healthy appetite could have handled. He knew about rationing and shortages, realizing that whatever he ate was taking food from someone else's plate. He ate sparingly, the same way he behaved at the home of Mademoiselle Camusel, who in her motherly way nevertheless encouraged him to take heartier portions.

Hermine and Jeanne are friends of my family, Lily explained. *My father and their father are also friends.*

Lily hadn't often mentioned her father, who was under arrest and missing. He didn't know what to say.

The food is good, very good. Thank you.

It wasn't turkey—Bob didn't think they had turkey in Belgium—but it was good meat, more than they'd had for a while. The meal was topped off by birthday cake and coffee.

Bob's French was improving, but not so much so that he could clearly understand what the girls were saying, nor even their names and their relationship to Lily—not that it mattered. And if there was a birthday wish, Bob hadn't understood. But everyone had the same wish, a variation on the theme, that they all be safe and that the Germans would soon be defeated.

The party broke up early so that Bob and Lily could race back to Mademoiselle Camusel's ahead of the 10:30 P.M. curfew. Bob thanked Hermine and Jeanne the best he could.

Isn't it dangerous to travel around so close to curfew? The Germans are everywhere.

We'll be fine, said Lily.

Hermine and Jeanne were still twittering about having such a handsome guest.

Well, the pilot communicates well enough, as long as he keeps his mouth shut when strangers are around.

Don't worry.

Alors, bon anniversaire, the girls said, kissing him on both cheeks as Lily and Bob rushed out the door.

They scurried back to the streetcar line, avoiding crowds of Germans who were standing around until the tram arrived. They jumped aboard; but just as the conductor came around to collect tickets, a platoon of German soldiers surrounded the tram and ordered everyone out for an identity check.

Cartes d'identité, s'il vous plaît. Identité.

It was never clear who they were looking for. There were both uniformed soldiers and men in plainclothes lingering in the shadows. Bob figured they were looking for deserters and people from the underground—and escaped pilots, just like him.

Bob and Lily didn't even have a chance to look at each other as they hustled to the sidewalk. But Lily was keeping an eye on him. As their sergeant stood by, three soldiers perused papers and patted down each passenger in the drab line of people hunched over, waiting to go home. As Bob stood to be searched, he palmed one bit of incriminating evidence—he hid his lucky bullet fragment in the crook of his raised right thumb and index finger, and they never saw it in the dark. He handed over his papers and was searched without incident. No one spoke as he followed the sullen file of passengers reboarding the tram. Suddenly, one of the soldiers poked a rifle in his ribs.

Avez-vous montré vos documents? asked the soldier. *Have you shown us your documents?*

Bob's stomach dropped and his mind churned at the speed of light until he realized that he understood the question.

Oui, oui, he replied. The soldier nodded, letting him pass.

He reboarded the tram, and it went on its way. Lily sat down next to him; the danger had passed. But all the while, she'd been too close. It was not what they had agreed to.

You should have moved away, why did you do that? He whispered. *They could kill you.*

She looked up at him.

I was worried that they were going to ask you something. I thought you would need help.

They weren't supposed to be talking on the tram, even in a whisper.

But I was worried about you too.

Not long after that, the illusion of safety and the remoteness of the occupation came crashing down. The Gestapo picked up Jane Macintosh, one of Lily's helpers—and Lily had just given her Mademoiselle Camusel's address. Jane was a British girl, one of those unfortunate souls who had been caught on the Continent in 1940 during the Nazi invasion. She had been visiting relatives on holiday, and now she was stranded for the duration of the war. Lily's address was in her coat pocket and Lily had to assume that the Nazis would find it. Despite all the precautions, Hélène Camusel's house was no longer safe.

Bob was waiting for Lily as always, with little to do except wait for the beer man and practice French with Mademoiselle Camusel. He was improving, but Mademoiselle Camusel continued to repeat words louder when he didn't understand something.

Lily stepped off the closest tram stop and turned onto the rue Marie-Christine. She had taken a circuitous route in case she was being followed, putting on an air of being nonchalant and not in a hurry. In reality, she'd never before been so worried.

Bob heard her walk up the stairs.

We have to move.

Lily began speaking rapidly to Mademoiselle Camusel.

We're not safe. Jane had the address. We have to leave right away.

Not at all, Mademoiselle Camusel said. *The Nazis won't come here.*

Mademoiselle Camusel refused to leave, but Lily took no chances. They cleaned up the apartment and left with the clothes they were wearing, nothing more. There was a hug from Mademoiselle Camusel and a half-understood wish for Bob's safety from this brave woman whom he didn't know how to thank adequately.

Bonne chance, she said, kissing him on both cheeks.

Merci, merci beaucoup.

Keep studying your French, she told him.

Lily and Bob went first to Jeanne and Hermine Biard's house, their hosts for the birthday party. The girls were happy to have the pilot with them again, but soon Lily found another flat across town on the chaussée Saint-Pierre.

Again, Lily and Bob were worried about each other's safety. Lily thought it would be more secure for him to hide out with her two friends, who were not nearly as active in the underground. Bob said no.

If you are in danger, I'm going with you.

This could be a bigger risk for you, she told him.

Bob said he didn't care.

I will stay with you until I leave.

Lily didn't protest too much. She thought it was a gesture of courage, characteristic of this solid, decent American. The new location, she promised, was clean and above suspicion. But the change was very isolating. She was away long hours, shopping and running errands and doing whatever else it was that she did. Bob mostly avoided going out during the day. There was nothing to read, nothing to see, no stimulation at all until she returned at night. On one round of errands, she brought home a supply of butter. To relieve his boredom, Bob decided to surprise her with a batch of down-home mashed potatoes.

He was trying to remember how his mother did it back home. He boiled some water, tossed in the potatoes until they were tender, peeled off most of the skin and then mixed the cooked potatoes with a large slather of butter that he found in the icebox.

The aroma settled throughout the apartment, as if it could re-create the fragrance of the kitchen back home in Cradock.

I cooked for us.

All the butter was all she said.

The culinary effort put Lily in a foul mood—he'd inadvertently used a precious month's ration of butter on a single meal. Bob was dismayed at his own mistake; he hated to impose or cause trouble.

A few days after Bob and Lily left, the Gestapo arrested Hélène Camusel and took her to St. Gilles Prison. Lily had been right; they'd tracked them down through the address in Jane's pocket. But the resistance had cleaned out the incriminating evidence. So when the Germans searched Mademoiselle Camusel's two-room apartment, there was nothing unusual: no daybed in the kitchen, no men's clothes in the closet, no shaving brush and no medical supplies. She persuaded the Gestapo that she was just a poor, perhaps eccentric, even crazy old spinster who had an occasional visit from the beer man. They released her, but her apartment was no longer useful to the Comet Line.

As Christmas 1943 approached, there was little to celebrate. The evening walks and the occasional gatherings with Lily's friends continued for a while as Belgium faced a fourth cold and joyless year under German occupation. On the strolls with Lily, Bob remarked that the frequency of bombers overhead was increasing; he hoped the boys were hitting the Germans hard and often.

———

Bob and Lily made one last visit to Dr. Rouffart's clinic. As always, they avoided the most direct route, worried that someone might be tailing them. It was a treat to visit Rouffart, because he spoke fluent English and he was a man.

The leg is healing well.

It feels strong. We walk every day.

I think you're fine now. Good luck to you.

Bob took the doctor's visit as confirmation that he was ready to move. There'd been no conversation about Bob's future. Indeed, he was under no pressure to leave. Lily avoided the subject; both of them knew that some airmen opted to ride out the war undercover in Belgium and France. But staying put wasn't in Bob's makeup. He heard the bombers and knew where he belonged.

Bob waited for a meeting with Madame Brusselmans, the helper who had gotten medical supplies from her pharmacist after his operation. They met at a café, and he was able to discuss his predicament in full English sentences. Madame Brusselmans also had been educated in England.

I don't want to cause any trouble, and the hospitality is great, but I'm ready to move.

Is your leg all right?

Oh, yes, I think it is, thanks to Lily. I don't want to give anyone the wrong impression about the hospitality, but I've been here six weeks and it's time for me to get going. I'm a pilot and I have to get back.

All right, then.

The strolls with Lily continued a few more days. Any break from the routine was enjoyable. Once, Bob was delighted to go with Lily to the market. The staple items weren't very good. Potatoes were sold singly; so were eggs. The bread was becoming blacker and blacker, more like cardboard than wheat. Coffee was a rarity, and when they got it, it was mostly some kind of a grain mixture that looked and tasted like muddy water.

About a week after his talk with Madame Brusselmans, Lily came up the stairs and spoke without expression. *You're leaving tomorrow.* Bob figured that Madame Brusselmans had explained his mixed emotions about wanting to get back to the war. They didn't discuss any of the details, just that he'd be leaving from the train station.

The next morning was bright with a bit of winter chill. Lily and Bob walked without speaking to the tram stop and waited for the line that would take them to the Midi-Zuid Station downtown; it was the start of Bob's hazardous trek down the line toward Spain. There were final instructions.

My friend Marie will take you. You can trust her. You will travel for an hour to the border. And then you go to France.

Bob kept silent as usual for fear that someone would hear his English words.

At the station, he wrapped her in a bear hug and gave her a kiss. She looked up at Bob, admiring the strength and plain decency she saw in him.

What could he say? Thank you, Lily? Was that sufficient? She'd saved his life.

Lily was also thinking of what to say. *One becomes more attached to some than others,* she thought. She was thankful for the strength of character that Bob showed all their time together. All that and he was just twenty-one years old. How could she communicate that to him? So she shrugged and said nothing, nodding to the woman standing nearby who would guide Bob on the next leg of his journey out of the Nazi-occupied territories.

That is Marie.

When he turned a second time, Lily was walking away, out of the station, and Bob felt alone once more.

CHAPTER SIX

Intrigue and Mist

San Sebastián, Spain. October 1943.

Xirimiri (SHE' REE MEE' REE), Euskera, noun. Also, Spanish, siri-
miri; 1. a persistent mist of rain.

Throughout the fall of 1943 the Nazis were pressuring harder than
ever for Francisco Franco and his government to fulfill the debt
owed Hitler for help in defeating the Spanish Republic and winning
the Spanish civil war. And the United States and Britain were pressing just as hard for Spain to guarantee its neutrality in the war. San
Sebastián, so close to the fighting and still recovering from the civil
war, had become a center of espionage and rumors, a crossroads for
diplomacy and a convenient stopover to and from occupied Nazi territory. The atmosphere of intrigue was as thick as the persistent misty
rain that the people of the Basque country called *xirimiri*.

If the xirimiri were to dampen the heart and spirit of the Basque
country, there would be no life at all. Xirimiri tumbled upon Basque
fishing villages, mountains, and cities—a never-ending drizzle from

the heavens that bathed the countryside, resulting in green fields and moss. First the clouds appeared over the horizon, then the wind churned up the Bay of Biscay and the waves came crashing to shore. Even the heat of summer was deadened by a cool fog that had no season. Light was extinguished, and every sound turned to an echoed grayness that could not pierce the mist. The xirimiri was confounding and before one realized it—though it seemed hardly to be raining at all—everything was soaked.

The xirimiri was falling as Jean-François walked into San Sebastián. His wool jacket was becoming waterlogged by the unrelenting mist. He would not attract attention as he crossed down from the outskirts toward the city for his rendezvous with Michael Creswell. Crossing the bridge over the narrow tidal river that borders the center of town, he saw a low skyline of French-inspired architecture, the tree-lined avenues of Paseo de Los Fueros and Paseo de Francia on the Río Urumea, with tile-roofed apartment buildings as a backdrop—France as it would be if France were free, if there were no German occupation. Of course, neither San Sebastián nor anywhere else in Spain was really free. Here there was the memory of a deadly civil war, and its proximity to a world war made the scene somber in the gray morning.

In the Parte Vieja, the old city of San Sebastián, the xirimiri made the stones of the Plaza de la Constitucíon slick and glimmering. Children chased mangy dogs and pigeons, just missing the feet of the Guardia Civil, who walked in pairs, hands behind their backs, in their ostentatious green uniforms and shiny, black triangular caps, an occupying force in the Basque country.

Jean-François walked into the basilica of Santa Maria; there was not a church anywhere that did not attract his devotion. He made his way to the altar, which was part of a process of centering his energy and his commitment. He remembered talking about his faith less than a year earlier, when he had spent Christmas 1942 with Dédée in San Sebastián.

Will you go with me to midnight Mass? he had asked her.

No. I'd like to, she'd told Jean-François. *I cannot, I don't believe. You go along. I'd like to believe, but I just don't.*

So he'd gone alone to Christmas Mass at the Catedral del Buen Pastor, the Good Shepherd Cathedral, one of two major churches in San Sebastián, which stood face-to-face about a mile apart on the central axis of the city. This was the other, in the shadow of Monte Urgull, in the heart of the old city.

No matter about Dédée's beliefs. To him she was the most devout, most spiritual nonbeliever he had ever met. Then, as now, he knelt at the altar and prayed for peace. He prayed that Dédée, her father and their dozens of allies would survive the imprisonment and torture of their Nazi captors. And he prayed that he could continue his resistance by sending many more Allied soldiers back to battle the Third Reich until the evil propagated by the Nazis existed no more.

Jean-François walked on after leaving the cathedral. The mist was still in the air; it never stopped. Xirimiri would outlast both the Nazis and the occupation of the Basque country—it was the rule, not the exception. The citizenry sat in the vast arcades that surrounded the town square, sipping coffee and extracting scant bits of information from their ragged newspapers.

San Sebastián had been spared the fire and bombing of other Spanish cities during the civil war. Basque nationalist fighters had repelled an onslaught by anarchist fighters who wanted to torch the beautiful old city. The fight came within a block of the beach, but the anarchists were repulsed. Eventually, San Sebastián fell to Franco's forces on September 13, 1936, and half of the city's 80,000 inhabitants fled. Franco's forces executed at least 3,000 of those who remained—and tens of thousands more in the entire Basque country and throughout Spain. Sixty years later there would still be unsettled claims, inquiries and searches for mass graves.

The Germans had helped Franco win the civil war, and they used the Spanish countryside as a testing ground for their modern weaponry. Infamous among the attacks was the daylight German bombing of Guernica, the town between San Sebastián and Bilbao that is the heart of the Basque nationhood. The laws of the Basque country, *los fueros*, were promulgated under an ancient oak in Guernica; a peace treaty held that the kings of Spain would swear in perpetuity their respect for Basque laws and independence.

Waves of planes from the Nazi Condor Legion converted the market day afternoon of April 26, 1937, into an inferno. The scorched-earth bombing leveled the city of 7,000 inhabitants, killing an estimated 1,658 people and wounding 889. Franco orchestrated the attack as a frontal and highly symbolic assault on the Basques. For the Germans, it was target practice and an early exercise in aerial bombardment for the coming world war. In his perverse cynicism, Franco contended for decades that it was not the Nazis but the Basques who dynamited their own city. That would not explain why the Condors received plaudits and decorations on their return home. Hitler contended that Franco owed the Third Reich mightily for engineering his victory, set the figure of German aid during the civil war at $200 million and expected the debt to be paid.

Part of the repayment was to let the Germans operate along the border, to provide supplies and ammunition to the German army and to allow German soldiers to take their rest and recreation on the Spanish side of the border. Franco and most of his military command were unabashedly pro-Nazi. As a result, German soldiers were everywhere.

Always lurking behind protests of Spanish neutrality was the Nazi presence. A few blocks from the beach where Jean-François walked was an undistinguished building at Calle Prim, 21. It was in the basement of this building, ceded to them by the Spanish government, that the Gestapo interrogated and threatened Spanish citizens and foreigners.

And just as often the Gestapo ran roughshod, operating right out of Guardia Civil headquarters. German business used easily detected fronts to ship legally and, when pressured, to smuggle war materials from the Basque industrial center of Bilbao through San Sebastián into France and beyond to Germany. Spain was feeding and supporting the Nazis. Under military law, the Guardia Civil could accost anyone on the street and demand identification. As in occupied Europe, Spanish citizens were required to carry domestic passports and travel documents that showed they were authorized to leave their home cities. The Comet Line produced forged documents for Jean-François and their other members so they could circulate without problem.

The Bay of Biscay was a logical center for commerce and espionage. For centuries the narrow coastal plain between the ocean and the foothills of the Pyrenees had been the best connection between southern and northern Europe. It was also a prime spot for spying and illicit transits. Mata Hari had passed through San Sebastián and into Hendaye during World War I. Kim Philby, who covered the Spanish civil war for the *Times* of London, often passed through San Sebastián and met with friends just over the border near the Hendaye train station. Philby cultivated a reputation in the 1930s as a conservative and perhaps even a Nazi sympathizer. Who would have thought that his soirees in Hendaye were to meet with his KGB handlers, reporting back to Moscow on the latest troop movements?

Unusual diplomatic events were taking place this day in San Sebastián. Gleaming Mercedes-Benz and Bavarian Motor Works automobiles pulled up along the corniche, fetching and discharging German and Spanish envoys at the regal entrance to the Hotel María Cristina. Ongoing negotiations concerned Nazi insistence that the Spanish step up and expand supplies of raw materials to the Third Reich. German officials from Berlin were there; so were embassy officials from Madrid. The German envoys told the Spanish foreign minister, Count Jordana, that Spain's help in defeating the Allies was taking a central role in the future of Europe. Spain would have a prominent role in Europe under the Reich. But the Nazis also reminded him that there was the practical matter of repaying the $200 million debt they calculated Spain still owed Germany.

As San Sebastián woke up, people ambled onto the streets, looking for meager rations or buying the local newspaper, *Diario Vasco*, for 25 centimes, and perhaps poor quality cigarettes, which could be bought at a kiosk or tobacco shop and were sometimes sold one by one. When there were no cigarettes or no money, men could be seen scavenging the trash and the gutters, looking for half-smoked butts.

On the day that Jean-François came to San Sebastián, the newspaper ran four pages and reading it was a chore, in part because of the absurd daily elegies to Spain's exalted leader. Besides its pro-Axis slant and its emphasis on puffery about Franco and his commanders, *Diario Vasco* made do with poor quality newsprint that sometimes did not feed properly into the printing press; the result was an elongated, unclear typeface that in many ways was appropriate to the distortion of the news. There was no free press in Spain under Franco.

The front page of the newspaper reported the week-old bombing of Schweinfurt by Bob Grimes's colleagues of the Eighth Air Force. From Washington, the U.S. Secretary of War, Henry L. Stimson, acknowledged that 600 airmen were missing after the bombing. "He added that photos obtained after the operation show that the majority of the factories were destroyed." He issued a warning about respecting the rules of the Geneva Convention. "We cannot permit losses of 600 valiant soldiers and we hope that we find them safe and sound, even if they are in enemy hands."

Jean-François knew that with such losses, more and more Allied airmen would be in need of assistance. The coming months would be crucial.

Meanwhile, the invasion of Italy was going so well for the Allies that even Spanish cheerleaders in the editorial offices and government information ministry could not disguise their enthusiasm. The American army was engaged in Italy and the Germans were desperately trying to hold the line. The newspaper reported the opening of the Battle of Rome on October 16. "The Allies are converging on the Italian capital from the north and the south," the paper reported.

This was the scene in San Sebastián on October 20, 1943, as Jean-François prepared for his trip south to Gibraltar. *Diario Vasco*, in its gossip column, "Xirimiri," offered a sprinkling of local society news. The newspaper also gave the latest film reviews and advertisements. *Suspicion*, with Cary Grant and Joan Fontaine, was playing at the Kursaal. There was a Boris Karloff movie at the Príncipe. The Victoria Eugenia was playing *Terror-GSU*, an anti-Soviet propaganda film by the German director Karl Ritter. As the most prestigious theater in town, the Victoria Eugenia often was forced to run films by directors like Ritter and his colleague Leni Riefenstahl, whose job it was to produce movies that extolled the virtue of the Nazi cause.

Most provocative for the xirimiri on the street was the report that the warriors of the touted Blue Division—the 17,924-member Spanish volunteer force fighting in Russia on the Nazi side—were returning home. Heroic parades were planned, though the truth of what happened did not warrant a parade.

Franco was an opportunist. But despite the inclination to support Hitler and the Nazis, he also was a pragmatist—or at least his advisers were. Spain needed foodstuffs and fuel to maintain control of the country. As the fortunes of the European war began to wane for the Nazis in 1943, Franco continued to pay lip service to Hitler, but he also began to realize that the thousand-year Reich might not survive. In many ways, he was hedging his bets all along, trying not to antagonize either side too much.

Accordingly, Spain and Germany agreed in early October to disband the Blue Division, officially designated as the Wehrmacht 250 Infantry Division. In its twenty-seven months in the field, about 45,000 volunteers fought in this Spanish force, none of them conscripts. The fighters were rotated in and out of battle so that anyone dying to serve the Führer would have an even chance of doing so. About 4,500 Spaniards were killed in action, and an estimated 16,000 were listed as wounded or taken prisoner.

Jean-François always felt a relief when he arrived in Spain and compared the occasional security problems in San Sebastián to the dangers of operating directly under the Nazi yoke. But the more time one spent in Spain, the more obvious it was that Franco maintained his own brand of repression.

Life in San Sebastián was a question of survival—physical and otherwise. Marisa Ferrer, a seventeen-year-old girl, got in trouble while hiding in a doorway one day when a crowd gathered to hear the city orchestra strike up patriotic tunes on the square in front of city hall. When the music ended, a policeman spotted her standing at a distance and arrested her for what one could call a lack of demonstrated patriotism: she failed to give the Fascist salute and to shout the obligatory "Long Live Spain." Fortunately, Marisa was able to get word to her mother through a friend, who ran to the Ferrer house near the Plaza de Guipuzcoa. Family connections got her out quickly.

The presence of the Germans was always visible. All week, German staff cars were lined up for an official function at the Hotel María Cristina. The Nazi officers were resplendent, if absurd, in their uniforms as they greeted their Spanish counterparts. How well the German and Spanish generals got along! It was rumored that Heinrich Himmler had come to town recently. Admiral Canaris, the head of German military intelligence, also visited from time to time.

135

If there was a general air of repression and danger in San Sebastián, the feeling of domination increased markedly once or twice a year. Franco had adopted the city as his own. Although his home was in Galicia far to the west, Franco sailed to San Sebastián in his private yacht, the *Azor,* and took up residence in the grand Ayete Palace, inland from Ondarreta beach, during the summer and whenever else he could. Agustín Lacort, who lived down the beach from Ayete on the Calle de Zubieta, could see the yacht sail into the harbor. He was disgusted when he saw the crew training boats in the bay, which were obliged to row out and raise their oars in unison to salute Franco. "The King himself never had anything like this," he snorted.

Franco, this limp little man who personally signed every execution order over coffee and breakfast toast, did indeed script his arrival just as if he were the successor to King Alfonso XIII, entering the city with his fawning entourage. When he arrived, hundreds of soldiers cordoned off the streets; when Franco went to Mass in the old city, sharpshooters stood with rifles drawn on the rooftops, and residents on the Calle Mayor were ordered to close their shutters.

Actually, security fears were greatly reduced when the dictator came to town. Joseba Salegui, a Basque nationalist who was imprisoned after Franco's victory, survived a Spanish concentration camp, escaping a death sentence. He told friends that it was easy to monitor when Franco planned to visit San Sebastián. In preparation for the Caudillo's arrival, the city always ordered workers to transfer the swans from the pond at the Plaza de Guipuzcoa to the Ayete Palace, so that Franco and his wife would have a more pleasant view from their window. The crating up of the swans became a signal for antigovernment militants to go into hiding. With Franco's arrival, the Guardia Civil always rounded up as many known opponents to the regime as they could, along with those who had been held in Spanish concentration camps immediately after the civil war. When Franco left San Sebastián, the dissidents and the swans were released from custody.

Occasional protests of frustration came to naught. At one point, Alberto Elósegui, perhaps emboldened by the example of his outspoken teacher, Father Jakob Gapp, who was seized by the Gestapo and taken away, climbed Monte Urgull and posted the outlawed Basque national flag over the city. He eluded capture by nearby garrisons, then fled Spain to avoid being killed. Protest and practicality were separate items. The Basques and other Spaniards who detested Franco hoped he too would fall when the Third Reich eventually fell.

And the Basque National Party worked toward that end, organizing an intelligence service to feed information to the Allies. They tracked German spies and their commercial fronts, reported on gun emplacements on the roads between France and Spain and used hundreds of subagents to monitor shipping, as well as agents and Nazis who transited the region to carry out foreign adventures.

Such was the atmosphere in San Sebastián—so close to the fighting, but like the rest of Spain, yet to emerge from the social and economic trauma of the civil war. There were vast shortages of basic foodstuffs and supplies. People bought rotten lentils from the countryside, electing to sort out the stones but leave in the worms. "A little protein," they would joke.

The monthly ration was one kilo (about two pounds) of potatoes, a quarter liter (a cup) of cooking oil, 200 grams (less than half a pound) of sugar and 100 grams (about 4 ounces) of coffee. The quality was awful. The coffee tasted like pasteboard, the bread seemed a mixture of chaff and sawdust. Automobiles were of two sorts, those driven by officialdom and those of the common folk. The official cars were late models, including American cars and German BMW limousines. The other cars were adapted most innovatively. Spare parts were nonexistent so replacements were made in makeshift machine shops or fashioned out of tin and cloth.

In return for Spanish neutrality, the United States was sending gasoline to Spain. U.S. and British intelligence reported that some of the fuel was being diverted to Germany—American petroleum products feeding the Wehrmacht. It was a deal with the devil—in the person of Generalísimo Francisco Franco—to keep him out of the Axis fold. Oil products kept industry running, fueled government and military traffic and made for a lively black market. The common folk figured out how to adapt their internal combustion engines so that they could run on coal. Portable coal-burning stoves lashed to the trunk fed a low-octane fuel by-product into the carburetor as a substitute for gasoline but gave almost no acceleration or power. Chevrolet bodies on top of Chrysler chassis with rag-worn tires on mismatched rims were common throughout Spain.

Yet for Jean-François, arrival in San Sebastián was a staggering letup from the war. There was electricity, at least for a few hours most nights; food, rationed though it was, seemed comparatively plentiful to someone coming from occupied France. There was anonymity and relative safety on the streets, even though uniformed Nazis lounged about everywhere.

The Germans did not have the same type of journey that Jean-François endured each time he crossed the frontier. The trip from Saint-Jean-de-Luz was an hour or so by the main highway, compared with the twelve-hour, death-defying trek through the mountains. The Wehrmacht rewarded its charges with day passes as long as the soldiers were well behaved and demonstrated the best face of the Führer's Reich. These young German boys walked jauntily and unimpeded and sometimes were even applauded by the citizenry along the promenade. Between the boulevard and the beach at a diagonal from the casino was an open play area for children, where they could jump on swings or play tag among the contorted tamarind trees.

A group of young soldiers strolling one day saw Agustín Lacort's eight-year-old daughter, Merche, playing there, her hair and skirts flowing as she frolicked. Perhaps she was a reminder of the idealized Aryan child back home. She could not help being blond. But she bolted quickly when they approached her, frustrating their attempt to snap a photograph.

The Germans were polite enough, but she'd been afraid of them ever since the day she went to gym class and the teacher, Señora Ullman, was crying. Merche didn't go to public school, because Franco had forced all formal education to be religious. Her parents wanted her to have a secular education. Teachers like Señora Ullman— math teachers, science teachers, literature teachers and gymnastic teachers—taught private and semiprivate sessions when they could.

Arriving for class one day at the Kursaal Theater, along the breakwater in Gros, Merche was surprised to find the teacher dressed in a blouse and skirt instead of her usual teacher's smock. "There is no class today," Señora Ullman said; her eyes were red and swollen. The little girl pretended to be playing in another corner but listened to the teacher describe what had happened. The Phalangists ordered her to appear at Calle Prim, 21; there, the Gestapo, who already knew she was German, accosted her. "They said that my little boy had to be sent away to join the Hitler Youth," Señora Ullman said. That very night, the teacher left for Málaga, hoping to hide from the Nazis. Merche wondered how the Germans could make people run away.

Merche never forgot Señora Ullman and her little boy. She screamed whenever she saw German soldiers, and their laughter would ring out while she ran away as fast as she could. She did not want to be sent away to Málaga, nor did she want to be forced to join the Hitler Youth.

CHAPTER SEVEN

The Autonomy of the Line

The Rock of Gibraltar. October 27, 1943.

As Jean-François headed south by land for the meeting in Gibraltar, a KLM commercial flight from London was arriving via Lisbon. The plane made a deep bank and descended quickly toward the airstrip, giving passengers a breathtaking view of the British colony. One of the passengers was Airey Neave, an army major turned British intelligence officer. If not nervous, Neave was at least relieved to be looking down on British territory once more—there were risks in flying commercial aircraft along the coast, and he was well aware of a recent German attack on a civilian flight in June. The actor Leslie Howard, on a goodwill tour, was one of the passengers killed. There was speculation that the Luftwaffe—which didn't usually attack defenseless civilian craft—had believed that Winston Churchill was traveling on the plane.

Neave was based at the British military intelligence Escape and Evasion MI9, operated jointly with its American counterpart, MIS-X. Even though he was an active military officer, he wore civilian clothes and carried a passport that identified him as an attorney. His cover story was that he was traveling to represent a British subject facing prosecution in the Portuguese courts.

Neave was no stranger to escape and evasion; indeed, he was selected for this division because of his firsthand experience in these operations. The twenty-seven-year-old major, wounded at Dunkirk as British Expeditionary Forces helped defend France and Belgium from the Nazis, had escaped four times from the Germans. His final, successful escape, carried out during a snowstorm in January 1942, was from the infamous Colditz Castle, where the Reich kept its most intransigent prisoners of war. Disguised as German officers and later as Dutch workers, Neave and a friend walked through a courtyard, then hoisted themselves over a twelve-foot castle wall. They managed to reach safety in Switzerland after a harrowing four-day trip. There followed the problem of leaving landlocked Switzerland. He waited three months until finally arrangements were made to sneak across France and then from Marseille to Gibraltar. So he had been here before.

After Neave got back to England in mid-1942, Brigadier N. R. Crockatt, deputy director of military intelligence, decided that this was exactly the type of man who should be organizing escapes in Europe. He summoned him to the War Office.

"You've seen the people who work for us behind the lines. They need money and communications. Do you want to help them?"

Neave did want to help and took the job. Now, about a year after escaping himself, Neave was back in Gibraltar on an important mission. He hoped to convince Jean-François that the Comet organization needed the training and protection that full entry into the British intelligence service would offer.

Humorously, Neave's arrival in Gibraltar was causing problems before he even got there. The British and their resistance allies used code names for all their contacts. Neave was "Saturday"; Donald Darling, the MI9 man in Gibraltar, was code-named "Sunday"; and

Creswell, in Madrid, was "Monday." The problem was that Jean-François was known throughout the escape network by the code name "Franco." So when Neave left London, saying he was off to an important meeting with "Franco," "Sunday," and "Monday," some colleagues thought he was jumping protocol and scheduling a clandestine weekend soirée with the Spanish Caudillo, leaving the Foreign Office and the British ambassador out in the cold. Neave made great fun of the confusion when he heard about it. At Whitehall there were looks of severe embarrassment, along with throat clearing and harrumphs at the Foreign Office.

In his approach to Jean-François, Neave wanted to appeal to the Belgian's sense of duty. But he also wanted to provide moral support and avoid harming an operation that was in full swing with brave partisans putting their lives on the line every day. On his orders, Jean-François was given the rank of a British officer for his stay in Gibraltar. There would be no doubt about the respect that His Majesty's government had for the work of the Comet Line.

Neave looked forward to meeting Jean-François. In terms of manpower needs and morale, the value of rescuing pilots and sending them back to London could not be overstated. The Comet organization had already saved more than 200 Allied airmen. For the first time, men whose belongings had been taken away in the night from their bunks in England were reappearing. There was a change in morale and a change in the odds. Clearly, there was an ever-growing need for experienced flight crews. "By the end of 1943," Neave said, "when the big raids which preceded the D-Day landing were taking place, there is evidence that an airman who evaded capture if he were not severely wounded, had more than an even chance of returning home."

Some miles from the Rock of Gibraltar, which was visible in the distance, brazen against the sea, Creswell found an isolated spot and pulled off the road. Jean-François climbed into the trunk. Any problem with his papers—false documents from Creswell—would cause unnecessary problems. Knowing the record of the Spanish military, the Nazis would also be informed about any such mishap. It couldn't be risked.

The Spanish guard post barred the way in La Línea, a village that borders the sand spit no-man's-land dividing Gibraltar from the mainland.

The car slowed to a halt.

Documentos, said a voice.

Sí, sí, sí, Creswell replied.

Jean-François could hear the Spanish guards questioning Creswell. He was perspiring heavily, though not from any sense of danger: even in October, the outside temperature was in the 70s, and the sun-baked trunk was a furnace.

¿Algo a declarar? said the voice. *Anything to declare.*

Nada.

Muy bien. Servido, señor, came the reply.

In seconds, Creswell was accelerating once more. There were perfunctory greetings in English soon after that, and in five minutes the car braked to an idle. Jean-François heard a door sliding on hinges, and then the car rolled ahead a few more feet. There was silence and total darkness until the trunk opened and he saw Creswell's smiling face.

We're in Gibraltar.

Gibraltar is a two-and-a-half-square-mile bastion of rock, one of the Pillars of Hercules that stand vigil between Africa and Europe, gateway to the Mediterranean Sea. Held by the British since the eighteenth century, Gibraltar—El Peñon, the Spaniards called it—was a perpetual affront to Spanish sovereignty. No less so, when Hitler dangled the possibility of capturing El Peñon as one reason to join the Axis.

If Spain ever were to enter the war, here was where the gauntlet would drop. The importance of Gibraltar, overlooking the nine-mile strait, was obvious. In 1943 the Allies were firmly stationed on the northern tip of Africa, and they used Gibraltar as a sea and air shuttle for troops, information and supplies.

The British military gave Jean-François a uniform and an official identification card—for once, a valid document with his own name on it—and told him to relax and treat his four-day visit as an opportunity for rest and recreation. It was sorely needed. Though well-nourished, Jean-François had been moving nonstop between Bordeaux and the border and over the Pyrenees, with numerous trips north to Paris and south to San Sebastián. He was weary of mind and body, though never of spirit. He'd developed a painful boil on the back of his neck, just above the collar, which was infected and angry-looking. He had been living for months under pressure and constant danger, and didn't realize the difference in tension level until, safe in the bosom of Mother England—albeit a thousand miles from Britain proper—he caught a blissful, safe night's sleep.

The next day he set out for a hike around the protectorate. London bobbies, identical in their brass-buttoned uniforms and helmets, marched off to their beats in Gibraltar town. Beyond one avenue lined with palmetto palms, he came to the Alameda Gardens, which looked out toward the port and the navy docks down the slope to the sea. The harbor was filled with the gray Allied warships of the Mediterranean and Atlantic fleets. There were warehouses with supply docks and trucks moving supplies so they could be loaded onto small boats to carry out to ships anchored in the harbor; dredging equipment; ferries; sailors and workmen—both British and American—and local seamen. Jean-François sat down and watched the constant activity, chaos that added up to organization, thinking about the size of the force that was operating at this solitary foothold on the Western European mainland. He was a part of this war effort. Surrounded by all that was British, it was quite odd when one turned away from the water and walked downhill onto a street that was the image of old Spain, set between the Rock and the harbor, which led to the old cathedral.

Many of the civilians who regularly lived on Gibraltar—and all of the women and children—had been evacuated from the Rock when hostilities broke out. Some civilians manned the stores and kitchens; strolling around were groups of khaki-clad British Tommies, and Jack-tars who wore blue-and-white-striped sailor suit linens that flapped in the wind. Jean-François wandered down to the recently broadened airstrip on the site of the old Gibraltar racetrack. Twin-engine recon-naissance planes came and went, and an occasional biplane as well as DC-3 airliners brought in a few passengers en route to and from Africa, Lisbon and the British Isles. There was no regular service be-tween Spanish cities and the Rock.

As he looked across the rolling hills, rock outcroppings and brush-covered vegetation, Jean-François felt a sudden rumbling. What appeared to be a stony mound suddenly gave way to a sliding pedestal and he could hear the sound of gears and motors. Suddenly a two-man gun emplacement rose out of the earth, with two helmeted British gunners at the controls. This was no ordinary field. What had appeared to be a natural landscape was actually a stage set for antiair-craft guns. The soldiers surveyed the terrain, looked about the horizon and then, with grinding and rumbling, began to sink again into the bowels of the earth. Within seconds, the false setting of hills was restored, perfectly camouflaged to the eye. This was the result of a maze of secret passages below the surface: about 150 caves were woven through the Rock of Gibraltar; the tunnels included a fortified infir-mary and impregnable defenses in case of attack.

Aboveground, one occasionally spotted one of the Barbary apes—not really apes, but monkeys—jumping from cliff to precipice around the fortress. Winston Churchill had been here several times—most recently in May 1943—and was dismayed to hear that the population of apes was dwindling; he ordered that urgent measures be taken to protect the primates. It was now the British Army garrison's responsibility to feed and care for the Barbary apes, a symbol of the empire. And as everyone knew, the empire would control Gibraltar as long as the apes survived: it was a matter of national sovereignty of the highest order.

When the time came for the meeting with Neave, Jean-François was received at Government House. A Gordon Highlander, in full kilt and regalia, stood guard at the door. The governor, Lieutenant-General Sir Noel Mason-Macfarlane, greeted him with pomp and ceremony. Jean-François managed to keep his wits and avoid chuckling at the sight of Mason-Macfarlane.

He was an old man, with a shock of white hair, who looked like the stereotype of a British officer from the movies. Because it was hot, he wore a billowing military shirt, culottes and socks with tassels that stopped just below his knobby knees.

"I am asked to thank you for all your brave work," Mason-Macfarlane said. Jean-François was still focused on his funny legs.

". . . and to convey to all members of the Line the gratitude of the Allies. Tell them the day of liberation will soon come."

Jean-François was grateful but impatient. The war wasn't over. He had pilots waiting to move south. He set the tone to let them know he was not working for England alone.

"We are doing our duty for Belgium and France and the Allies," he told Mason-Macfarlane.

So much for the ceremony. Shortly, they went to a meeting room. Neave, Creswell and Darling—code names Saturday, Sunday and Monday—sat down to talk with Jean-François, code name Franco. Interestingly, no Americans were present. Jean-François never saw any

American officials, even though a majority of the fliers being rescued were from the U.S. Army Air Forces.

The Americans had come late to escape operations, and MIS-X, the American counterpart to MI9, was understaffed. It was under tight control and constrained in its open activities in Spain because Carlton Hayes, the U.S. ambassador, didn't like U.S. intelligence operations.

Neave felt the dilemma of his mission. He wanted to give every possible support and encouragement to Jean-François. But he and other officials in London thought that more organization and structure were needed. The Nazis had decimated—almost incapacitated—the escape organization, destroying it mostly by use of informants for the Gestapo and the Luftwaffe's secret police.

He thought that field training, better communications and rotation of agents would protect the members of the Comet Line and keep it going. Before him, Neave saw the dark and impassive visage of an exhausted, sickly young man. The meeting room had an expansive window that opened to the Mediterranean Sea, and the view was an unavoidable counterpoint throughout the meeting. Neave sensed that anything was possible.

How have you been treated? he asked.

It was delightful. I did not expect to see the governor in shorts.

He meant all he said to you.

Jean-François looked at the expanse of the sea.

To be here in this great fortress, if only for a day, has given me great hope. I feel for the first time that the forces of evil will not prevail.

Neave told Jean-François that his goal was to find a way to prevent further losses by German treachery. He thought London could do more to support Comet, and he wanted to try every possible angle.

With your permission, I'd like to send someone to help you in Paris. He is an officer, a Belgian, like you, and he will have to come overland.

The new British-trained operative was Jacques LeGrelle, code-named Jérome. Jean-François didn't like the idea. He feared Britain was sending a military commander to take over.

It still remains a Belgian line. You are not trying to control it?

No. You must give the orders. We provide money and communications. We have always respected that, since the days of Dédée.

Jean-François said he would accept, but he was not comfortable with dictates from London. He reminded Neave that Dédée had defined Comet as an independent organization: it was not a branch of any army. It was a young people's movement, born in Belgium, and it would stay that way. In her honor, and in agreement with her, Jean-François would never accept British supervision.

It is understood, said Neave. *There will be no interference.*

Neave hoped the assignment of Jérome would be a turning point for Comet. While he sympathized with and respected Jean-François's independence, he was responsible for the security of the line. Although Comet was an independent operation, London needed this lifeline. He would be able to go back to London headquarters and report success—that Jean-François had accepted Jérome as the Paris supervisor. They would worry later about the operational details.

Neave was as impressed with Jean-François as he'd expected to be. And yet he was saddened: none of the Comet members had professional training; mistakes had been made. It wasn't just Dédée and her father—dozens of them had been captured and killed; perhaps schooling on evasion techniques would prevent more disasters. Up to now, the brave amateurs had shipped several hundred Allies through enemy territory. But the Germans were increasing the pressure.

Our only intent is to provide you with operational safety.

He looked at Jean-François. The frustration was tremendous, because MI9 thought it very likely that the Nazis would soon capture Jean-François. In addition, there was the question of his physical health. A day or two of rest in Gibraltar wasn't enough. Jean-François "was dreadfully exhausted. Boils which had broken out on his neck were giving him pain."

You are ill. Come to England and rest for a few weeks. We can return you to France later, Neave said.

No. This is my work. This is war. There are scores of pilots to bring out, and I am responsible. I promised Dédée and her father that I would carry on.

Neave sighed and turned away to the panoramic view of the sea. He "looked out of the window for a moment at the dazzling waters of the bay of Gibraltar. We would remain safe on British soil, but [Jean-François] must soon return over the mountains to the unknown perils of his mission."

Neave could only plead and beg Jean-François to be careful; he did not have the power to order him to protect himself. These were friends and allies; the disagreement was operational. Jean-François was assuming all of the risk.

For his part, Jean-François minimized issues about his health, as he always did, reminding his British friends that he was young and strong. Faith and passionate commitment to the fight would see him through.

Jean-François also agreed to reopen the Elizondo crossing, as long as he wasn't the one to run it. They were now moving twelve men a month across the river, but Allied crews were backing up all along the line. The second route, if it worked, would offer doubled capacity and would be particularly significant, as increased air raids meant more pilots parachuting into occupied territory. Jean-François would assign an old Belgian friend, Antoine d'Ursel, code-named Jacques Cartier, to reopen the Elizondo operation.

The next morning, Jean-François cheerfully climbed back in the trunk of Creswell's car. Neave and Darling accompanied them a short distance in a separate car. There was a snap-to at the gate, where a sentry waved them through and back into Spain. When they reached a reasonable distance from Gibraltar, Jean-François, no longer in the trunk, and the other men stopped for a farewell drink.

"It was difficult to be cheerful as we drank a bottle of wine," Neave recalled. "At sunset, I shook hands with him and watched 'Monday' speed along the dusty road towards Madrid. I felt certain I should never see [Jean-François] again."

Jean-François left the Gibraltar encounter still laughing about the pomp and ceremony and Mason-Macfarlane's legs. He also was amused by the way that Airey Neave, in a measure of class-consciousness, kept referring to him as "the baron." The British had gotten it into his head that he was a Belgian nobleman, possibly from bad intelligence reports. It was true that Jean-François's father had been much taken by the idea of having a family claim to nobility and in the Belgian fashion purchased the right to be called a count of the Belgian court. Jean-François was a good and loving son and had forbearance for his father's peculiar interest. He laughed as he told the story to friends. "My father asked me and my brother if we also wanted to be nobles; you know, the title wasn't hereditary, it was a matter of buying it. I told him, no, thank you very much, I don't want to have a title."

Nevertheless, if the British saw him as a baron, Jean-François could not correct the error. Even the faux title didn't get him an audience with the British ambassador when Jean-François rode back with Creswell from Gibraltar. The ambassador spent his official time maintaining friendly relations with Francisco Franco and his ministers. When he wasn't doing that, he was busy keeping up his hobby of bird-watching in the gardens behind the British embassy.

Jean-François was satisfied that he'd held fast on keeping local control of the escape operations, though he admitted to himself that it had been hard to resist Gibraltar and the offer to go to England. But the freedom of his home and his life and the future of Europe were at stake. He couldn't conceive of stopping or resting or doing anything but what he was doing. He answered the growing volume of pilots by working harder than ever and recruiting even more people to work with him.

His friend Jacques Cartier agreed to take over the revived Elizondo escape route. Cartier, who had been stationed in Indochina, was an old family friend. He had been running operations in the north until now. He would travel with Jean-François to discuss plans with Creswell in San Sebastián.

Meanwhile, after a shaky start, all seemed well with Jérome, the new British-trained agent. Jean-François had an early run-in with Jérome, but he wrote it off as proof that a bureaucratic relationship with MI9 was bound to create trouble.

Jérome, suffering the effects of a back injury from parachute training, was flown to Gibraltar in November and rode to San Sebastián in a British diplomatic car. He went north across the border from Spain to France—"waltzing" was what they called moving an agent in this way—and onward by train to Paris. Jérome, in effect, would replace Dédée's father, Monsieur de Jongh, who had been arrested in June by the treachery of the clandestine German double agent, Jean Masson. Jean-François explained every aspect of the operation, taking days away from his own duties farther south to make sure that Jérome was comfortable with the handoffs from the Belgian side of the operation and then onward.

They found a new safe house, an apartment in a middle-class section of Paris. One day, as Jean-François prepared to resume his duties in the south, he saw a written message on the table that Jerome was preparing to send to London. It began: "Jean-François is an excellent operative, absolutely reliable . . ." Jean-François grabbed the letter angrily and threw it in Jérome's face when he returned.

I will not have you preparing reports about me; I will not have you communicating with London at all without my knowledge. You are going to recognize me as the leader of this organization or you are out. Decide now.

I'm sorry, Jean-François, I didn't . . .

Jean-François stared down the older man and interrupted his sentence.

Apologies are not necessary; trust and complete understanding are what I'm talking about. We will be friends and we will work together and there will be no more telegrams. Understood?

Yes, Jean-François.

That was the end of it. Jérome was a great addition to the Comet Line, and he and Jean-François became fast friends.

PART THREE

December 1943

CHAPTER EIGHT

By Train Across France

Paris, France. December 22, 1943.

A fter leaving the shelter of life in Brussels with Lily, Bob Grimes followed Marie, but he did so with some trepidation. He would not have gone at all had Lily not promised that Marie was a trusted friend. Soon they boarded a local train, and Bob sat quietly among Belgian passengers, while Marie stood in the corridor, meeting his occasional glance. Their destination was only about an hour—thirty miles southwest—to Tournai, not far from Lille across the French border. The time and the distance, however, were not the point. A succession of male and female helpers, none of them much older than Bob, led him on a circuitous route that was mapped out carefully to avoid checkpoints and surveillance of any kind. Marie walked a discreet distance ahead of him as they exited Tournai station. December 19, 1943, was a Sunday; the air was brisk but not biting. Church bells pealed an incessant, unexpected greeting, for Tournai is the city of 100 steeples and 400 bells. Bob had hardly focused on the day of the week until then: he realized he was back in the world, starting to count time. The day began slowly; there were people strolling at the Place Crombez, but there was little commerce on this day of rest.

Marie and Bob walked to an unmemorable café on a street where there was hardly any traffic—quite a contrast from city life in Brussels. They joined a couple already seated at one table. Something about the man told Bob that he was an American. They looked at one another but did not dare speak. After a cup of coffee, Bob and the supposed American were on a meandering route, sometimes back in view of the train tracks, evading all border controls, until they reached a farmhouse in the countryside.

There was another guide now; the helpers kept moving in and out, communicating only when necessary, watching in case someone approached with some random question that might give them away as foreigners.

Now, Bob was told, *you'll stay until tonight. Then we go.*

The farmers at the house had hidden their stores of food from the Germans and were able to prepare a sumptuous country dinner. He'd forgotten what abundance was like. He slept deeply, anticipating that freedom was at hand. They left sometime after midnight and followed a dark path through farm fields and isolated stands of trees. After a while there was another safe house in the woods.

"Welcome to France," said a man who called himself Jacques. There had been no indication of a border crossing at all—these helpers knew what they were doing.

Bob gave them his Belgian identity card and in return he was handed French papers already sealed with his photograph. There was also a train ticket, booked third class for Paris. It was still dark when they arrived in a city whose name Bob could easily remember.

Lille read the sign on the train podium. "Reminds me of Lily." Only a day had passed, but already life in Brussels seemed far away.

————

It was Monday, and the highway to town was busy. Men were off to work, children fought and played, shoppers lugged sacks from the shops or went along looking for scant Christmas supplies on the black market. The risk was low for two more young people merging into the crowds. The scene must have been repeated a thousand times around Europe that day. The Germans were not able to track every path leading to every border crossing; there were too many people for them all to be stopped and searched. The frontier between Belgium and France was ill-defined and, for the Nazis, somewhat moot, because they held both sides.

The train to Paris was a sudden party. Bob crammed into a car filled with young people, boys and girls his age, a cacophony of laughing and shouting as they rode to Paris for the start of a new workweek. Elbow to elbow, bodies were leaning and jostling against him; the air was filled with the scent of soap and women's perfume. Girls melted you with a look if you pressed too close or touched them in the wrong place. It was glee and pandemonium in a blacked-out railroad car for three hours before daylight. Had everyone forgotten that there was a war on?

Paris was instantly recognizable, of course, at the dawn of a cloudy day, even to an American who had never been there before. The train approached the Gare du Nord, where the Belgian passengers arrived. Bob had no idea how much danger the train station represented.

Once inside, there was another handoff with Bob Grimes as the football. A man motioned him to the street, and they walked several blocks to a nondescript apartment building. A woman opened the door: *Here you will stay and rest for the journey ahead.* Bob was disappointed to be in fabled Paris without being able to see the sights. At the same time, he was relatively relaxed, because the Comet helpers and his inability to communicate fully were cushioning him from the danger that lurked nearby. He had been forewarned that the most dangerous leg of the trip was that night, from Paris down to the heavily patrolled Spanish border. Other Americans would be with him. Bob did not sleep nor did he speak, those ten hours in Paris. He ate some food and was told to rest and wait.

No names were used, but the man leading them in Paris was Jacques LeGrelle—Jérome—the agent sent from London to organize the Paris section of Comet under Jean-François. Jérome suffered from a constant tension that would not subside until the day was over and he got away from the train station. There were uniformed Germans, surely plainclothes Luftwaffe security, SS and Gestapo officers; the Gare du Nord had been the site of many tragedies and petty horrors over the last year. It was here that Jean Masson arranged the capture of Dédée's father. It was here in August that Ron Pearce, an escaping Australian airman in the British air force, saw a Nazi soldier beat down a man who ill-advisedly lunged to enter a train car reserved for soldiers. Had Ron attempted to stop the German, he too would have been beaten and captured if not shot. The man lay prone and motionless on the platform; passengers stepped around him as they moved to other wagons where civilians were allowed to board. There was nothing good about loitering at a train station in Paris.

Throughout the day Jérome, newspaper clamped under his arm as a signal, picked up the airmen: first Arthur Horning and Robert Z. Grimes; then James Burch and Lloyd Stanford.

Horning was the man Bob met at the café in Tournai that day, but Bob couldn't remember the details. Horning's memory of that portion of the trip was decidedly more pleasurable. He had found himself walking across from Belgium to France arm in arm with one beautiful girl after another, each strolling with him like a lover. Horning could be excused for being enthusiastic about the treatment. At Lille he was quite literally delivered into the arms of Amanda Stassart, code-named Diane.

Art was from Pittsburgh, and at twenty-eight, he was a bit older than most of the American Army Air Forces pilots. He'd never been on a train like this. It was not first-class travel, but it was elegant all the same, like something from the movies. Lacquered, fine-grained wood doors and walls, the feel of a luxurious mahogany drawing room, brass handles and fittings on the doors and windows and individual compartments. Diane and Art sat apart from everyone else in the eight-passenger compartment. Art was at the window, Diane at his side. He was disoriented and spoke no French in any case, so was unable to ask a question that troubled him. He'd surrendered his Belgian identity card to his resistance escort, but no one had provided French documents. Why hadn't he been given new identification? Had something gone wrong? Perhaps that was why he was traveling separately from Grimes. If Diane spoke English, she wasn't letting on, and he wasn't going to ask her on the train. She was simply beautiful—auburn hair tied back, rich brown eyes and lavish red lipstick, smiling and patting his hand.

The conductor came along, and they showed their tickets; then Art was distressed to see uniformed German soldiers walking up and down the aisles. He heard them slide open the door in the next compartment. How would they get out of this?

All the while, Diane knew about the problem with Horning's identification papers. There had been a mix-up, and they'd left Paris without them. But she was prepared for the Germans. She hopped into Art's lap, draped her arms around him and started slobbering him with kisses. Those lips, licking his ear red, wet on his mouth, pretending to whisper and caressing him for real. He had to keep reminding himself it was an act. She looked at him again with that sly look in her eye. The German guards peered through the glass and passed them by without opening the compartment door.

Why change something that works? The train south to Paris made the 135-mile trip in three hours, and Horning and Diane—two lovers in a compartment—were locked in a passionate embrace that no one disturbed. At the Gare du Nord, Diane led her sometime beau to a cement stanchion at one side of the station. "Wait for a person with a newspaper." She was gone but never forgotten.

Lloyd Stanford, a twenty-three-year-old second lieutenant from Augusta, Georgia, and Lieutenant Jim Burch, from Texas, had been in Paris for about a week. They were from the same flight crew—Burch, the copilot, and Stanford, the bombardier. Both had been injured when they bailed from their B-17 after being shot down over Holland on October 10. Stanford's injuries were superficial cuts, but Burch had been laid up with a deep bruise the length of his leg. He kept the problem to himself, but Stanford was worried about him. Just as with Bob Grimes, the Comet operatives had delayed moving them down the escape line, hoping that the leg would improve, since Burch had no external sign of injury, just deep bruises. But the leg didn't improve, and by early December they set out for Spain anyway. They had many checkpoints to evade, first from Holland into Belgium, and then into France before arriving in Paris.

Three evenings before Christmas in 1943, the operation got rolling. Jérome signaled the guides to meet him at a prearranged time. The four young, fair-haired lads—a head taller than everyone else—entered the Gare d'Austerlitz, which handled train traffic south of Paris. The young men wore identical, threadbare black wool suits, and they strode across the cavernous hall one by one, each escorted by a conservatively dressed young man or woman who wanted nothing more than to blend in with the other Parisians going about their business. Their gait was determined yet not hurried; they avoided eye contact with other travelers and pedestrians, and on the whole worked at conveying a relaxed, pleasant appearance.

Bob Grimes, feeling strong and somehow confident after his six weeks in Brussels, was shocked when he looked around the platform. He spotted a young redheaded man much taller than everyone else. He'd seen him somewhere—he had to be an American. There were others—a skinny guy who could also be an American and another young fellow nervously looking around him who certainly was an American; all were coming his way. It was a good idea to pretend to be distracted and not think about getting caught.

Obeying furtive hand signals from his guides, Bob was directed to a seat on a train bound for Bordeaux. The compartment had tight quarters and was full. There were several other men and not much luggage on the racks. Bob again surmised he was sitting with Americans and knew the best thing to do was to act as casual as possible, so he pretended to be asleep. Could anyone hear the roar of his heart thumping away double time when the ticket collector came along? No problem, though. No questions, not a word spoken.

There should have been another tolling of bells or a fanfare when the train pulled out of the station. Instead it was a soundless, almost imperceptible, gliding motion that tugged the train slowly ahead; Bob squinted one eye half open at the window and saw the rail yard and, beyond that, the lights of Paris rapidly retreating from view. Jean-François and Jérome, meticulous in their planning, chose this night train because it made many stops and they believed the Nazis would deem it too inefficient to serve as a means of escape. The Germans were not as vigilant as they were on the mainline express trains—first-class rail service that sped south through Lyon and then onward to the

Basque country. Often, in contrast, there were no police on the local trains at all. So why did this night have to be different? The helpers had placed Grimes and Stanford in one compartment, Horning and Burch in an adjoining section. They were not separated from the rest of the passengers, because in third class, the compartments were open. There was no glass separating the cubicles from one another or from the aisles, just groups of benches that seated six comfortably or eight packed in. Seating was back-to-back with a narrow corridor on the right side of the car.

The route passed through villages and fields, mostly in open country. The miles were becoming a blur and Bob was just watching the scenery slip by through a half-open eye, still pretending he was asleep with his head against the window. The Germans used the rail lines for transport, and trains were increasingly the object of Allied bombs, so the cars were routinely blackened out. Occasionally troop trains or long lines of freight cars passed or were sidetracked on one side or another, sucking air as they rolled by and then vanished. The notorious Drancy detention center, where the Germans held Jews and other prisoners before transferring them to concentration camps, was on the route. Also there were two camps for Allied prisoners of war close to the rail line: one at Beaune-la-Rolande, the other at Pithiviers, on the way to Orléans. It must have been close to midnight when the train passed a field with dim lights. Bob saw low wooden buildings, a tower and an area close to the tracks surrounded by barbed wire. The train was braking and moved smoothly until it jerked to a halt along a short platform. He heard the doors open and the sound of commotion. Voices in French were hard to make out; he thought he heard something about Americans escaping. He hoped he was wrong—perhaps there had been a break from the camp he'd just seen.

The train lurched forward again, and the conversation of the two officials grew louder. Grimes continued to lean against the window; his heart was pounding. As the conversation continued, he feared the

Germans were talking about escapees and would capture him. He half opened an eye to size up the situation. After six weeks of practice in Belgium—including those close calls with the German soldiers—he could just tell the look of the Gestapo. The man in civilian clothing was certainly that. The other was a uniformed German officer. Why did they have to stop at the side of the compartment where Grimes and Stanford sat? Neither American acknowledged the other, nor did they dare to look at anyone else. Both were petrified, praying that no one would try to talk to them.

The two officials spoke in French, which meant that the plain-clothesman was not a German. Bob could make out that they were talking about security—about catching people. Bob's rapid heartbeat competed with the clacking of the rails. The Nazis decided they would take a sample identification check. Why not start right here?

Cartes d'identité, s'il vous plaît, said one.

The other passengers complied; Bob felt elbows and forearms around him reaching into coat pockets. He kept his eyes closed and kept leaning against the window, occasionally smacking his lips and snorting. The Germans checked each of the documents and now focused on the remaining passenger who hardly budged, deeply asleep.

Monsieur, carte! the German repeated, and this time he was addressing Bob alone, who still didn't move.

Eh! came a snarl, and Bob felt the man's breath as he reached over to give him a punch to the shoulder.

Identité!

Acting now and measuring slow movements, Bob lifted an eyelid as if in a stupor and felt his pocket for the ID card he had received earlier in the day, handing it across without looking up and closing the one open eye again. His heart pounded out of his chest, and he could hardly breathe as he waited for a response, eyes closed. The guard grunted, threw the card back at him and moved away.

The Nazis worked their way down the corridor and continued on to another car. Feigning sleep all the way, Bob remembered the trip so unclearly that he was surprised when Stanford said later they sat facing each other throughout the ride. Stanford was alert and knew who his comrade was. The guide he called the Little Lady in Black took him to a café in Paris earlier in the day and said there would be others, and mentioned a man named Robert. Surely this was him.

They arrived in Bordeaux at daybreak and switched to an even lower profile train for Dax. This train was carrying workers for their morning toils. No one would be escaping on such a local route. There was a certain comfort level here, and it was much easier for the four men to be gathered up together, although no one yet dared speak. Seated in one open compartment were the four airmen and their guide, who'd introduced himself as Max—Max Roger, a trusted friend of Jean-François. The boys worried every time the local train stopped at a siding; after about two hours, Max motioned them to get off at a station that looked like nothing more than an old railroad switching yard. This was Dax, which had been the last border post in the south between so-called Free France, under the Vichy government, and the German-occupied zone. That distinction held until 1942, when the Germans occupied the entire country. But it was still an occupation outpost; nearby thermal springs and Roman baths made it a popular recreation spot for German officers. Travel in the vicinity could be difficult.

Max directed them to a bicycle shed at one end of the station, where a rickety old girl's cycle was waiting for each of them. Stanford had noticed a young guy shadowing them ever since they got off the train. He didn't show his rising concern, but he worried and looked around at the others. The man followed them until the station was out of sight. Max turned around and introduced him—it was Jean-François—to this latest crop of escapees.

Jean-François spoke to them in heavily accented English.

It is very dangerous trip now. We must to ride one and one, keep a dis-tance apart, he said. *I go at the front, then all the pilots, and Max behind.*

Depending on how one viewed the situation, it was either the height of inexperience or extreme confidence that led Jean-François to keep a complete list of the Allied crew members he helped. The names and faces, in the dark and racing by in the reflected glass of grimy train cars, tended to blend together. On December 17 it had been a Cana-dian named Witherbridge, Davies of the Royal Air Force and an American named Morris. Four Americans came through on December 20: Whitlow, House, Ashcraft and Combs. (Whitlow was the pilot and Ashcraft the radio operator on the crew with Stanford and Burch, but neither pair knew the whereabouts of the other nor, for that mat-ter, that any of their other mates were still alive.)

In the succession of Allied aviators who Jean-François helped cross the border that late fall of 1943 was one especially interesting fellow, a thirty-year-old army sergeant from New York named George Watt. Jean-François knew none of this, but Watt had perhaps one of the more colorful histories of any Allied airman. Watt was one of the several thousand idealistic young men who came to Spain in 1937 to form the Abraham Lincoln Battalion. Without U.S. government approval—indeed, with official disdain—Watt and his American allies fought on the side of the Spanish Republic against Franco and his Nazi benefactors in the prelude to World War II. Watt had been a member of the American Communist Party—he'd quit the party, as did many others when they became disillusioned with Stalin. Watt was inspired by the call of the Spanish independence fighter named Dolores Ibárruri, who they called La Pasionaria. "No pasarán!"—*They shall not pass*—she exclaimed, and it became a revolutionary rallying cry for generations afterward.

None of Watt's fellow airmen knew this, nor did many know that he was Jewish, thereby making him doubly scared of being captured by the Germans or by the Guardia Civil lest, somehow, they realize he'd fought against Franco.

Watt left Spain in 1938, fleeing for his life from an ambush at the Ebro River on April 4, as Franco's Nazi-powered army marched toward total victory. In his memoir he recalled, "We walk stark naked and barefoot over a seemingly endless stretch of sharp stones and burrs that cut our feet. A minute or two later a small black car screeches to a halt. Out come two men. We're damned happy to see them. One is Herbert Matthews, *New York Times* correspondent. The other is Ernest Hemingway. . . . The Lincolns are the lost battalion, they tell us.

"They ply us with questions.

" 'What happened . . . '

" 'How many got out . . . '

" 'Where are Merriman and Doran . . . '

"We tell them briefly what we know . . .

"Merriman and Doran ran into an ambush. We don't know whether they got away. There are hundreds of men still across the Ebro. Many are dead; some are drowned . . .

"Matthews is busy taking notes. Hemingway is busy cursing the Fascists."

When the war was over, Watt returned to the United States. He showed up to enlist in the U.S. Army when World War II began, but members of the Abraham Lincoln Battalion were banned until a change of policy in early 1943. Watt was finally given the right to fight for his country, and he became a gunner and assistant flight engineer on a B-17. On November 4, 1943, he was shot down over Belgium, two weeks after Bob Grimes. That was how he had found himself riding up the road from Dax with Jean-François and Max Roger on December 8, 1943, two weeks before Bob Grimes and his three companions arrived. Watt, who was older and slower than the other bikers, lagged a bit on the ride over the hills to Bayonne but made it to Spain without trouble. He didn't even remember the river crossing that night; the water was only calf-deep, and they crossed in a minute without thinking twice. The Guardia Civil was not organized enough to identify him, so he was just another escapee rescued by the British embassy and sent back to London via Gibraltar.

Jean-François knew nothing of George Watt's story, nor did he need to reminisce about past successes. He recalled that only the week before, there had been yet another American, older than the rest, who couldn't pedal fast enough to keep up. The bicycles, so crucial to evading capture near the border, were always a problem.

Now he had these four: Stanford, Horning, Burch and Grimes. Jean-François studied their bike-riding habits as Max led them out of the train station. He wanted to make sure they were capable of making the twenty-five-mile, two-day trip to the coast.

This bicycle segment of the escape was not an ideal mode of transportation, but it was crucial. Jean-François adapted to the fact that the Germans were in hot pursuit. The only alternative was this new method, via back roads. It was a grueling bike ride to the coast, and the young fliers were also exhausted and frightened; but there was no choice. Jean-François was handling twenty bicycles in three groups of six, with two spares, so that they would always be present when a new group of airmen arrived at Dax or Bayonne.

There was an elaborate deal set up to prestation six bicycles at the railroad station. It had not been easy. The bikes were as good as one could expect, serviceable mid-size bikes that Americans referred to derisively as girls' bikes, because they had no center bar.

With so much movement, the travelers had no choice but to trust that the Frenchmen would not turn them in. There was no question that guardian angels were protecting them all about. On an earlier trip, Jean-François was in another compartment when a beautiful woman chanced in on one of the second-class compartments and asked one of the airmen in French if she could sit down. The pilot, a British air squadron leader named Wally Lashbrook, responded with the little French he knew: *Je ne sais pas, mademoiselle.*

Oh, an English pilot, she replied, smiling, and left him alone. The woman must have known that failure to report even this mild encounter was a crime punishable by death.

The true nature of things was also evident to the platform supervisor in Dax. Jean-François never found out the man's name, but they looked at each other with the knowledge of what was going on—perhaps not on a single occasion, but several rounds of seeing the stealthy Jean-François leading four other young men sporting caps and proper clothes were a little too much to miss. These were escapees, but the platform man never got in the way until one day in midsummer when Jean-François was horrified to discover that he was missing the paperwork to take one of the six bikes from storage.

But it is my bike, monsieur, he told the platform employee.

It is impossible was the reply. *You cannot prove it. See the station manager.*

There followed an hour of arguing with the station manager about rules, responsibilities, regulations, the difficult times, the limits of authority, human charity, forgiving and overlooking the mistakes of others, offering second chances and helping one another in these trying times we live through, culminating with the station master relenting. *Take the bike and go.*

Merci, monsieur, he said, and headed down the path, laughing to himself. *I guess I was patient enough to wear him down.*

———

On a subsequent trip, Jean-François made a short detour to the station manager's office. The door was ajar; he looked inside and saw no one. He took out a parcel from his sack, filled with Spanish delicacies—fruits and sausages and cheese—impossible to find in Nazi-occupied France. He placed the sack on the stationmaster's desk and then ran to catch up with the others. These Dax railroad officials were now being solicitous in every way. They hardly looked at the documents when the bikes came back as baggage from Bayonne or Saint-Jean-de-Luz. They were quietly and anonymously protecting the American airmen and the helpers. Jean-François was sure that the station manager would realize who had left him this care package.

Jean-François was not looking for adventure, but sometimes it found him, even on a bike ride across the province to Saint-Jean-de-Luz. One of the American pilots actually didn't know how to ride a bike. This seemed impossible. What kind of lives do they live in the United States? Do they still ride horses?

Here he was, sending Max with the other three riders away up the road to wait, while he gave the pilot—he couldn't recall his name—a two-hour crash course in bicycle riding. Fortunately, there were enough dirt roads so that the man bruised his ego more than his knees or elbows every time he fell. Triumphant though wobbly, he and Jean-François caught up with the others on a grassy knoll. The girls from Saint-Jean-de-Luz, Denise Houget or Auntie Go's daughter, Janine, brought along cheese and bread to eat at wooded enclaves along the way.

Then the riders set out toward the coast. Jean-François led the way as scout, and each of the pilots spaced his way several hundred feet apart to make them look like part of the normal transit—there were no private cars, and bicycles on the road were normal. Max Roger brought up the rear, just close enough to catch hand signals from Jean-François, letting him know if anything was amiss.

The novice bicyclist made it an adventure, and the others needed to coax him to keep up. He wobbled his way along fairly well until a German army vehicle approached in the distance; the unsteady rider, certain that he was about to be captured, ran off the road and fell. The Germans, though, saw nothing unusual—no more than a silly Frenchman being scared and falling down, and they laughed and whistled and hung their heads out the window as the hapless American sat, helpless but safe, on the side of the road.

The guides always kept away from the airmen, leading and trailing them by 300 feet, so the Germans never realized what they were doing. The pace was slow and deliberate. They stopped in Bayonne overnight and then continued the following day before dawn via secluded side paths up to Saint-Jean-de-Luz.

Jean-François never improvised along the way unless some emergency developed. A fixed route would let the other helpers know how to find the entourage if necessary. But over time he gradually altered the itinerary. Instead of taking the main road, they would often ride country lanes, weaving on and off the route either to bypass checkpoints or to avoid possible detection by increasingly commonplace German patrols.

Bob Grimes had been worried about how his repaired leg would hold up on the bicycle ride. Fortunately, he felt strong, and the trip down from Dax inland to the coast at Saint-Jean-de-Luz wasn't so difficult. The four airmen, with Max in front and Jean-François at the back, were spread a hundred yards apart and riding single file on the road. When they stopped for breaks, they sat away from the road, in the fields where they would not be spotted.

One of the other Americans, Jim Burch, was causing problems. He didn't have the energy to keep up. His partner, Lloyd Stanford, was falling back to stay with him, and Jean-François had to signal frequently for the others to stop so Burch could catch his breath. Jean-François figured that the Americans weren't used to such strenuous physical activity. They had been too busy flying in planes all the time.

Bob had also noticed the way Burch and Stanford were slowing them down and how they were always muttering. He figured they were slackers. He didn't have time for it. They had to focus on getting home.

There was very little private motor traffic on the occupied coast of France. Trucks and buses carried forced labor gangs; commercial vehicles were liable to be stopped at random and occasionally a German military car drove by. All civilians encountered in the occupied zone were subject to arrest unless they could produce two forms of identification—standard French occupation papers and special coastal zone documents—giving them permission to live, work or transit through the area. German regulations made it clear that local trains would be easier to handle and less subject to control.

Jean-François's goal in moving the airmen was to blend in with the workers and the commerce of the region; at that time the task of checking identification would open holes in German security. The schedule had them arriving at Saint-Jean-de-Luz when the streets were busiest, usually in the morning. After dropping off the bicycles at a set hiding place, where they would be picked up and brought back to Dax, the men meandered casually down the main coastal road and across the bridge, joining inconspicuously the ranks of the day laborers and marketgoers, who crossed there. There was always a soldier stationed at the crossing, but at peak times the Germans did little more than look over the heads of the crowds in case they could spot anything suspicious.

Sometimes, Jean-François stopped to chat with the soldier, who might not even speak enough French to get beyond basics. But for a grunt soldier of the Wehrmacht, imagine the excitement. He was deployed all alone at a bridge near the Spanish border. His platoon sergeant tells him to look for anything suspicious. What would be suspicious? How could he tell? Now when the young guy comes up to him and asks questions, he can practice French, be friendly with the locals, and show his importance as a military man who might be able to answer a question of a member of the local populace. Jean-François discussed the weather and the fishing and the market and how many hours the soldier had to be at the bridge. Didn't he get tired? Jean-François asked. Jean-François said he'd like to be a soldier one day too. Meanwhile, the airmen easily wandered by in the crowd, not looking up as they crossed the bridge down the hill to Kattalin's house. Bob Grimes and the others were just hours from reaching what they imagined to be freedom at the Spanish border.

CHAPTER NINE

The Life of a Traitor

Paris, France. December 1943.

The Nazis had rounded up dozens of members of the Comet Line in Brussels and Paris, but now they had new intelligence indicating that Jean-François had restored operations and was increasing the number of airmen being moved to southern France. They turned to their most successful infiltrator, Jean Masson, the Belgian traitor who had been lying low since the arrest of Monsieur de Jongh and friends in June, and he prepared to dust off his identity as a resistance operative and hit the streets of Paris once more.

Looking out on Paris from the balcony of his apartment near Montmartre, Jean Masson could enjoy some level of satisfaction. His loyalty to the Third Reich and his success in penetrating escape organizations like Comet had won him a certain cachet. His hours were his own, so he could wake up at leisure and look with pride at his two little boys, whose names were a clear mark of his self-regard and his idolatry of the Führer. The children were two-year-old Jacques Junior and ten-month-old Adolph.

Masson was an ardent Nazi, and his love for the Führer was now reaping dividends. He enjoyed a high lifestyle and had as much money as he needed. By all accounts he doted on his children and their mother, his mistress, Marie-Thérèse Laurent. Marie-Thérèse's husband was off in Africa and not likely to come back soon—if ever—as long as the Nazis controlled France.

Masson lived in the ninth arrondissement at 29, rue de Douai. He kept two apartments there: one for his family and the other for his Gestapo cronies and their operations.

If a delivery of escapees was scheduled, Masson sometimes conducted business right at the apartment. The pilots were delivered by one of his accomplices, often Colette—Marie-Antoinette Orsini was her real name—with whom he sometimes traveled up to the Franco-Belgian border. If Marie-Thérèse suspected a liaison with Colette, what of it? Did Masson owe allegiance to any one woman? His only allegiance was to the Führer.

Airmen described arriving in Paris relaxed and confident, certain they were about to be sent back to England. Several of them recalled the shifty smile of the rather diminutive man whose name they often did not quite remember, Jean or perhaps Jacques. He was not a memorable character. Promptly, Masson escorted them to the adjoining apartment, where Captain Schnurr and his assistant Lieutenant Brandstetter were waiting. Sometimes the Gestapo officers held them there and administered an initial beating. The concierge of the building heard the screams. Once, she said, she heard someone shout out: "Don't shoot them in the head because they don't talk after that. Shoot elsewhere." The neighbors might or might not have heard that, but they certainly knew what was going on. They also were powerless. Even moving from the building could cause suspicion. But Masson and his friends didn't always conduct business there. Occasionally the Gestapo men called for a car and transferred the airmen directly to headquarters.

If the morning was free, Masson could walk the mile or so to Gestapo headquarters by foot. These were heady days for the Gestapo. The autumn air of 1943 was filled with the omnipresence of Nazi power. The half-hour walk in the neighborhood was a stroll through the captured heart of Paris. Masson walked past the nightclubs of Pigalle that had returned to some form of normalcy, near the cradle of impressionism and where currently Picasso kept his mouth shut and still painted, along rue de Clichy where the nineteenth-century stone façades were always festooned with flowers, and finally he made his way down the Champs-Elysées.

Gestapo headquarters was at the old offices of the Sûreté—the French secret service at 11, rue des Saussaies—not far from the Elysée Palace. It was in the heart of the city; and the Nazi flag rippled in the breeze. A promenade along the Seine at lunchtime on a crisp fall day was not out of the question.

Evenings, Masson frequented Paris's hottest nightspots in the company of beautiful women and influential members of the local German occupation hierarchy. Before going home, he often stopped in at Jimmy's Bar, where he was seen drinking too much and regaling anyone in earshot with tales of his bravado in fighting the enemies of the Reich. One of his closest companions was a fellow Gestapo officer and his nominal superior, the notorious Prosper Desitter—"the man with the missing finger"—and Desitter's equally infamous mistress, Flore Dings.

Before wandering up to the Gestapo offices and interrogation center, he could stop, if the fancy struck, at the fashionable café just down the street. A coffee took the edge off a previous night's hangover. Masson was a heavy drinker. The Gestapo headquarters and its neighborhood did not attract those who had no business there. Perhaps the screams of prisoners submitted to various forms of torture could not be heard through the thick stone walls of the building. But Parisians knew well what faced those who entered there. Seized along with some acquaintances and charged with crimes against the Reich, for example, M. Rabate, a mechanic, was told by a menacing inquisitor: "Here you will have to speak." Your friend "came in here arrogant. He went out crawling." If a prisoner went out at all. "The cooks, whose quarters were on the second floor, were often disturbed by the screams of the victims being interrogated on the fifth floor."

Jacques Delarue was a Sûreté officer who clandestinely enlisted in the French underground when the Germans took Paris in June 1940. When his anti-Nazi activities were discovered, he was imprisoned and tortured.

"There were cells in various parts of the building," he wrote in an account of the headquarters and the methods used by the Gestapo. "The largest were in the basement, while various little box rooms on all the floors were summarily transformed into barred cells. Five or six prisoners were sometimes herded together for hours on end in a small airless cupboard. The handcuffs were left on their wrists the whole time and some were chained to a ring in the wall.

"As a general rule the first interrogation did not take place until ten days after the arrest except when urgently necessary. The methods employed to make the victims talk were always the same. They were forced to kneel on a triangular bench while a torturer climbed on their shoulders; they were suspended with the arms tied behind their backs until they fainted. . . . Their teeth were filed, their nails torn out, and they were burned with cigarette stubs and on occasion with a soldering lamp. The electric torture was also practiced; a wire was attached to the ankles while a second wire was run over the most sensitive parts of the anatomy. The soles of the feet were slashed with a razor and the wounded man was then forced to walk on salt. Pieces of cotton wool soaked in petrol were placed between the toes and fingers and lit. The torture of the bathtub consisted in plunging the patient into a bath of icy water, his hands handcuffed behind the back, and keeping his head underwater until he was on the point of drowning. He was dragged to the surface by the hair and, if he still refused to speak, was immediately plunged underwater again.

"Women were not exempt from these tortures, and it was usually upon them that the torturers used their most odious refinements."

Masson occasionally looked in on the terror and interrogation sessions. He was all too happy to stop by when a resistance fighter—who might not yet realize that he had been captured through Masson's treachery—was being submitted to the bathtub torture.

That was the case with Monsieur Adeline, who had inadvertently set up Masson's introduction to Comet in April 1943 by introducing Masson to Camille Spiquel. Camille had brought Masson to Monsieur de Jongh's apartment on the rue Vaneau. Masson gleefully intervened directly during the Gestapo's interrogation of Adeline, who denied any participation in helping airmen escape.

I know nothing, Adeline said, issuing repeated denials.

But my friend, I saw you in the apartment. We were together . . . you are lying, Masson replied with a scornful smile.

Yet the best of the Nazis' tactics were sometimes foiled. The patriot Pierre Brossolette jumped from a window on the fifth floor, killing himself for fear that he would not be able to withstand the torture and would begin compromising friends or revealing operations.

And there was Lily's sister, Nadine Dumont. She was one of the first Belgian resisters to be caught by the Nazi intelligence net. She was a year or two older than Lily and defiantly entered the fight against the Nazis. "They have no right to occupy our home," she said. "They will be punished, and we will fight them until they are defeated," she had told her fellow members of the resistance. She was seized in Brussels on August 11, 1942, along with her mother and father, and thrown in St. Gilles Prison. She was beaten when she refused to talk, yet she stood before her captors, eighteen years old, all of five feet tall and 105 pounds, and was surprised at her own attitude. "It was my nature: I stayed calm. I don't know why. Before I was arrested, I said I would try not to speak. I didn't know if I could do that. My focus was on not speaking. I was lucky maybe, I don't know."

Everyone had heard rumors of endless interrogations and tortures. Yet Nadine was calm, telling herself—wrongly, she later realized— that the Nazis wouldn't kill a woman. During her interrogation, she was determined not to give the torturers the satisfaction of seeing her fall down. She stood there and looked at them, devising explanations that would not implicate her mother, her father, or any other member of the resistance.

For each interrogation session, Nadine was taken from St. Gilles, a Gothic-spired stone edifice that inspired revulsion, to the equally feared Nazi headquarters in Brussels on the avenue Louise. Each time, she summoned the courage to hide her fears and spoke evenly and calmly to her captors. As the sessions went on, she was analyzing the interrogators, looking for ways to appear cooperative while continuing her lies.

It was apparent that there were two classes of interrogators; and one day, she recalled meeting a different sort of Gestapo agent, one who had an air of breeding compared to some of the brutes she had faced. "I feared him more because it seemed to me that it was easy to trick fools into believing your story." He began to ask questions about Nadine's friends and associates. As they spoke, she looked out the window into the courtyard and noticed a pear tree in full fruit.

"I don't know how I did it. I should have been afraid, but I wasn't," she recalled.

A Nazi was asking her questions, and Nadine was daydreaming about freedom. She knew she would be imprisoned until whenever the Nazis were defeated.

Isn't that a lovely pear tree, she said. *Have you tasted any of the pears?*

She turned to look at him. The man was astonished. And she just started to laugh. She was calm and measured.

You must enjoy having fruit trees in your garden.

He threw up his hands in disgust and called to the guards. *Send her away; she'll never talk. She's got nothing to tell us.*

He left brusquely. Eventually, they sentenced Nadine to prison and shipped her off to a succession of prisons and concentration camps in Germany. Even some of the Nazis acknowledged her spirit, though her absolute conviction that evil would be destroyed was beyond them.

But Nadine was an aberration and this did not trouble Masson. Most people broke under torture and provided the information that pleased Masson's superiors. He could be proud at having come up in the world. It was December 1943 and he had just turned twenty-one years old.

With his panoramic view of the city from the balcony, Masson could look down on daily life as if it were all controlled from here. He had been assigned to the Gestapo since 1942. It was technically known as SS Section IV-A, a division of the SS. Colonel Helmut Knochen was in command. There were problems, of course. While Masson's superiors in Paris gave him independence and support, the center of their attention was the deportation of Jews, which was monitored directly from Berlin. It gave them little time for Masson. His section did not have all the logistics and manpower they might have needed to crush the Comet Line. Each SS command in the occupied territories was expected to deport a quota of Jews to collection sites and onward to concentration camps. In France this was no easy task. As strange as it might seem to the SS leaders, some French officials under occupation did not cooperate with the deportation of their Jewish-French compatriots. In July 1942 Knochen's subordinate for Jewish matters, Captain Roethke, had to go directly to Adolf Eichmann to explain why he could not fill evacuation trains with the required number of Jews. Eichmann ordered all efforts to focus on reaching established quotas for arresting and transporting Jews. The trains to the concentration camps had to be kept filled.

Knochen exemplified the kind of specialist that Heinrich Himmler, the head of the SS and the Gestapo, wanted to have in the field. He was well educated, spoke fluent French and appeared quite urbane. He had almost a professorial style, which seemed to belie the tough image usually associated with a hardened Gestapo chief. No matter the image, Knochen empowered his subordinates to crush resisters with all necessary force.

With such momentous headaches being dealt with at high levels, it was clear that Masson had a mandate to act on his own. He was content with modest victories on behalf of the Reich. But there were concerns.

Throughout the Gestapo, the SS, the Abwehr and the various branches of the army, rivalries and petty jealousies slowed things down. The Gestapo section did not enjoy the cooperation required to rout their enemies in an efficient manner. Such rivalries existed among the regional branches of the Gestapo and the aligned and often indistinguishable SD (*Sicherheitsdienst*) that they rarely even exchanged information. That was to say nothing of the border police, also part of the SS, or the Luftwaffe secret police, under Hermann Göring, or the Abwehr—military intelligence, under Admiral Wilhelm Canaris—or the Geheime Feldpolizei—the army secret police. Everyone wanted the glory, and no one saw any benefit in helping anyone else receive credit for a capture or a kill. It was even more unlikely that Gestapo liaison officers in Spain would offer any help in tracking down Comet operatives.

Still, Masson did the best he could. It was said that both Reichsmarschall Göring—second only to the Führer—and Himmler realized the damage of the escape organizations and were keenly interested in stopping aircrews from ever fighting again in the war. Hence the refrain that the Gestapo recited so often to its captives: "For you, the war is over." For the sake of his adopted fatherland and for his own glory, Masson wanted to make it so.

Even as Masson's confidence was building, Allied military intelligence was piecing together details about him, based on resistance reports and cross-references from airmen who had managed to evade his clutches. "It was his task to collect the evaders in the provinces and to transport them to Paris," according to a joint British-U.S. intelligence report. "He is evidently a German Intelligence agent with a long and bloody record of penetrating resistance and evasion organizations. In this evasion service he began his activities in the Eure et Loire and gradually extended them throughout."

At times Masson worked on side cases. In Belgium and sometimes in northern France, he had the good fortune to make friends with the enemies of the state, whom he crushed—those who dared to help Allied airmen evade capture. He used them to interrupt communications and that was the most important thing. The goal was to break the rhythm of the escapes while letting the inhabitants of occupied Europe know they would be tortured and killed if they harbored enemy fugitives.

All was going well; if anything, Masson's fault was that he had been too impatient. He so wanted to please his superiors that he moved too quickly against Comet. He always operated under the fear that his superiors, acting on orders from Himmler, would want to see quick results. Ultimately, this is what saved the Comet Line. If Masson had kept up his deception for a few more weeks in June, everyone in the escape organization could have been obliterated along with Monsieur de Jongh. If he had gained more of their trust and penetrated further into the organization, he might have completely shut it down. Sometimes he used the name Jean Masson; that was how Dédée's father knew him. But he also used the alias Pierre Boulain.

Helpers could be quickly shot; perfunctory trials were sometimes necessary. None of that was Masson's concern. His assignment was to disrupt the ability of the escape networks to operate. Sometimes the airmen that Masson captured provided a helpful amount of information. They might cooperate on the mere threat of torture, knowing their positions were precarious. If an Allied airman carried his dog tags, he could hope that he would be treated as a prisoner of war. On the other hand, frisked by the Gestapo, he was immediately recognizable, despite the escape line's best efforts to provide false identity. If he didn't carry military ID, he could be a common enemy of the state, subject to summary execution.

Masson was developing a virtual map of the Comet Line based on his own experience, seized documents and the testimony of captured fliers and others who had been tortured into providing bits of intelligence. In fact, in time the Nazis produced a detailed map showing routes and way stations the resistance movement used on the way to Spain.

As 1944 approached, Masson reaffirmed his goal of breaking the various escape lines for airmen. He had been most successful with the so-called Brandy Line. Working with his helper, Marie-Antoinette Orsini, and other accomplices, he fetched Allied aircrews regularly from the Brandy Line and shipped them directly into Gestapo custody.

But the Comet Line was proving difficult. Several times, Masson thought that all of the leaders were already under arrest, but it wasn't true yet. He had not been able to locate Lily, who had moved underground and had eluded him so far—also the one they called Franco. He was perhaps the overall leader of the organization. His real identity was unknown—the Germans had not figured out that Franco and Jean-François were the same person.

In the early days of January 1944 Masson had received intelligence that aircrews were being delivered to a location in the sixteenth arrondissement. Young men had been seen in the vicinity going in and out of the rue de Longchamp. Masson and his team were staking out an apartment building and were almost ready to pounce. Masson moved slowly. If he worked methodically, he might be able to lure the top remaining Comet agents into his trap. That would certainly cripple Comet's operation in Paris. With a major branch of Comet cut, Masson would be tantalizingly close to realizing his goal of creating a kind of parallel operation. He would return to Belgium for a while to create the illusion that everything was operating normally. He would pick up airmen in Brussels with the promise of moving them quickly with false papers across the border. And the fools in Belgium would have no way of knowing what would happen. Once in France the airmen would be arrested and interrogated. Some would be shot, others would be sent to concentration camps. In fact, fewer of the captured aircrews were being sent to prisoner-of-war camps as specified by the Geneva Convention. It was too much trouble.

Saint-Jean-de-Luz, France.
December 23, 1943.

While Masson and his fellow Nazis were arrogantly predicting the demise of the Comet Line in Paris, the Basque section of the line was able to flourish. Auntie Go, Kattalin and Florentino were doing more than just moving dozens of pilots to safety—they were also gathering and delivering key intelligence for the British and the Americans.

The Nazis were so inflated by their intelligence successes that they completely missed the fact that the Basques at the extreme southern portion of the Nazi empire should have given them extra reason to fight the Comet Line.

Every time Florentino crossed the Pyrenees, he carried more than contraband in his backpack; mixed in with his cognac and French perfume were rolled-up reports bound for the Allies from a network of Basque informers. Changes in troop strength, the location of gun emplacements and photographs and maps of coastal defenses were duly noted and sent via this overland courier service.

Dozens of members of the Basque information services—workers and wives and schoolchildren—wandered the occupied coast, providing a steady stream of information to the Allies. The material was delivered to gathering points and then shipped across the Pyrenees with Florentino and other guides.

The furtive Basque information network was created under the auspices of José Antonio de Aguirre, the Basque homeland's *lehendekari*— president in exile. The charismatic Aguirre was one of 150,000 Basques who had been forced to flee Spain when Francisco Franco secured his victory in the civil war. Aguirre sneaked across Europe, even hiding in Germany, before taking up residence in New York, declaring, "The territory may have been conquered; but the soul of the Basque People has not; nor will it ever be."

Aguirre coordinated the espionage effort through J. Edgar Hoover's Federal Bureau of Investigation, which in the early years of the war handled international intelligence for the Americans on behalf of the OSS.

Kattalin, when she wasn't providing logistics for Comet and the escaping airmen, was a link for the underground messages. She made weekly trips to pick up the latest reports, though sometimes agents delivered material to her. It was a dangerous enterprise. There were tough checkpoints that Kattalin needed to cross to get to the eastern part of the country from the occupied French coastal region. She operated clandestinely on these trips, taking back roads and secondary trains to Pau, a French town eighty miles southeast of the coast.

While Jean-François was leading Bob Grimes and company down from Paris, Kattalin was receiving the latest batch of clandestine intelligence material. Besides the photographs, she had detailed maps and overlays showing bivouacs and the latest armored equipment. She had drawings of new insignias on the uniforms of SS officers, in case the Allies needed to produce a replica for one of their agents.

They had detailed reports on troop movements, about the progress of construction projects on the beaches, stolen documents describing logistical concerns, hundreds of pages of material all dutifully bundled up or sometimes—if the enterprising technicians at MI9 had their way—even stuffed as microfilm into toothpaste tubes and other supplies.

The latest material was high-quality, but the identity of the person who supplied the photographs and maps of Nazi installations will never be known. It must have been somebody who was innocent enough in appearance not to attract suspicion. Perhaps it was a young girl; at other times, the Basques sent out an old woman or an old man who didn't seem to pose a threat.

Whoever it was walked right along the beach in Saint-Jean-de-Luz, taking a shortcut off the highway, and was innocent enough so that the soldiers and forced laborers looked up from their work and didn't think twice. They paused and looked right into the camera hidden in the person's clothing.

A helmeted guard stood at ease. Members of an antiaircraft platoon were standing by their half-buried gun. Six men wearing steel helmets looked right at the innocent girl, one of them loading a practice round. Several of the soldiers stood nearby on the hard sand at a portable radio tower. There was even an officer, jacket half undone, almost posing with a hand on one hip. How were any of them to imagine that their snapshots would soon be in the hands of the Basque information services and on their way to British and American military intelligence?

The secret photographer walked beyond the gun emplacement and then paused also to look out to sea. A wider angle gave a view of the coastline. To the south, the Spanish peninsula at Fuenterrabía was clearly visible. One picture showed German lookouts scanning the horizon from the line of bunkers, as well as a web of telephone lines that led from the bunkers, which were part of an early warning network to command headquarters in the event of air or naval attacks by Allied forces. Barbed wire and other obstacles surrounded these installations. Machine gunners peered from narrow horizontal openings facing the ocean. The concrete construction, virtually the same along the line, featured six-foot-thick steel-reinforced walls designed to withstand bombardment.

The photos also showed reinforcements and a new round of troop deployments. For some time, the Germans had been digging in; there was now extensive construction all along the coast. Forced laborers had built a long dock into the sea at Saint-Jean-de-Luz, a mile or so from Kattalin's house. Workers had built artificial sand dunes to cover gun emplacements and bunkers. This was part of the defense system the Nazis were creating in preparation for an Allied invasion, which could come anytime after the winter of 1943. They called it the *Todt* (death) wall, and it stretched five hundred miles, from Normandy south to the Spanish border. Forced French labor with some German military engineers put this and thousands of other border fortifications together, preparing what Hitler hoped would be an impenetrable defensive barrier.

One recent report showed that about 14,000 German troops were in Saint-Jean-de-Luz, mostly either Luftwaffe or navy. U.S. intelligence in Spain estimated through its Basque operatives that there was a total of about 40,000 Germans in the entire Basque country, including Alpine forces, the SS and tank corps. The reports also described a steel antisubmarine net that was stretched across the entrance to the port. All along the beach, squads of gunners and radio operators milled about, wearing their short-brimmed field caps and ankle-length wool coats festooned with dark green lapels and shiny black belts.

Some of the intelligence material that Kattalin collected from her crew of helpers and informants were negatives of pictures taken with hidden cameras; sometimes, they sent along small photographic prints attached to detailed maps. "The Germans at Saint-Jean-de-Luz carried out another requisition of gasoline-powered vehicles, principally trucks," said one report. "Twelve vehicles were taken. Only the public services and food dealers were exempted. Despite this provision, the town was obliged to give up half its trucks and three fishmongers were deprived of their vehicles."

The reports were bundled as soon as Kattalin gathered them, and Florentino carried them as quickly as possible over the mountains to British and American operatives in San Sebastián. The material was delivered in turn to people like Steven Comiskey, of the American OSS, in San Sebastián and Arthur "Pat" Dyer, of Britain's MI6, in Bilbao and, when relevant, onward to Washington and London.

The contraband was quickly disposed of in San Sebastián; beyond the port was a British safe house on Calle Marina, a possible drop-off point for the latest round of intelligence documents. Then Florentino would head immediately back to Kattalin's house, where he received new assignments, picked up and delivered parcels or waited for airmen to arrive. The routine varied little. In the afternoon, he met them, tied their alpargatas and led them overnight up and down the paths and across the river.

In the waning days of 1943, Florentino was moving frequently across the border. Even when he wasn't leading Allied airmen—*ingelesak*, as he and his fellows called them—to safety, there was urgent intelligence material for the underground mail delivery service.

The Basque resistance operated literally right under the nose of the Nazis. How could it be otherwise? The Basque connection was a network of friends, relatives and kinsmen who spoke the same impenetrable language and shared the same trusted roots and traditions. Kattalin recruited some of the Basque support workers—it was one nestled resistance operation within another.

Florentino's conversations were limited, even with his own people in his own language. He spoke about gathering up supplies of food for the pilots, about how many packets had to be shipped down to Spain, about the weather on the trail. Words of love did not enter into it. The gossip among the young Comet people was that Florentino was infatuated with Kattalin. "I always thought he would like to marry her," Jean-François said.

No one ever heard Florentino complain about working so closely with women. If he wasn't staying at Kattalin's house, he could be found at the bar at the Hotel Euskalduna, right across the main plaza from the Saint-Jean-de-Luz train station. Kattalin worked at the hotel along with her cousin Catherine Muruega. The hotel bar was a meeting place for smugglers and resistance operatives. Nazis also stopped by for a meal or a drink but never realized what plots were being hatched there under a steady diet of beer, wine and cognac.

Florentino and his friends reveled in their ability to evade the police. For him, the river between France and Spain was no more than a current between two Basque provinces, with no boundary at all. It was a question of *hanhemenka*, here and there. The current occupiers were a nuisance to be bypassed, nothing more. Different evasion techniques were needed to get around various authority figures, like Franco's *Guardia Civil* and the Nazis. The packs of smuggled goods, cheese, wine, fine meat, lace and cotton were double-wrapped in oilcloth, and paper within paper. Florentino was accustomed to carrying such parcels—they could weigh seventy pounds—for long distances, in the same way that he could hoist a pilot on his back and carry him across the river.

He marched along with a *makila*, the traditional walking stick the Basque mountaineers used to negotiate mountain paths and counterbalance the merchandise on their backs. To increase the number of trips and lighten the load, the smugglers had other artful alternatives. There was a swift-flowing canal that offered all the advantages of hands-free, natural delivery. The canal coursed a straight shot from Oyarzun down the hill to Irún; Florentino could arrange with one of his friends to send shipments floating downstream in the dark. It was improvised and ingenious. If the Guardia Civil happened to spot and waylay a shipment, no harm was done. The guards would confiscate the goods for their own use and perhaps look the other way on another occasion. And the smugglers were in less danger of being arrested. Always mixed in with the lace and whiskey and cheese and linens were the tight-packed intelligence parcels.

On December 23 Kattalin was at work rolling the material into tight packets so that they could be mixed with contraband food, linens and cigarettes duly carried in backpacks by Florentino and the others almost every time they led Allied airmen out of France.

Kattalin had told Florentino that Jean-François was bringing down four more escaping airmen that evening. Florentino had a job to do; he felt more comfortable anyway in the hills that were his real home. Even so, he was not moving as quickly as he usually did. He was bone weary. He tried to shake it off, but he was getting a fever. It was not the drink. In the last days of 1943, Florentino was coming down with a case of the flu.

CHAPTER TEN

Death and Survival

Saint-Jean-de-Luz, France. December 23, 1943.

Bob Grimes was concentrating on keeping his mouth shut. He looked at the other guys, Art Horning and the two newcomers, and decided that he would say nothing. He was suspicious, and he didn't know who these people were. What if they were spies?

During this bike ride, the men were spread too far apart to talk, maybe a hundred yards between each bike, so the Germans wouldn't get suspicious.

Bob found himself daydreaming again.

What if I had just turned that damn plane around when I lost the engine?

No, you weren't supposed to do that. You were supposed to complete the mission.

What had happened to Art Pickett?

You gave him enough time to get out. Kellers said everybody had enough time to get out.

He was riding a girl's bicycle, hardly feeling the muscle in his left leg at all. But his mind was at 22,000 feet, looking at the oncoming Fw 109s and seeing the strange apparition of the German pilot pausing to look at him.

Why not just bail out?

When they reached a little house in Saint-Jean-de-Luz, they left the bikes and went inside, where there was a kind of bar area. Someone brought them soup, some thin beer and bread. The helpers told them they could rest for a while. Bob couldn't tell whether he was awake or dreaming as his thoughts went from floating down to the ground in a parachute to the sound of the bullet clinking in the hospital pan and the chatter of the streetcars in Brussels.

And then the four of them were walking again; he had no idea where he was. Two days before Christmas, Bob was still wearing the same ratty clothes he'd used all the time in Brussels. He kept walking along with Max and Jean-François and the other airmen. They came out of a bend in the mountains and crossed the highway out of Saint-Jean-de-Luz and down a hill.

It was raining and foggy, but for the first time in six weeks, Bob saw the Atlantic Ocean. It reminded him again of flying his airplane across the English Channel before parachuting into Belgium. He saw the hills along the uneven coast and the little port of Saint-Jean-de-Luz down below the road. It looked like a picture postcard.

Jean-François had the pilots walking along in scattered groups to minimize attention. They kept on walking, blending in now with all the people going to market. The men ambled across the bridge from the main road above the village, with the coastline and the Bay of Biscay always in view. Bob saw German soldiers and a private with a rifle guarding the little bridge at the bottom of the hill. Bob remembered that a good Frenchman doesn't put his hands in his pockets or clink his change, and he always keeps his beret right on top of his head. So he kept walking, trying to look as French as he could. After a while the airmen were led onto a side street, where Bob saw a stout lady, with steel-colored hair pulled back in a bun, leaning out a window. It was Kattalin the widow, watching for their arrival.

Kattalin could see rivulets of water running down the slope along the narrow cobblestone street. Her house was a three-story white stucco-and-wood structure in the Basque chalet style. They turned down the side street, meandering over the narrow walk before slipping into the door of Kattalin's house on the left. Kattalin didn't smile as the tall blond pilot walked into her house. All afternoon stragglers had been arriving as steady as the winter rain.

But now, her mood was getting darker as the number of men in her house totaled ten.

"Too many people," said Jean-François, agreeing with her. "Too many to cross the river." But there was no choice.

Kattalin was hardened but not oblivious to the constant danger of being captured, and she was always looking out for potential traps and mistakes. So was Jean-François. Attention to detail was essential. The four airmen had come in and were downstairs drying off. Jean-François was there too, and he brought with him two more Belgians and a Frenchman. One of the Belgians was Daniel Mouton, a big, barrel-chested fellow with a jolly laugh and a mustache. Daniel was a former Belgian soldier who'd been imprisoned by the Germans and escaped. He was a gregarious type and used his disarming friendliness as camouflage for his shrewd analysis of everyone and everything going on around him.

The other was Jacques Cartier, Jean-François's friend who had agreed after the meetings in Gibraltar in October to reestablish the Elizondo Line to the east. Cartier was a solid-looking fellow, but much older than anybody else there; he looked as if he was fifty years old. He had deep pockets under his eyes and a baleful expression that reflected the loss of friends and family during the three years of Nazi occupation. He wore a jacket and a tie and carried himself like an army officer. At the other end of this trip, Jean-François would take Cartier to meet Michael Creswell and discuss the strategy for Elizondo. Careful plans had to be made to avoid any more arrests on the border. Jean-François still had his misgivings, even though Cartier was an experienced, intelligent veteran of such operations. He'd slogged through the jungles of Southeast Asia when he was a younger man, picking up a case of malaria that bothered him from time to time.

The Frenchman was Roland Bru, code-named Richard. He was a member of the Résistance en route to Madrid. Little was known about who he was and even less was known about his mission. But Résistance members and Allied special forces occasionally moved in and out of occupation zones with Comet.

There was careful timing on every departure. They were waiting at Kattalin's house for it to get dark, about four or five o'clock in the winter months. That would get them to the river around midnight. After crossing the river, they would arrive at their Spanish safe house in Sarobe at dawn.

Kattalin had another problem. She was spending more time than usual upstairs tending to Florentino. Her friend was always impassive, even now as he suffered with a full-blown case of the flu. It was a cause for worry because influenza was a serious illness; there was no cure. People in Basque country fearfully remembered the epidemic of 1918, which came to be known as the Spanish flu and killed millions all over the world. Nobody knew how many thousands of people had died in the Basque country, but everyone had a friend or relative who was cut down by the epidemic—men and women in their prime, not just old people and babies, dying from one day to the next. Now again, people on the French side of the border got the ominous news that many of their friends in Irún were getting sick this Christmas season. Kattalin could only pray that her teenage daughter, Fifine, would be spared, that Florentino would get better quickly and that no one else, herself included, would be immobilized by the flu.

Florentino was bundled up under blankets, trying to sweat out his fever. There was aspirin; there was cognac. Perhaps a trustworthy doctor would come to spray some antiseptic into his throat—that was how one fought the disease. It was crucial to stay in bed, drink liquids and take cold compresses if the fever went too high.

Tonight the boys had to go without him. There was no question about this; even if Florentino raised the idea of abandoning his sickbed, neither Jean-François nor Kattalin would hear of it. They needed him healthy and alive, although they could not wait for him to get better. Kattalin summoned two other Basque mountain guides, Martin and Manuel, who had worked with Florentino before and knew the way. There could be no delay. At all costs, even in the rain, even with Florentino ill, the underground railroad had to keep moving. In two days, four more pilots would be arriving; the Comet Line was stacked with escapees all the way back to the countryside outside Brussels. Men were waiting to be transported and delays or backups increased the possibility that the Gestapo would discover them.

On the main floor, the Americans sat in groups looking like frightened rabbits. Kattalin and Jean-François were used to that. They'd seen this in the past and knew the Americans were weakened by the journey and did not understand exactly where they were or what was happening. These young American boys were completely dependent on Kattalin and her friends. The language barrier was always the problem. Kattalin could only look at them, perhaps say "allo" or "yes"—the only words she knew that even resembled English. She prepared dinner and smiled. Would they remember her? For the sake of security, she hoped not.

Mostly the airmen sat around dozing or looking off into space. After what they'd been through already, there was a general lack of trust in the people around them. So it went. Each of them had been briefed on the danger of divulging information. They'd also been tested to see if they were Nazi plants. Caution was prudent and hard to shake, even when they were dying to talk to other Americans after the long ordeal. Fighting the monotony, boredom and anxiety, one or the other started talking to break the ice. One heard, in between periods of snorting and snoring, the obvious sound of whispered English.

Horning was the most talkative. He was obviously older than everybody else. He started the conversation.

I'm twenty-eight. How old are you? he asked Bob.

That seemed ancient to Bob Grimes, who wasn't even twenty years old when he started training on B-17s back home.

Horning was a likable guy, of medium height, with a pointed nose and thin lips, and dark, wavy hair that sat on his forehead in a widow's peak. It made him look somehow European.

I'm from the 401st Squadron, 91st Bomb Group, based at Bassingbourn, England, Horning said.

He had been the navigator on a B-17 flight over Münster on October 10. They dropped their bombs okay, but their engines started burning on the way back. It sounded a lot like Bob's problem. His engines worked fine on the ground, but the superchargers acted up as soon as he got into the air. Horning's pilot, Lieutenant E. Richard Verrell, had had problems with the plane on their previous mission. The engines were overheating, but nothing was done about it.

The thing was, Horning said, "the airplane was given a ground check, but no air check." The Flying Fortress was barely airworthy. The pilot gave the call to jump.

Free-falling before he pulled the rip cord, Horning had his parachute leg harness on backwards and was worried about slipping out of it. "Glancing up . . . I could also see the aircraft with smoke and flames pouring out. . . ."

At least Horning wasn't badly hurt. He twisted his knees and ankles when he landed, and had lost his boots, but that was about it. He was glad that none of the Germans shot at him as he floated to the ground. Fortunately, too, no soldiers were close to his drop site, near Goor, Holland, about thirty-five miles from the German border.

Horning wandered from farmhouse to field in Holland, finally arriving in the arms of the Comet Line. There were lots of helpers. In particular, he remembered Charlotte Ambach, who shepherded him around Belgium just as Lily had helped Bob Grimes. Charlotte was a beautiful young woman. She and her mother, Elise, wanted the pilots to know how much they hated the Nazis, and how they'd do everything they could to save pilots. Horning was grateful and always astounded by how a young girl like that could risk her life to help him, when instead she could have played it safe.

"In all the traveling," he remembered, "Charlotte stayed right with me, sitting alongside me as though we were close friends. Such a pretty girl could attract a lot of attention and she placed herself in jeopardy."

But the pretty girl that Horning really wanted to talk about was Diane, the girl who jumped into his lap on the train from Lille to Paris. The story got better, and her flaming red hair got redder every time Art told the story. How would he ever get back in touch with her? Diane wasn't even her real name.

Stanford and Burch were sitting by themselves. They didn't say much at first. Stanford was scribbling down notes. Burch was sleeping and lazy. They tended to be stragglers when they rode their bikes, and loafers when they walked down the road. They weren't letting on why—Burch was suffering with a bone bruise and could hardly walk. The Comet operatives had known about the extent of Grimes's injuries, but Burch had apparently decided to tough it out. Stanford was dragging to take care of his copilot. Stanford worried about him. The bicycle trip from Dax was rough for Burch. Horning and Grimes didn't have much patience with the two of them. They didn't know that Burch was wounded; they hadn't seen the blackened bruise all along his leg.

Stanford finally started talking. He said that he and Burch were part of the same crew. Burch was a B-17 copilot, and Stanford, the bombardier on the same plane.

He said they also remembered Charlotte Ambach. Horning was right; she was a very pretty girl. She took them around Brussels too. Funny thing, the airmen couldn't recall having seen one another until Paris. Their paths must have crossed more than once on the way south.

Stanford and Burch were a couple of years older than Grimes. Stanford had a job back home in Augusta, Georgia, as a Bell Telephone installer. Burch was from Terrell, Texas. While the other boys had sweethearts back home, Burch was married. He figured that his wife, Olga Johnson Burch, had already gotten a letter saying that he was missing in action. Burch's mother and father also lived in Terrell, and they had another boy, also a pilot, who was flying P-38s in the Pacific theater.

Stanford and Burch's last mission had also taken them over Holland. Stanford told the story in detail, reliving it. Bob knew what that was like.

Suddenly we dropped out of formation, Stanford said. *It happened three times. I don't know why.*

Each time their pilot, Whitlow, dropped out of formation, he had to push hard to catch up to the rest of the aircraft. The crew was worried. The consequences of dropping out of formation were obvious.

I saw ME 110s firing at us, Stanford said. *I think they put the wing gunner, the tail gunner and the ball turret gunner out of commission.*

That was one way of saying it. The three men were dead.

We almost caught up to the formation but there were more fighters. There was a 110 below us. I turned down on him and fired. I saw a flash from his engine and he delta-spiraled down and turned flat again. I saw him go down.

197

Then I saw another fighter come in from the nose. He was firing tracers by us. Then I noticed the number three engine was out. We kept trying to get back to the formation on three engines. But when they saw us flying around but not firing, and eight or nine 110s circling, the others turned to get away from us as fast as they could. Can't blame them.

Then there were eight or nine more fighters circling their B-17. They were hit again. The pilot gave the order to abandon ship. It took Stanford only seconds to gather his chute, but before bailing he went forward on the narrow catwalk to the flight deck. It was an eerie sight.

The plane was flying itself, the two seats in the cockpit were empty. The pilot and Burch had bailed out already. The plane was buffeting and jolting. Stanford held on tight and attached his parachute.

The g-forces were pretty good, but I got to the hatch and jumped end over end away from the wing.

Stanford agreed with Grimes about how peaceful it was when they jumped. After the firefight, it was quiet, and he was just sailing through the air.

But I had this new kind of British chute. I couldn't steer it away from a stand of trees. I was about six or seven feet off the ground. I had to cut myself out of the harness and jump the rest of the way.

Burch and Stanford came down a mile or two from each other, near Holten, Holland. Burch's parachute was among those that Stanford saw just before he did his header out the bomb bay. Burch wasn't talking about his own experiences. But when he and Stanford walked along, he told his story and Stanford filled in the gaps.

Burch never explained what was wrong with their plane, but it was clear they had fallen out of formation. He jumped when the pilot gave the signal to bail out. His leg probably scraped along the lip of the fuselage when he jumped. He also had some other injuries. He told Stanford that he lay dazed in a hedgerow after he landed, then walked for several hours, in pain from his injured leg. A Dutch boy named Jon met him and took him to a clandestine shelter, where partisans were also hiding some Jewish refugees. He was hurting and unable to move. Burch stayed in bed hoping he'd regain strength. Three or four days after the airmen came down, one of the Dutch helpers stopped by and took Stanford for a drive. It was a reunion at another house with Burch, who was still nursing his wounds.

After a few days of hiding in a barn, a doctor came to look at them. He said he couldn't do much for Burch's leg. He also brought news about another member of the crew, Richards, the tail gunner. He also had parachuted down near Holten. German soldiers found him quickly and took him to a hospital. They would send him to a POW camp before long. There was no word on the other men.

Stanford was determined to look out for the copilot. Burch had suffered some burns and scratches, but his real problem was that leg bruise. The doctor said there was apparently no entry wound, just a contusion that needed rest. He prescribed two more weeks in bed, but even after that Burch was just not right. Both men were cared for by a succession of friendly faces in alternating safe houses.

Stanford said the Dutch constantly asked for information about the war.

We were the first Americans there. I made a point of telling them that we were bombing the occupied territories but with great reluctance. I talked to them about the war from our viewpoint. I think it did a lot of good for them.

When the time came to leave Holland, there was a novel scheme to move them. The underground had a contact in the Dutch civil government who transported supplies in a three-wheel converted motorcycle. The airmen were smuggled to Belgium in between some boxes. Once in Belgium they joined the growing number of men, mostly Americans, awaiting passage with the Comet Line.

Bob turned to the other men.

Wait a minute, he said. *I'm a pilot, Burch is a copilot. Horning's a navigator, and Stamford's a bombardier. All we need now is a plane.*

At one point, Daniel Mouton came over and told his war stories. He was animated and entertaining, a friendly guy. But how much could one believe? How many times could a man escape from the Germans?

I escaped three times, Daniel said.

Three times captured, and three times escaped. He laughed and slapped them all on the back.

Boys, he said, *I'm not going to let them catch me again.*

Daniel had an infectious laugh. He was not as tall as Bob, but he seemed bigger and stronger, broad across the shoulders. He was the kind of guy who talks to loosen everyone up and make them feel at ease. His English wasn't great, and Horning complained that he was difficult to understand.

Why did Daniel Mouton keep repeating the word *pineapple*—he pronounced it *peen-abble*—and talking about Jesse James and Al Capone? Maybe they were the only Americans he'd ever heard of.

"He would repeat those words over and over," Horning said.

The boys were not allowed outside; but it was raining, so it didn't matter. They had gotten used to waiting. Outside the room, there was much activity, and they froze whenever they heard a knock at the door. Jean-François came and went; Kattalin and her daughter, Fifine, served a meal, then disappeared up the stairs. Martin and Manuel, the guides, arrived around dark. Jean-François approached the Americans. He told them what he always told the pilots:

We are leaving. Go single file—do not talk, do not make noise, follow our commands immediately.

Stay close, do not fall behind, Jean-François told the men.

We will rest, but the march will be very long. You must be very, very quiet and follow our orders. There could be Germans anywhere. We will march all night.

The helpers gave walking sticks and pairs of alpargatas to each of the men; the Americans took off their sturdy shoes and were told to string them around their necks. They chuckled as they donned the flimsy, rope-soled shoes, which were tied by cloth ribbons.

Jean-François inspected the alpargatas, gave them walking sticks for balance, and mostly offered encouragement with a pat on the back and his unwavering look of confidence. The pilots took their cue from Jean-François. If he was worried about the increasing frequency of Nazi patrols or any other thing, he betrayed nothing to the Americans. This evening was going to be nothing more than a walk in the woods.

The rain let up for the moment, but the air was heavy. As the day dissolved into a black, moonless night, Jean-François was complaining to himself. "Ten people is too many. We should have fewer men." But he couldn't figure out what to do about that. The Frenchman from the Résistance needed to move out, and Daniel Mouton and Jacques Cartier were crossing for a meeting with Creswell in San Sebastián. At this point, the Comet Line had never been so well tuned: twelve pilots a week—constant motion and activity.

Jean-François looked for the positive. The weather was terrible—that meant it was also perfect, just as they liked it. The rain was good, because few soldiers would venture out on a night like this. But of course heavy rain was another matter, because it made the hike treacherous. And it was discomforting to move so many people without Florentino. Martin and Manuel had crossed with pilots before, and Jean-François trusted them. But Florentino was the anchor, the man who would sacrifice everything to succeed.

Kattalin kissed each one of them on the cheek at nightfall when they left, and watched as the men paraded somberly up the hill.

Zorion! Agur!

Bonne chance! Au revoir!

The airmen followed Jean-François and the two Basque guides up the street; Jean-François made sure there were no cars on the highway. They moved across briskly, starting up the hill into the obscurity of the countryside.

Bob Grimes surveyed his surroundings on this last march to freedom, taking advantage of the light, such as it was. There was still a bit of pale illumination from the receding day and the paltry glow from the low lanterns in the mostly blacked-out village. The road closed abruptly onto a series of winding farm lanes. This first part of the walk was less than two miles to Urrugne, the French village where Dédée had been arrested. It wasn't very difficult, because it followed a country lane through gentle hills. There were curves and slopes, but nothing requiring a walking stick.

Along the hard-packed dirt road, Bob saw barnyards and farm animals, whitewashed farmhouses, rough-hewn wooden shutters half opened and revealing a bit of lantern light. There were horse carts and cone-shaped haystacks in the fields, where people carried sad-looking packages of bread and slabs of butter and cheese in baskets on the way home for the evening.

The trees seemed to amplify the sound of the rain, but at least they provided some shelter from the drizzle. The sky was lifeless and the clouds obscured the crescent moon. The men were on an endless mechanical march through an unseen cathedral of leaves, fog and spray.

Around one hill, they came to Urrugne, which had been established by the Basques a thousand years ago. Jean-François led them along the periphery, because Nazi patrol cars or French gendarmes sometimes came this far. Against the pale gaslights, there was a barely discernible shadow cast across the road. It was the old church tower of Saint Vincent, in the town plaza. The church was built in the twelfth century, and the clock tower was added much later. In daylight, a sober inscription could be read beneath the clock as it marked the time: *Vulnerant omnes, ultima necat*, which means "Every hour wounds, the last one kills."

From Urrugne, the route turned into a series of winding, hilly lanes. They climbed over a half-collapsed livestock fence and then inched along a path between two fields. This would take them a bit farther inland to the foot of the mountains. Then they would climb into the Pyrenees and descend again to the river. They still had four hours to go.

The men now kept closer together, perhaps catching a flash of the backpacks that Manuel and Martin, the two guides, were carrying. Once in a while, they stopped to rest and sat against a tree. One of the guides unlashed the ropes around his pack and passed around milk, a bit of hard bread and cognac.

Bob Grimes could see nothing in front of him; it was blacker than black. He guessed he must have been seeing something, because he knew he was following someone. But sight could be defined differently; it was an assumption of vision rather than actual eyesight. It was the combination of senses, internalized so that he could judge distance and maintain bearings. The senses were translating all other measures into the perception that he could see something that was beyond him.

The intensified blackness of the shrouded night offered no diversion but the slurping sound of their steps or the slight cricking sound when a branch snapped back at them on the trail. Bob was guided by the sounds and variations in the tone of emptiness, a ripple of clothing, combined with a rustle of wind from a swinging arm ahead of him. And sometimes, in fact, the men bumped into one another. It hardly paid to have your eyes open at all. It was better to rely on this sense of sound, the sloshing of the alpargatas—both his and the others'—that also served as a form of seeing. He could see and measure that sound and follow it.

There were internal sounds; he could sense the pumping of his blood, his heart pounding, the sound of his breath, in and out. Such was the depth of silence around him that he could isolate his internal rhythms as he plodded along. Occasionally there was a snap or a slap from a branch. More than once, a man hit a low branch, bending it forward, and it flung back, stinging at Bob's head. Other times, he bumped into the others, who were holding down some brambles with their forearms, so they wouldn't boomerang in the others' faces. There was a bitter, decayed taste in his mouth—even the water had that bitter sting to it. This was an ancient track that skirted grazing land. In the mild mountain winter, there were occasional encounters with sheep grazing a few feet from a stone fence, preceded by the sound of dull, clanking bells as the animals ambled along.

Bob could feel the cold, biting air at the inside of his nostrils. It was not too cold to smell the animals and the manure and leaf compost that caked the path. At intervals one could perceive gradations of air and openness in the blackness of the night. The sky was blotted out by the fog; unseen below was the expanse of terrain as they traversed their route, clinging to mountains overlooking the bay and the surrounding hills that dropped steeply off just feet from where they walked. It was cold, yet he felt more weighed down from the dampness than the temperature. Bob still wore the same suit he had found on the rack with Lily in Mademoiselle Camusel's apartment in Brussels. It felt like a gritty, grinding, soggy sack, washed only by his sweat and the elements.

Was he conscious? By what terms? He knew to move ahead, he was thinking about this much—the next step, one foot in front of the other. There were dreams to take him out of this place as he walked.

The daydream about Mary Helen, the girl in Arkansas back at flight school, or trying to land his trainer with the feel of the stick, trying to touch it down onto the ground, or the experience of flying the B-17 and the nagging thought that there must have been some way of keeping her airborne. He reminded himself again that this wasn't so. A plane with a shot-out tail doesn't fly. Snippets of memories, girlfriends, hiding in the fields, limping into the barnyard in Belgium, too much butter for dinner with Lily in Brussels, then back home at basketball practice or running when he thought he could run no more.

He thought about survival. Take it one step at a time, he told himself. He looked at it as an obstacle course. It's all the same as training to fly an airplane. First you fly a one-engine plane, then a twin engine; you work your way up. You pull together a crew, you get assigned a mission, then another. If something goes wrong on the plane, you try to improvise. You keep going. Don't plan ahead, he told himself. Take one step at a time; be prepared for anything. Be logical and get home safe. He was almost there.

Daniel Mouton was ahead of him. They were wide awake. If adrenaline wasn't enough, a few of the others took Benzedrine tablets during the crossing. That helped them count their steps one by one, kept the body functioning and insured that the mind would stay, if not alert, at least responsive to stimulation. The march to freedom was an uphill climb, a fight each step of the way. As they moved on, Jean-François whispered his French-accented encouragement—wait, now go, and now stop for a while.

He imagined the two stragglers tailing behind; Stanford and Burch were always begging for rests and slowing them up. They were awfully quiet, not acting like team players. Jean-François was back with the stragglers; occasionally their lethargic pace forced everyone else to stop. Bob didn't like the way they were slowing the rest of them down.

Seems like Burch and Stanford are always lagging, Bob was thinking. They must have been together since they came down. *Horning and me are always pushing.*

What else was Bob thinking about? Lily should be proud of a job well done. Thank you, Lily. He could walk and he was going to make it. He could feel his foot and his toes wriggle on the soft rope soles of his alpargatas. In his mind he could see the toes, and then up his leg, as if the sinews and reddish striations of muscles, tendons and connectors were straining with each step. He could almost see the image as Dr. Rouffart was looking at it through the fluoroscope with Lily standing constant guard. The wound was now healed, but not completely normal. Where the layers of muscle should be adhering tightly contoured along his thigh, there was a foreign space, filled by scar tissue from the bone radiating outward; for such was the feeling, somewhere between pain and burning in his left leg, each step that he took. If he were to sum up the effect of these steps, it would be approaching exhaustion. But there was a determination and need to survive and move on, so he did move on. Each step was confirmed by the slapping of his feet in the alpargatas alternating on mud, stone, leaves or a piece of undergrowth, climbing step after step; not counting minutes or hours, they walked through the unknown wood to the unseen promise of a safe haven.

The way was steep, undulating and deceptive. Sometimes a path climbed around a curve and brought them to a short descent, followed by an even steeper upward grade. There was no idea when they might reach the crest of the mountains. Other times the path dissolved into runoff from a stream that crossed along from the side of the hill. Bob now realized why Jean-François had given them walking sticks, and he used the long wooden staff the rest of the night for balance.

Occasionally, there'd be a bird whistle from a guide in front, and Jean-François came back and had everyone crouch in the underbrush. There were sounds; you might hear other brushing footsteps passing by in the opposite direction. Bob Grimes could not know that other smugglers were coming across from Spain to France and were signaling to one another in the night by way of greeting.

It was the final walk at the end of a great journey. Each airman had been ripped from the sky, had jumped for his life from a moribund airplane and had suffered some degree of injury in the process. Each man had to strip away clothes and identities, hide in the bushes from the Nazis and their patrol dogs and depend on the goodwill of people who had no reason—other than their inherent sense of duty and humanity—to risk their own lives by getting involved.

Horning was pushing on, and he was complaining. He was tired and thinking more about the cold, although for December it was reasonable—not quite freezing—and there was no snow. But the wetness permeated everything, and they were all sick of their dirty, old clothes. Every ounce of extra gear and moisture weighed them down; the soggy clothes, the feel of the shoelaces cutting into their necks from the shoes dangling at their chins. Every bit of weight—every ounce—and every unwanted movement was a torture on the road to Spain.

Jean-François walked up now, slowing them down and patting each of them on the back.

It's okay, we will be there soon, he whispered. *We will rest again.*

They sat down in the brush, and the guides broke out more food from their backpacks. The ground was caked with torn leaves and pine needles. There was the scent of crushed lavender; there were brambles and the spiny husks of Spanish chestnuts, still sharp enough to scrape their ankles.

Stanford, for his part, downed a Benzedrine tablet with his milk. He was worried about the pace. He listened more than talked, and took note of everything that happened. He wanted to stay awake, and he was more worried about Burch, who was moving very slowly.

Burch was lying on the side of the road, not moving very much. He whispered now to Stanford.

Lloyd, he said. *Promise me something.*

The copilot was solemn, like a soldier gets before engaging the enemy. Was there any battle here? Perhaps Burch's dignified, uncomplaining personal struggle to keep up with the march was the battle itself.

If anything happens to me, go talk to my parents and my wife. Go down to Terrell, Texas. Tell my mom and dad, and Olga, my wife. Tell them everything that happened.

Stanford promised. It was an ominous request. The war was far away. They were almost free. The other men didn't say anything of the kind. Who wouldn't promise something like that? Who could say that any of them wouldn't make it?

Horning swallowed a Benzedrine tablet too, but he was still asleep on his feet. The guides gave him some sugar cubes, and that seemed to give him energy, at least so he wouldn't complain so much.

Bob didn't think he needed the Benzedrine. He was focused on getting home. He felt wide awake.

Jean-François roused the men around midnight. There was a drizzle on and off, but it didn't matter much because they already were soaked and muddy. The men were sheltered in a little flat area of the woods and still saw nothing. Bob could remember no landmark, nothing other than the sound of his feet and the leaves and the sensation of hiking uphill and suddenly having to use the walking stick to avoid sliding downhill. He was right when he guessed they'd been walking half the night.

It is very good. Spain is right here. We must cross the river, Jean-François said.

River, said Bob. *Nobody told us about a river.*

Neither Bob nor the other American airmen knew that the frontier to neutral Spain and freedom meant wading through a river. It hadn't occurred to them. But it didn't seem like a big deal. They took their cues from Jean-François, and he was calm.

Jean-François had sent the two Basque guides down to the river while everyone else was resting. They came back with their report, meeting them on the road. As expected, the rains had swollen the Bidassoa River high in its banks, but it was still passable. There was no sign of the Nazis down there, only the faint light on the other side of the river at the Spanish border police station. It was a guard shack a few hundred paces from the point of the river crossing, a spot that is named for the little train depot there: San Miguel.

This last piece to the river was downhill, so steep that it almost made them jog, and in the dark that made it even more dangerous and slippery. Going downhill was deceptively difficult because it pulled on different muscles. Bob could feel the burning in his patched-up thigh.

The dirt path widened a bit. Running water had turned the ground to mud on the rutted, rocky path; sometimes the water turned the path into a stream. The men needed their walking sticks to probe the unknown contours ahead of them. After a while, the distant sound of rushing water became evident, ever louder.

Bob was thinking of his good fortune. His leg didn't feel so bad. He was almost home free.

Stanford was propping up Burch. The copilot was in trouble.

They paused at a little crest, about twenty feet above the river. Their eyes, accustomed to the night, picked up the phosphorescent sheen of the water rushing over the boulders.

When they came to the final descent to the river, Jean-François and the guides led them to a natural stairway. Smugglers and previous escapees had worn down a series of steps around tree roots, flat stones and dead tree trunks rotting along the way. It was a twisted jumble of eroded mud and gnarled wood. The guides stood at the most difficult points, reaching a hand out to the airmen and to Jacques Cartier, who also was showing signs of weakness. Everybody slipped in the mud. There was a deep hole between the trees that forced them to sit or kneel on exposed roots, extend downward with their legs and shift position to avoid toppling from the edge. When they got to ground level, they found the bank was strewn with small, slippery rocks that twisted their ankles and pressed their toes in the light alpargatas. Burch fell down more than once, and Stanford helped him up.

Jean-François spoke to them now:

Very quiet, very quiet. No talking. We will cross the river. It will be to here, he said, holding one hand to his midsection to show the depth of the water. They could barely see one another.

Remove your trousers. You will do like this.

The men took off their pants and the guides showed them how to tie the pants legs together and hold them at their necks. In this way, they formed a rope chain, one man linked to the next.

They were on their haunches, with their backs to the sound of the river, while Jean-François asked the guides to check the river one more time. They waded in halfway, maybe ten or fifteen yards to the center, reporting they could do so without problem. A strong current, the guides concluded, but passable.

The river was about twenty-five yards across; more than two hundred men had crossed at this very spot, three days a week when Florentino led airmen to safety. On a good night, it was not memorable. Back in London, being debriefed, a number of the British and American crews didn't even remember crossing the river. But in the wintertime, it was cold enough to remember.

Just as on the night almost a year earlier, when Dédée was arrested because flooding had forced her to delay crossing, rain over recent days had swelled the mountain tributaries that fed the Bidassoa River. There were unseen holes in the riverbed at this normally tranquil spot. From the crossing point, the river twisted around boulders and churned downhill in a surge of medium white water. Farther downstream, the river was calm, but that was near to the Pamplona Highway, too close to possible detection by any Germans on the road or by Spaniards at their border posts.

The Basque guides, Manuel and Martin, led them to the edge of the river. They crossed in clusters. Manuel led the way, Horning followed him, then Martin, followed by Richard—the Frenchman—and Bob Grimes, Stanford, Daniel Mouton and Burch. All trudged down the embankment and started wading across. Jean-François stayed back for a moment with Jacques Cartier, who would go last.

Stay here, Jean-François said. *We'll come back after the rest of them cross.*

Cartier said nothing.

Wow, we've got it made, Bob thought. *We'll be home free.* He took one step. The wind-brushed misty rain made it seem colder, more so when he stepped forward into the river. It was scarcely possible to see Richard just in front of him, even though they were tethered by the tied pants legs. Bob took a few more steps. The water reached his ankles, and he could see that he needed to step gingerly to avoid slipping on the irregular stones of the river bottom. The alpargatas were waterlogged and dragged his feet through the current. By touching gingerly with his feet, he could distinguish the different contours of rock under the water, between the shiny flat stones on the riverbed and the rough pebbles that pushed into the soles of his feet, throwing his knees off balance and the larger rocks that forced a side step for fear that he'd not be able to pry his feet loose.

Steadying himself with his staff, he moved forward; his knees, then his midthighs, were covered by the cold water. The rushing torrent drove against his legs and made it harder to choose which rocks to step on. He slowed down to keep his balance, the staff in one hand, Richard's pants legs in his other hand. The current was pushing harder. It was an increasing struggle to maintain his footing; the flaps of his suit jacket were ballooning out on the surface of the water, now covering his waist. It was almost possible to swim, but the current was so strong, he felt he would get pulled away from the opposite bank. He could just see the outline of Richard in front of him; he heard the water roaring far more than it seemed this small river should roar. The river got deeper still, and the current was progressively stronger. When it reached above his waist, the walking stick felt useless—more nuisance than providing the balance he needed—so he let go, and it floated away. He took one more step; the ground was uneven. Then the water was up to his chest as he walked all the while in tandem with Richard. He was holding on now, clinging for safety to those pants legs, a lifeline around the other man's neck. One foot in front of the other, step by step, Bob repeated the phrase that carried him along. Keep it moving, each step is one closer to home.

All he knew was to hang on to Richard. When he moved, Bob moved. Suddenly he was aware that no one was holding on to his own pants legs. Wasn't Stanford supposed to be back there? This wasn't good. Nobody had said anything about a river. He thought he heard someone yell, but he couldn't see a blasted thing.

The water was almost at his shoulders, but he kept up with Richard, who also maintained a slow, steady pace. But Bob suddenly lost his balance or stubbed his toe on a rock. Everything began to unravel—it wasn't right. This is difficult, this is deep, this is . . . he stepped badly, lost his footing and felt all sense escape him—everything receded in an instant as his head slipped under the violent current that started washing him down the river.

It was like jumping out of the plane—the crashing dissonance, the need to move forward, hardly remembering where he was—and then Bob felt an instant of profound silence and lassitude. Time was compressed in a free fall. Bob Grimes slipped beneath the water.

He paused only for an instant, then spun around with a rush of adrenaline, thrashing, half kicking, half swimming and reaching for anyone or anything to hold on to. He got a solid grip on Richard's coattails. He could have pulled this other man down with him, but he felt like he was holding a taut, unyielding lifeline and had grabbed a solid trunk of a body that gave him enough stability to stand up: the other man didn't move. One step more and just as quickly he was out of the worst of the current. Water drained off him: he was able to wade in water at his knees around a few rocks, stable on his feet and out of danger. He found shallower water now; the current receded, and he waded to the Spanish shore. It was dark and hard to tell where anyone else was. He lay prone on the bank trying to dry off and catch his breath.

Meanwhile, Stanford, the next man in line, had, in fact, lost hold just before Grimes stumbled and went under. But Stanford had better luck with where he stepped. The water was rough and deep. Stanford felt strong, and he was taking it slowly. He heard one of the men splashing behind him, but he focused on making it across the river. There was more splashing and a scream, indistinct sounds that were drowned away by the churning current. Stanford had the sense that his copilot wasn't there anymore, but he had all he could do to keep his own balance, struggling toward the shallower water. He waded onto the shore and waited. There were other men there with him, but Burch wasn't among them.

Daniel came next in line, then Burch, holding Daniel's trouser legs, wrapped around the neck. They walked slowly, because Daniel could tell that Burch was truly exhausted. The center of the river was deceivingly shallow, about up to their waists. But then they had to walk a step or two upstream to avoid boulders. Daniel inched his way forward, feeling the way to avoid holes where they could lose their balance.

Daniel moved deliberately so that Burch could stick with him. When the water went above their waists and the pressure from the current was strongest, he suddenly felt Burch's balance give out. The American held on to the trousers around Daniel's neck and started to drag both of them under the water at the mercy of the driving current. Daniel had to worry about his own balance; for an instant, Burch slipped from the grasp of the hefty Belgian. By instinct, Daniel swam toward the sound of Burch's struggling movements and managed to grab him, haul him upright and retreat to calmer water. They paused for an instant, with Daniel steadying them both, close to the shallower water on the French side.

Daniel knew they couldn't stop now, so he balanced himself with Burch at midstream, and they set out a second time. Again, they moved forward, with Burch still holding on, wading into the rising course of water. They paused for balance, took another step, then paused again; and in this way, they inched across the river. But Burch was exhausted. The weakness of his damaged leg, the eight-hour walk over the mountains in the dark and the coldness of the night had left him enervated. When the water rushed above his waist and his stumbling feet hit the irregular river bottom, he slipped again, choked and screamed for help, and pulled Daniel under again. This time, Burch's desperate movements were so strong that Daniel had to break free to avoid drowning. If he went under, he'd be upended by the rapids and smashed against the rocks. For a second both of them flailed and were dragged toward the sound of rapids rushing downstream. Burch yelled and called for help. Daniel thrashed into the shallows at the same moment that the sound of a rifle shot boomed through the valley, a sharp explosion of sound against the roiling river. Daniel froze in place. A second shot reverberated. It came from the Spanish shore. A third shot and a fourth. The gunfire was alien to the night, and its sound contrasted with the rushing water. Daniel waited for the echo to recede. The final report of the gunfire ricocheted from the shore to the mountains and back. Then it was silent again.

Daniel managed to recover his balance and kept low, looking for Burch. But there were no more shouts, no further sign of him, just the sound of the water. Daniel searched and tossed about the river hoping to find Burch, but the treacherous, deeper water pushed him back. He finally swam against the current to shallow water and reached the safety of darkness on the Spanish riverbank. He was almost certain that Burch could not have found his way to the shore, that guards somewhere had heard the commotion and fired and that the poor, exhausted young American had surrendered to the flood of water and been washed away in the current. Daniel himself had come close to drowning despite all his strength. Crawling low along the bank, he reached the other survivors on the Spanish side, each of whom had gotten there separately. By sheer luck, Horning had just a mild experience crossing; he was never threatened seriously by the current. The same with Stanford; neither one of them came close to drowning. Grimes shook off what happened to him. There were holes and ridges in the riverbed that some encountered and others did not.

Jean-François waited behind with Jacques Cartier for a moment while the other eight men waded into the river, then started crossing himself. He told Cartier to stay a while longer on the riverbank, that one of the guides would return for him shortly. Jean-François made it across quickly and without slipping into one of the holes in the riverbed. The current was forceful, a much more violent flow than he anticipated, but he crossed without a problem. Jean-François was much shorter than Bob Grimes, but he was never in water that was any higher than his waist. It was a matter of the haphazard contours beneath the surface.

Jean-François climbed up onshore and found some of the other men and the guides trying to dry off. He told Martin to take the men with him away from the river. He wanted them to climb away from the water, cross the railroad tracks just above the shoreline and hide by the embankment beneath the Irún-Pamplona highway. It was fifty yards or so to the railroad tracks and another one hundred yards to the embankment.

Wait for the rest of us there, Jean-François said.

That would be the collection point. Once everyone had reassembled, they would sneak one by one across the highway and then continue up the Spanish hills for the final leg of the march to the safe house at Sarobe.

Jean-François sent the other guide, Manuel, back across the river for Jacques Cartier.

Go now and I will wait for you here, Jean-François told Manuel.

Jean-François crouched low on the riverbank, while Manuel slogged quickly back across to the French side, found Jacques Cartier and started to lead him like all the rest with tied-off pants legs around his neck.

Manuel and Cartier had made it partway into the current when they heard the same rifle shots that had startled the others. There was a scream. The shots upset Jacques Cartier and caused him to speed up his pace against the current; it was easy to stumble on the rocks and irregularities of the riverbed. He lost his balance in the stream and started to pull Manuel down with him.

Manuel broke free and regained his balance but couldn't find Cartier. He appeared on the Spanish shore alone, pointing downstream as he crawled up from the river to find Jean-François. Jean-François, who had been pinned down on the Spanish side, had no idea who fired the shots that had whizzed over their heads in a thunderous report. It was silent now, and he whispered back to Manuel:

Go with the others to the highway. I'll find Cartier.

He ran back into the river, close to the strongest currents, circling back toward the center of the flow in search of his friend. He stopped where the water was shallow, whistled a birdcall signal, listened and whistled several times more.

No answer.

He whistled several more times and ran along the French side and then swam across to Spain, creeping up and down the shore. It was so dark he could have tripped over a man before he saw him. Finally, there was an answer. It was Jacques Cartier, signaling back from the

French side. Jean-François waded to the shore and stayed close to the water, whistling until he found Cartier, who had been thrown by the current but had managed to fight his way back to the starting point in France.

Thank God, he said. A miracle. *He is safe.*

But Jacques Cartier was shivering more than Jean-François had seen anyone shiver. And he had lost his trousers when he was swept downstream.

Malaria, Cartier said, unable to control the trembling. Apparently, the stress had triggered the malarial fever that he had contracted when he was a soldier in Southeast Asia.

Jean-François looked at Cartier, whose face was white and drawn, the skin around his eyes pouched and wrinkled beyond his age.

Listen, let us go back to the town, Jean-François implored. *We'll wait for a few days. We'll come back when the river is lower. You shouldn't go now.*

They rested for a few moments. Jacques Cartier gathered up his energy and forced himself to stop shaking. He firmly rejected his young friend's proposal to go back to Kattalin's house.

No, we go tonight. Now to Spain, Cartier said.

But there is no hurry, Jean-François said, pleading with him to reconsider. *Let's stay here for tonight. The current is too strong for you.*

Cartier would not be dissuaded; he was stubborn even in his weakened condition. He absolutely refused to retreat.

Jean-François pondered what to do. His friend was twice his size, twice his age. *And he has three times my life experience*, Jean-François thought.

Jean-François stopped arguing. Once again they went into the river. The crossing was diabolical. In good weather, it was a short walk in shallow water. In the dark, in the downstream deluge, it took endurance and luck.

They moved slowly and deliberately; Jean-François felt each step of the river bottom.

Halfway into the current, there was another rifle shot, followed by two more. Who was shooting? Would the men be able to evade capture under the darkness of the night? The rifle blasts from the Spanish shore rumbled above the sound of rushing water. The report trailed away, the echo splattering both sides of the shore.

What is that? Jacques Cartier asked, still moving cautiously toward the deeper water.

They're shooting at the boys, Jean-François said; he kept going.

The deeper the water, the more concern Jean-François had for his friend. He wanted to turn back, but Cartier goaded him on; he wanted to escape the Nazis now, this night. They moved more quickly, but when they reached the center of the river, Jacques Cartier faltered. There was a rock, followed by a pocket in the riverbed. Cartier was spent, his energy fading despite his determination. He shivered and quaked and was swept off his feet. He instantly dragged Jean-François down with him, simultaneously flailing and losing grip of their makeshift lifeline. Cartier slipped free and disappeared in the current. Jean-François righted himself and dove back into the water in desperation, looking all around. With fear and horror in his stomach this time, he swam to the French shore. He signaled once; there was no answer. He signaled a dozen times, and he heard nothing. He searched the riverbank, but there was no sign. An eerie feeling descended upon him that his friend was neither captured, nor swimming, nor safe at all on either shore. He was certain at that moment that Jacques Cartier had drowned.

Bob hadn't stopped long enough to comprehend how close he'd come to being swept away. He'd hung on for dear life back in the river. He had rested on the shore for a while, shook off the water and managed to get his pants back on over his wet legs. He waited until Jean-François had ordered them to get moving. He ran, head down, with the others behind Martin, low to the ground, sometimes crawling on his hands and knees. Seconds after moving, Grimes heard some sounds close to the river—an indistinct scream or a call for help.

There was an incline, then railroad tracks in the open; they continued for some seconds more until they reached the muddy edge of the highway. There was a ledge about six feet high, with the road above it. Bob could dig his fingers into the mud, smearing his face against long tufts of grass. He heard the sound of men talking. Four shots rang out, zipping over his head, the report bouncing from mountain to valley and back again. Bob clung to the face of the embankment. As the sound ricocheted away, he was holding his breath, focusing on a sound close to his ear. Someone was standing inches above him on the road, so close that he could hear the person's boots crunching as he shifted his weight from side to side on the gravel.

When the shots rang out, the men scattered. Richard, the French agent, ran off in the night and escaped in the Spanish mountains on his own. Manuel and Martin, the only members of the group who knew where the Spanish guard post was, dropped their backpacks and crawled away in the opposite direction, down the riverbank. That left the four of them, Daniel Mouton and the three remaining Americans—Bob, Horning and Stanford.

Pinned against the embankment, Bob counted seven gunshots in all. Four in a rapid volley and then three more a couple of minutes later. He realized that there were soldiers standing just above them on the road, talking and shifting their weight inches from their heads. Then one of the men shouted and went off into the distance. Suddenly, a blinding floodlight illuminated the men huddled by the road. One of the soldiers had come up behind them on their flank. Bob saw the shadow of a gun behind the light, and he saw for the first time that he was kneeling in the muck with three other companions.

Shielding his eyes, Grimes saw the light and the form of a soldier holding a rifle. Near him, in silhouette, he saw the faces of Daniel,

Stanford and Horning clearly for the first time all night. Above them looking down, his boots inches away, was the shadowy form of a second soldier, also aiming at them.

Boys, said Daniel Mouton. *This is when we put our hands up and surrender. We don't want them to shoot us.*

Jean-François, back on the French shore was searching so frantically for Jacques Cartier that he didn't notice the lights and the sounds of the airmen being captured on the Spanish shore. He whistled and swam and kept running back and forth along the riverbank as long as he could, looking for a sign of his friend. But there was nothing. When he knew daybreak was near, he retraced the five-hour hike through the hills to seek help from Florentino back at Saint-Jean-de-Luz. He burst into Kattalin's house at midmorning.

Nous avons perdu Cartier, nous avons perdu Cartier.

Kattalin translated for Florentino and the old Basque rose from his bed, cursing himself for not going along.

I'm going to find him, he told Kattalin. His French wasn't at all adequate. But no translation was necessary; Jean-François knew how Florentino would react.

Florentino left the house and headed for the mountains. Even though he was sick, he could move fast by himself. Adrenaline and determination must have taken him through the mountain trails. He searched in vain, well into the gloom of Christmas Eve. Below San Miguel, the river hooks toward the rapids, and the current then smashes against a line of boulders before it reverses back again downstream toward the sea. It was dangerous for Florentino to be out in the open at daylight. He returned to Kattalin's house, frustrated and cursing some more.

Jean-François, in his gloom, had already left for Dax. He could not shake the memory of the disaster on the river, but he faced the pressing reality that they had to keep the rescue line moving. He was tired, but there could be no rest. He'd gotten into the fight with all his fervor and religion, considering it a battle of David and Goliath. There was no thought of stopping. That was the character trait that united the people of the Comet Line. While Christmas was a sorrowful time spent unexpectedly in France, there was no brooding.

Max met him in Dax with four new airmen. They rode their bikes without incident to Saint-Jean-de-Luz on the afternoon of December 27.

Kattalin and Florentino were waiting, and Kattalin told him that word had just come down from Biriatu, an old village in the mountains that overlooks the river.

They have two bodies.

Impossible, said Jean-François. *Who are they?*

A German patrol had come down along the riverbank on the French side below Biriatu and discovered two dead, both males, one young and one older, washed up on rocks not far apart.

Jean-François could not understand what had happened.

The Germans had brought the bodies to the medical examiner, who filled out this report.

> There was an older man "Age, 50 years approximately; height 1 meter 80 [5' 10"]; blue eyes; hair, dark brown; nose, hooked; large ears; heavyset. Identifying marks: deep scar on lower abdomen. Wears a striped shirt, a crème-colored sweater and a matching vest. He was wearing espadrilles."

This was Jacques Cartier. But Jean-François wanted to know about the other body.

> The younger man, "age approximately 25 years. Height 1 meter 70 [5' 6"]; blond hair, blue eyes. Identifying marks:

small birthmark at the base of the nose. The cadaver was dressed in a dark gray suit, a matching vest with a shirt and collar and an undershirt bearing the label John Medley LTD 1942; wearing espadrilles; and two handkerchiefs, one bearing the initial 'F' and the other 'JB.' "

Jean-François kept a logbook signed by each of the airmen when they came to Kattalin's house. He checked his list and saw the names: Stanford, L. A.; Grimes, R; Horning, A.; Burch, J.

It was Burch, the pilot who had been so exhausted that night.

The local Feldkommandantur determined apparently that the 600 residents of Biriatu needed a lesson. The bodies of Jim Burch and Jacques Cartier were deposited under guard in the courtyard of the little church of the hamlet perched on a mountain overlooking the border they had tried to cross that night. The intended message: Thus always with those who defy the Third Reich. This was a miscalculation. The Basque villagers of Biriatu, whose bucolic life of farming and shepherding had been invaded by troops in their strategic perch over the border, had nothing but contempt and disdain for any communication from the Nazis. Indeed, at the Hotel Iribarren and the guesthouse known as the Bonnet-Lecuona, a separate resistance group hid and smuggled fugitives across the river whenever they could, right under the noses of the German garrison. The villagers responded to the public display by bathing the bodies of the drowned resisters in boughs and garlands of flowers. The Germans then moved in and took the bodies away.

We don't know where they are buried, Jean-François said.

At nightfall on December 28, Jean-François and Florentino took the next four airmen into the hills and arrived at the river around midnight. The current was low, the crossing was peaceful and all arrived safely at Sarobe by dawn. The airmen were safe and would never even remember the river.

Jean-François met Creswell and they exchanged information.

Jacques Cartier is dead, drowned in the river. One of the pilots also drowned in the river.

Creswell was somber.

But your other three pilots are okay, he told Jean-François. *They'll be free from the Spanish before long and on their way to Gibraltar.*

Now that Jacques Cartier was lost, the plan to open the second escape passage at Elizondo was once again postponed, if not discarded. Creswell might have begged Jean-François to take a break in England, but he knew that Jean-François would never accept.

Instead, Jean-François stopped at the Catedral del Buen Pastor in San Sebastián to say a prayer for Jacques Cartier and the poor young pilot, Jim Burch. And then, just after the New Year, he returned to France. More Allied airmen were waiting, stacked up along the escape line. There were more airmen parachuting into occupied Europe every day. Jean-François needed to go to Brussels to check on safe houses and deliver expense money provided by Creswell. He would find out about the status of the trains and surveillance down the line. He would check the Paris operation to make sure the transfers were operating efficiently. And then he would return to southern France to lead more pilots on the trip from Dax to the border. A blockage or delay in any one of these locations was a danger for each and every person on the line.

CHAPTER ELEVEN

Uncertainty in Spain

Irún, Spain. December 24, 1943.

Bob's eyes grew accustomed to the beam that the soldiers shined intermittently on them. A dim glow also cast bands of light from the guard post, just enough to distinguish shadows and dark images. Bob followed the soldier whose boots had been crunching the gravel above him. This man was the sergeant. Behind him came the other soldier, carrying a black-muzzled rifle, beads of water dripping off it. They motioned their captives to hoist up the two duffel packs and start moving toward the guard shack.

At some point, the guides, Martin and Manuel, must have shed the packs on the riverbank and vanished in the night. Richard, the Frenchman, was no longer there. The soldiers had no way of knowing that some men had escaped.

They motioned for the four captives to climb up and start walking along the hard clay road, forest on either side of them. This was not the royal welcome to Spain that the Americans had hoped for. Bob had no idea why they were being held as prisoners. The changing fortunes, exhilaration and adrenaline of the night crossing gave way to exhaustion; the hope for freedom met a closed door. He had many questions. For his own sanity, and in his own sense of determined logic, Bob just followed his primary instinct: take everything step by step.

Let's see now what these soldiers do. We'll analyze the situation at daybreak and then we'll know more.

The presence of the European war suddenly had come crashing down on the three young American officers—they were not individuals, they were captured soldiers in battle once more. Bedraggled and soaked, the prisoners shuffled in a line with their new guards to the customs post.

Knowledge about the military and an astute nature were helpful: Bob realized that anyone sent out on sentry duty at a border post in the dark would not be a bright light of military theory—especially on the day before Christmas. These guys would more likely be low on the totem pole and easy to confuse.

His immediate thought was survival, combined with a keen instinct for the possibility of escape. But that would have to wait until the day unfolded. The Spanish soldiers took them to a small house that they used as their border guard station. They motioned them to a room, where a sergeant started asking questions. Daniel Mouton was the only one who could communicate and he acted as spokesman for the rest.

We're Americans escaping from France, Mouton said.

What do you have in the knapsacks? the sergeant asked.

Mouton reached in and offered the Spaniard some stockings and other contraband. The sergeant wasn't interested. He told one of the soldiers to stand guard in the room, then motioned to the window to let the four men know there was a guard stationed outside as well. The sergeant left.

Daniel Mouton whispered urgent instructions to the airmen.

We've got a problem, there are maps, photographs and intelligence reports in the packs. We have to destroy everything.

Until now there had been no reason to tell the Americans about the intelligence operation that functioned along with the escape route, or that Kattalin's house was the post office for the Basque intelligence service, which was transmitting the latest reports on German troop movements, installations and details about the occupation.

We have to destroy the papers we have in these packs. Intelligence material with code names that could compromise operations in the entire southern sector. They could return it all to the Nazis. We'd be in a fix.

It was a double problem. First, they all knew what it meant to allow intelligence information to fall into enemy hands. Names and codes could be compromised. Agents could be captured. Second, they couldn't tell what the Spanish military would do with people carrying such information. They might treat them as spies, rather than escaping soldiers, and send them back to the Nazis.

They came up with a quick plan. They were held in a room with a table, a chair, a potbellied stove in the corner and a small side room with a toilet. Daniel and Art walked over to the guard, and Daniel started chatting away amiably.

Listen, will you let us start a fire to dry off? We can make a deal, Mouton said. *Tenemos regalos. We have presents in the backpacks. Mira como estamos mojados. We're all soaked. Let us light the fire.*

A sweeping look at the soggy quartet and some mournful glances was all it took. The soldier wasn't too sure, but Bob saw Daniel already reaching into the packs and taking out stockings, lace and all sorts of treats. He tossed the pack back on the floor and motioned to Stanford and Grimes to get to work. Stanford picked up some matches, and Bob ripped up the first roll of paper for kindling the stove. The men worked with theatrical nonchalance while Daniel practiced his Spanish with the guard.

Bob and Stanford pulled out the tightly bound, wrapped documents one by one. They burned the material as fast as they could, smiling over Daniel's shoulder to show how they were warming their hands and drying off. Some of the paper was soggy, and Stanford had to blow on the flames until he turned blue to keep the papers burning. In the heat of the fire, they took turns burning documents and blowing on the damp paper.

Keep burning the paper, Daniel whispered.

Stanford and Grimes worked stealthily, but by daybreak the job still wasn't done.

When it was Horning's turn to tend the flames, he had trouble with some of the soggiest material, so slipped it under his shirt and went into the toilet.

He closed the door, pulled out the roll of documents and started tearing sheets into small pieces, flushing the toilet as he did so.

He came back into the main room, which was noticeably warmer with the heat of the documents burning in the stove, and started unraveling more paper from the packs.

They were still using the papers for kindling when the sergeant came back about an hour later. The boys quickly rearranged the packs; Grimes and Stanford dumped the remaining two rolls down their shirtfronts and sat down along the wall.

They didn't understand a word, but they could interpret the pantomime well enough.

The ranking sergeant began screaming at the private who'd let them burn the documents. It was like an Abbott and Costello routine.

What did I tell you to do? What did I tell you? He slapped the soldier with the back of his hand.

You told me to guard them. They were cold and wanted to have a fire.

He pushed the soldier and slapped him hard in the face.

A fine soldier you are. Look at what you've done. What are they burning?

He motioned at Daniel and the Americans against the wall.

No se muevan! Don't move.

I don't know what they're burning.

He slapped the soldier again.

You don't know. Those could have been secret plans. You're a fine excuse for a soldier. I don't know what you'd do if I weren't here. You idiot. And put out that fire!

He gave the soldier a final forearm and left the room slamming the door.

Now prohibited from running the stove anymore, the men huddled in its diminishing warmth and started talking about what had happened at the river.

They asked Daniel questions. Why were they arrested? What did they know about the others? And in particular, where was Burch?

Bob said he'd heard some yelling back at the river. Where was Burch? Where were the others?

Horning said he had no idea what happened.

Stanford said he thought Burch was behind him and, looking at Daniel, asked if the three of them hadn't been crossing close together.

It was too dark to be sure, Daniel said. *Burch was very weak.* He had slipped and dragged Daniel under the water and down with the current. Daniel said he was able to grab Burch, and he had started to get his balance, but Burch slipped again and was dragged away downstream. He could have hit his head on the rocks.

Daniel said he couldn't find Burch after that. He feared the worst.

The Americans were silent and pensive.

It was already dawn. The soldiers gave the men some watery coffee and bread and then roused them for a march up the road. The demeanor of the Spaniards was somehow less threatening than it had been the night before. Their rifles were draped on their shoulders; there were two men in front. They'd obliged Grimes and Stanford to carry the backpacks, now much lighter since they'd given some of the goods to their simpleminded guard and burned the paperwork. Bob and Stanford guarded the remaining rolls of documents at their waists.

Once outside, the day was damp but not so cold for a morning in

December. There was occasional drizzle as they marched along the side of the road. The river was visible through the leafless trees below them, a spit of water that was cut by boulders and rotting tree trunks. This was the main road to the town of Irún, which twisted and turned away from the river through sloping woodlands and was bordered by a stone fence on their side of the road. Beyond the fence, the trees sloped down toward the river, which disappeared beyond view. Bob was preoccupied with the mission Daniel had given them the night before: get rid of the documents. He was still operating the only way he knew, one step at a time; at each moment, do what you're supposed to do. Be logical, and you'll make it home.

Bob kept his head down and faltered in his pace, pretending to be weak. Soon he lagged behind the rest. Occasionally there was an incomprehensible shout from the soldiers up front, who dropped back to goad him to keep pace. But he soon was trailing at the end of the line once more. He timed himself for the perfect moment. Finally, he was about 200 yards back and he saw a sudden dip and curve in the road, partly obscuring him from the others. He grasped the roll of papers under his waistband and, with a smooth motion, tossed the bundle over the stone fence; he watched it topple well down the wooded ridge into the underbrush, maybe twenty-five feet downhill. He managed to accomplish this without being noticed, then waited to see Stanford do the same.

When the soldiers yelled again for him to move forward, Bob caught up for a minute with Stanford, who suddenly dropped his pace until they were walking abreast. He wanted no part of spy work. Like a game of hot potato under the nose of the guards, he dumped the remaining intelligence material into Bob's hands and sped forward, so the only thing Bob could do was stuff this new roll of documents down his pants again. He pulled his jacket tight and glared at Stanford.

The jerk. What's he giving it to me for?

Again, Bob dropped back and prepared to dump the bundled papers before anyone noticed. The soldiers caught Bob trying to discard his last parcel, picked it up and shoved him forward, making him march at the front of the line.

The motley procession continued to the streets of Irún, a small border town whose population had been decimated since the civil war. About 15,000 people remained, and the memory of the war was still fresh. Everyone recalled the first days of September 1936 when presumed anarchists fled the town and set it ablaze at the feet of Franco's invading forces. The flames could be seen both from San Sebastián and from France. Seven years later, the destruction was still visible. There was rubble on the Paseo de Colón and on the Calle San Marcial. City Hall survived the blaze on the Plaza de San Juan and for a time stood alone in the wreckage.

At Irún, the captives were taken to a border patrol barracks, where a commander conferred with the soldiers for a while. He then turned to Daniel Mouton.

We're sending you to a hotel. Leave your things here, the commander said.

The Spaniards kept the knapsacks and obliged the men to turn over money and valuables. Bob and Stanford each were carrying 500 pesetas, worth about $50, given to them by Jean-François back in Saint-Jean-de-Luz. Stanford handed his over, and Bob motioned that that was all there was. He'd hidden his money under his clothes. Along the way, the Americans saw something they had never expected to see again: Nazi soldiers were strolling about casually everywhere they looked. The Germans looked like they had the run of the streets. Perhaps Daniel was the most disturbed. The Germans had already caught him three times. Now he was imprisoned just several hundred yards from occupied territory. How difficult would it be for a German to seize him and force him back to France? Daniel was representing himself as just another Allied soldier, a Canadian who spoke

French, English and Spanish. If he was revealed to be European—either French or Belgian—he'd most likely be sent back across the border—assuming they all weren't sent back. One of the guards approached Daniel, who translated for the others.

They say we're going to a hotel, and we'll see what happens after that.

As they walked along, led by their Spanish guards, people stopped to look. There were men and women walking with Christmas parcels; children dashed about. The men were dressed in dark suits, tieless with white shirts, and wore berets flat on their heads; they looked at the escapees curiously, squinting and impassive. The scruffily dressed captives were a novelty that attracted some interest.

The majority of people were dressed in black; old women hobbled on bowed legs carrying bread from the market; boys and girls on rickety old bicycles wove through the pedestrian traffic. Everything was in black-and-white, or a shade of gray.

Suddenly a woman broke forward through the crowds and walked alongside Bob for an instant. She looked at him earnestly, thrust a bar of chocolate into his hands and scurried away.

Why'd she do that? Bob wondered. *That was strange. These people are friendly. It's not so bad.*

Bob pocketed the chocolate in his jacket and kept moving. The boys were led to a nondescript stone-and-wood building like all the rest at the top of one street, and the guards shoved them through the door. The building was run-down and stripped bare.

Where are they taking us? Horning asked.

Bob shrugged. Stanford was quiet, probably still thinking about Burch. Daniel already was looking around for a chance to escape.

Bob realized what was going on when the guards marched them up a flight of stairs. They opened a rough-hewn door set in the peeling plaster walls of the corridor. There were a couple of men as bedraggled as everyone else sitting on the floor on a pile of straw. They looked up.

There was a nonlocalized putrid odor in the room, something old and rotten; the straw was musty with a vague odor of sweat and urine. The smell came from a witches' cauldron at the center of the room. It contained a yellow-brown viscous slop with fatty objects floating in it.

Some hotel. We're in jail, Bob said.

None of them had slept since the march across the mountains, and they were too far beyond exhaustion to think about what to do. They were also probably in shock after what had happened. The sudden danger of the river, being shot at, the capture and the endless march. And no one knew what had happened to Burch and the others. The four men fairly collapsed onto makeshift straw mats in the room and fell asleep, while around them the people of Irún prepared for Christmas Eve celebrations.

When the men woke up on the afternoon of December 24, they sized up their surroundings and discovered a few other prisoners and several other rooms. One was a Polish soldier, possibly a deserter from the war; a German pilot with a shiny Luftwaffe emblem on his undone blouse; and two Spaniards, one of them the local town drunk, who was there to sleep it off.

The German sat on the straw in a corner looking at them.

Who are you? one of the Americans asked the Luftwaffe pilot.

He didn't answer, looking back at them balefully. Why would a German be in jail in Spain? The German was not of a humor to join in their good-natured kidding—if he understood them at all.

Look, he's in the air force. He's got Luftwaffe wings.

Trade you for some cigarettes, Horning said.

But the German stared at them, not ready to part with any bit of his uniform. He did not speak with these new arrivals.

They drank some water and sat around dozing as evening descended. They were hungry, but the only eating was the candy bar that

Bob Grimes had in his pocket. The little woman must have known where they were going. Daniel and the three Americans sat in a corner and divided it up. Bob looked at the cauldron in the center of the room.

The gruel was horrible and crawling with vermin. The idea of eating it was sickening. They slept on and off until daybreak.

On Christmas Day, Daniel spoke to the Spanish guards. *We're all a bunch of Americans. We weren't escaping, we just got shot down and want to go home.*

Even with his bad English, the Spanish weren't going to know the difference. If they realized he was Belgian, that could be a ticket across the bridge back to the hands of the Nazis.

We are all Americans. Can we see the Red Cross or somebody from the embassy?

He didn't get a definite answer, so he kept talking.

What we'd really like is to go to church. You don't want to stop us from going to church on Christmas?

That struck a chord. War or not, God-fearing Spanish policemen were not going to have on their consciences that they had prevented believers from going to Mass on Christmas Day. No matter that Daniel was thinking about easing restrictions on their captivity and looking all the time for a way to get them out of jail.

On Christmas afternoon, two Spanish soldiers walked Daniel, the would-be American, and the three airmen down the hill to the closest church.

They were still wearing the clothes that had been theirs for weeks, wretched even before the trek from France, now mud-stained and crusty from the river crossing and sliding in the mud on the shore.

They marched the grimy and disheveled crew right into the closest parish, a tiny church where celebrants were shocked to see the Americans standing in the back pew. Daniel motioned when Bob, Horning and Stanford were supposed to kneel in prayer, and when they should get up. He was hoping the ruse of getting out of the prison would soften the way to more freedoms until they figured out a way to escape captivity. The Savior would forgive their act of diversion in His name.

Irún was a small town and everyone knew the Americans were in jail there. It was not usual, and the gossip was strong. People in the border city were divided in their loyalties. Some supported the Germans and Franco. Others hoped the Americans would win. They could read in the newspaper now that the Germans were on the run in Italy. People on the Spanish side of the border also heard about the way the Germans were pushing construction of battlements all along the sea. Many Basques were hoping the Allied invasion would come soon, force the Germans out of France and then depose Franco as well.

Even the supporters of the Reich in town could enjoy a good laugh at the expense of the overserious Nazi soldiers wandering about. Every year, the people of Irún celebrated San Marcial. Men put on their finest costumes: a head scarf or a beret set just so on their heads; a red vest over a billowing white linen shirt; a crimson silk sash about the waist and broad white trousers tied at the calf; white garters and woven alpargatas laced to the ankle. The finest horse in town—there were very few—was fitted with military buntings. All gathered to stage a re-creation of the Basque element in the Carlist Wars of the previous century.

This year, some wag told the Germans on the other side of the international bridge in France that Irún's officialdom was celebrating a military jamboree. The head of the Nazi Wehrmacht detachment in Hendaye thought that military decorum demanded an appearance by an officer of equivalent rank, a gesture to show what good neighbors had taken control of France. A colonel or *Oberhauptmannführer* donned his dress uniform, mounted his own steed and came across from France with all due pomp and ceremony to offer his respects to his Spanish friends.

The fellow who always played the old Carlist general in the San Marcial pageant was drunk as usual. When the Nazi officer crossed the bridge from Hendaye, no one stopped him from participating in the celebration. The Nazi was impressed, perhaps inspired by the display of military finery; everyone else played the part. The Nazi approached the Basque general-for-a-day, who managed not to slide off his horse and solemnly improvised an exchange of salutes followed by mutual oratory (each man's language quite incomprehensible to the other). And since it was only proper to include an inspection of the troops, the Basque led the Nazi officer as they rode up and down the line of the fine-fitted nineteenth-century Basque infantry. A final brisk salute, and the German officer turned about-face and rode back to occupied France, trailing heraldic trumpets from an orchestra intoning appropriate marching cadences. Certainly the Nazi officer had done his part and could report back to headquarters about the honorable state of cross-border relations. *Everyone was in stitches as soon as the Nazi was gone*, one of the citizens of Irún reported.

On December 26 a French Red Cross representative visited the motley group of Americans and Daniel—who was still successfully pretending to be an American. The Frenchman wrote down their names and drove down to San Sebastián, about twenty minutes away, heading for the British consulate. He reported that the Americans thought one of their fellow pilots had drowned in the river crossing. Michael Creswell and William Goodman, the consul, also received word from the Basque guides Manuel and Martin, who came straggling out of the mountains and reported what they knew about the Christmas Eve disaster. The details were still murky. There had been gunfire on the border, and Martin and Manuel also thought someone might have been killed.

Creswell had to move fast, because there were Gestapo and other German agents all around the border. Once the British and American legations registered the names of the Americans and expressed their interest in the case, it was unlikely that Spain would risk a diplomatic incident by returning them to Nazi custody in France.

Creswell sent back the Frenchman with money as payoffs for decent accommodations and food. Some of the money could have been used to make the Spanish authorities more disposed to treating the captives well. Bribery was never recorded on the books, but smoothing the way with cash would have been the pragmatic way to protect the captives.

Once he took care of that, Creswell still had the problem of finding out exactly what had happened on the river. There was no immediate word on Jean-François, Jacques Cartier and Florentino. Finally, on December 29, Florentino and Jean-François made it to Sarobe with a new group of airmen. Jean-François told Creswell about the night on the river. The death of Jacques Cartier was a serious blow to their plans to increase the number of crossings. A replacement would have to be found if they were to open the second escape route at Elizondo.

Meanwhile, official recognition and the Red Cross visit brought the immediate changes that Creswell intended. Grimes, Stanford, Horning and Daniel received more liberal treatment; they could go out for walks, although still under guard.

The soldiers allowed them a stroll every day into town and they progressively sought more and more freedoms. And Bob Grimes was making things even better: he still had most of the pesetas he had hidden, and he sprinkled them around to pry extra food and privileges from the guards. That wasn't difficult; a typical private's salary in the Guardia Civil was pennies, probably no more than 5 pesetas—50 cents a day. The only problem left was the boredom and the uncertainty about how long they would have to wait before they were set free.

Daniel, always tagging along but pensive on these outings, had an announcement to make one afternoon.

Boys, it's time for me to be going home. I have to get back to France. I have a plan.

He asked Bob and the others to give him all their pesetas, since the Americans and Brits would be caring for them now. And then he said to just watch him in action.

You'll be fine now; we won't have a chance to say good-bye.

On the afternoon of December 29, Daniel and the three Americans took their usual late-afternoon stroll into town and stopped at the local canteen. Only one Spanish soldier accompanied them these days, and his presence was far from intimidating—he sat at the table with them and joined in several rounds of beer.

When they were finished, the four men and their guard started walking back up the hill to their jail. The winter afternoon already was converting to night.

Halfway up, Daniel stopped short and turned to the soldier.

Wait, I left my beret back at the bar. Can I go back and fetch it?

This presented a brainteaser that was too much for the guard, who, after the free drinks, was even less alert than he otherwise might have been. Here was the problem: his orders were to cover these four men. One man said he had to go fetch his cap. Which was better, staying with the other three, or going back with the man to fetch his cap? He couldn't ask all four to wait while he himself got the cap. And he couldn't accompany the lone man back to the canteen, while the other three stood unguarded. That was stupid.

So, dulled by the beer and unable to think of a better way, he told Daniel to hurry back to the pub for his beret. The other option—not fetching the hat at all—apparently never entered into the equation.

Daniel winked at the three American airmen and said he'd be right back. He hopped back down the road, disappeared in the direction of the cantina and was gone.

By now, the Spanish authorities were hardly treating the airmen as prisoners at all, so they really didn't care that Daniel was missing. The foolish soldier only received a mild reprimand.

Two days later, in fact—Creswell could have been sending holiday money to the local Spanish police officials—the boys were released from custody entirely and were free to wander around Irún.

No longer was there apprehension that the Guardia Civil or the German soldiers on the street would send them back to France. They soon would be moving with diplomatic protection to Madrid, then onward to Gibraltar and back to England.

The Spanish soldiers marched them down the hill from the flea-infested house to a modest place closer to the center of town called the Hotel del Norte, where each had a small private room. It was the best hotel in town, although that wasn't saying much. But at least there was no more cauldron with crawling cockroaches, and they could even buy beer and loaves of bread.

Next, a young American consular official named Allison Wanamaker came down from Bilbao.

You're safe now, he told them. *It's just paperwork. Help is on the way.*

The boys wanted to know when they were going home.

Don't try to escape, you'll get hurt, Wanamaker told them. *Hang tight, and we'll make sure you get out soon.*

Conditions improved even more.

At the hotel, they met up with an Australian, who said he was a boxing champion down under.

The Australian was in the Royal Air Force, a tall, burly redhead with a walrus-size handlebar mustache the same color. He said he'd jumped from a British bomber and walked across the border from France by himself.

I'm not afraid of anybody, the Australian said. *I can beat up anybody.*

They looked for entertainment where they could find it. The Australian flier tagged along with them and was always causing a commotion. He'd encourage Bob to bribe the guards to take them downtown. There was a small shop where they stopped for coffee and pastry in the morning and a tavern where they drank beer and wine at night.

The Australian took a liking to a cute Spanish girl at the coffee shop. He leaned over the counter, spending a good while twirling his red mustache. He whispered sweet nothings—of which the girl understood not a word—while she blushed and made fresh pots of coffee. Neither could talk to the other, but what words were necessary? The Australian spent more time leaning over the counter every day, and the girl spent just as much time smiling and blushing sweetly.

One morning the Australian came in with a tattered Spanish-English dictionary. He leafed through the pages and found the phrase he was looking for, then tried it out on the girl.

"Relaciones sexuales," he said. "Relaciones intimas?"

His pronunciation was not close enough for the girl, still smiling, to understand, so he motioned her close and pointed at the translation of *intercourse* with a big fat finger.

A curtain came down over the face of the smiling, blushing girl, who stomped out of the room in anger and made sure she was never again anywhere near when the Australian came lumbering by.

With that entertainment gone, the Australian concentrated his efforts on the nights, drinking until he was soused and then threatening to beat up anyone in his way.

I was a middleweight champion, I can beat you up, take a swing at me.

No one was ever interested.

Those were the distractions while they waited to go home.

The British and American consular officials kept giving them money for better meals, although the Spanish idea of a good meal still wasn't appetizing to an American airman. One day they ordered fish at a restaurant and sat around a big table waiting to eat. The chef proudly brought out peppers and potatoes and onions in a stew along with fish heads, eyes and all, staring right back at them. They refused to eat it.

Strolling in the afternoon one day on one of the hilly streets that surround the city, Horning came to a bridge overlooking the rail yards just this side of the French border. He stopped to watch the activity below: tanker cars were pulling into the train yards, and men were transferring connecting hoses from the railcars to German tanker trucks. The markings were obvious. Spanish authorities were providing gasoline products to the Third Reich.

Bob later saw the same thing. It was taking place in plain view. Supposedly neutral Spain was giving fuel to the enemy. He could imagine the fuel being brought to an airfield in France and then loaded onto Luftwaffe fighters, which then would stage sorties to shoot down Allied planes. The helplessness was overwhelming. Give Grimes a B-17 and a crew, and he'd bomb the hell out of it—give him a machine gun, anything: the instinct was to destroy the operation taking place methodically and peacefully in front of them.

"We know," said the American consul when Horning blurted the news to him at the next opportunity. "Don't worry about it."

Bob Grimes and Art Horning had unwittingly seen a snapshot of the Franco regime's continuing support for Germany. British and American intelligence agents had been gathering ample documentation of Spanish subterfuge in supplying the Nazis. Reluctantly, the U.S. and British ambassadors finally informed Spain that their governments were initiating a total oil embargo. Samuel Hoare, the British ambassador, and Carlton Hayes, the American, still argued that diplomacy was a better method to deal with Spain, but Churchill and Roosevelt overruled them; there was categorical evidence that Spain continued to provide aid and comfort to Nazi Germany.

This finally and belatedly marked the recognition that Germany was no longer a threat to invade Spain and thus that Spain would have to start responding to Allied demands. Francisco Franco was insulted by the gesture, but his hopes for a German victory in Europe were evaporating. Spain began negotiating restrictions in tungsten shipments to the Third Reich. In particular, wolframite—tungsten ore—was provided only by Spain and Portugal, whose land shipments went through Irún and Hendaye. Without those shipments, Germany simply was unable to produce the hardened steel it needed for munitions and aircraft. Tungsten conceivably could have been used for nozzles on Germany's increasingly sophisticated experimental rockets. No one less than Franco's fellow dictator on the Iberian Peninsula, Portuguese leader Antonio Salazar, agreed with an intelligence assessment about the crucial factor of tungsten supplies. The report said that "Spain together provided Germany with almost one hundred percent of Germany's wartime supply of vitally-needed wolfram, the essential mineral in processing tungsten for steel alloys used in machine tools and armaments, especially armor-piercing shells. The strategic significance of wolfram was not lost on the Portuguese. Prime Minister Salazar himself acknowledged in early 1944 that denying wolfram to Germany 'would reduce her power of endurance, and the war would be accordingly shortened.'"

The Allied petroleum embargo worked where the mild and appeasing policies of the Allied ambassadors had not. Franco's biographer wrote that "the reality of the situation was that the oil embargo was pushing the poverty-stricken Spanish economy further back toward the Middle Ages. Franco's 1 April 1944 victory parade [commemorating his defeat of the Republic] had to take place without tanks or armored cars."

The economic pressure succeeded in forcing Franco to turn away German requests and curtail shipments of tungsten to a minimum.

This pivotal change in Allied policy and German fortunes was taking place while Bob Grimes and his fellow airmen waited in Spain for bureaucratic red tape to give way so they could go home. Every day in Irún was a day to hurry up and wait. Finally on January 10, Allison Wanamaker, the American consul, came back and told Bob and the others that they'd be pulling out of Irún. The following day they piled into a few cars with diplomatic markings and drove several hours southeast toward Zaragoza. To their surprise, they were taken to a resort complex in the town of Alhama de Aragón, renowned for its mineral springs. The Spanish government had agreed to house the Allied crews at the resort while Creswell and his American counterparts took care of paperwork. Bob stayed at the place about a week and remembered eating well and lounging about on the grounds. Alhama is an area of undulating countryside. He could see fields and little towns on the distant hills, but there was no exploring. He was fascinated by the sight of gypsies living in caves built into the sides of the hills, but it was impossible to get a close-up view of anything going on. The airmen were restricted to the resort—there was to be no mingling with the locals.

Before long, orders came through for Grimes, Horning and Stanford to ship out to Gibraltar. They took a diplomatic car and, unlike Jean-François some months earlier, did not have to hide in the trunk when they crossed into British territory. Awaiting repatriation there for a few days, they submitted to routine interrogations with Donald Darling, code-named Sunday, of MI9. It was a final line of defense to make sure enemy agents weren't filtering through the system.

After several days, Grimes, Horning and Stanford received their orders and hopped a plane back to London on January 29.

The plane flew out over the Mediterranean and took the long way to the British Isles, far off the Atlantic coast, to avoid enemy aircraft or ground fire over France. En route over the ocean, though, Bob jumped out of his seat when he heard the telltale sound of rocks being thrown against the side of the fuselage.

Flak, antiaircraft fire!

Don't worry; it's only ice, one of the plane's crew said, calming him down. As Bob knew well, condensation will sometimes freeze on an engine housing and then break free during flight. The ice slapped against the fuselage with that frightening thud, just as Bob remembered the sound of hot metal flak hitting the fuselage of his B-17.

He sat back and tried to relax. Bob was on edge, but their trip back to England was uneventful.

In London, the joint American-British military intelligence division at Room 900, Airey Neave's office at MI9, conducted a more extensive debriefing. American Brigadier General Curtis E. LeMay officiated at a ceremony, awarding Bob Grimes the Purple Heart for the injury he suffered on October 20, 1943, during his last combat mission over Belgium.

By now, everyone back home had gotten the word that he was safe, and eventually his orders came through: he was to return to the United States and serve as operations officer at a B-17 base in Florida. Bob had a final day in London before his scheduled departure by plane via Scotland. He took the train up to Edinburgh early rather than party one last night at the bars in town, because he was anxious to get home.

He'd been rooming at the officers' hotel in London with a fellow officer who did stay in the capital for that final night on the town. Bob and his roommate bumped into each other in Scotland just before the flight back to the States. The other officer showed up in crumpled clothes; his duffel bag looked like it had been shot to hell. It was torn and tattered; the gear inside was all shredded. It was a total loss.

What happened to you? Bob asked.

After you left, I packed and left my things on your bed and went out. I must have gotten back after midnight. I'd heard the air-raid sirens, but I didn't know how close it was to the hotel.

Bob, who usually went to bed early, looked at the torn bag. He would have been lying where the bag was when the shards of glass were driven across the room. Everybody joked about his heavy sleeping—he might never have awakened from that one. After all the escapes and near misses, that might have been the closest call.

PART FOUR

January 1944

CHAPTER TWELVE

The Gestapo's Trap

Bayonne, France. January 1944.

Jean-François crossed back to France; it was the New Year, and he had received some surprising news. The young girl Lily had come down unexpectedly from Brussels, and a rendezvous for the two of them was arranged. Jean-François had never met Lily; he knew only that she was one of the connections to Dédée and that she'd been successfully evading capture for more than a year since the Nazis seized her sister and parents.

Max told him that they would meet at Le Perroquet, the stylish café next to the palatial Bayonne city hall.

No problem, but how will we recognize each other? I've never met her.

One unmistakable way, Max said—though admittedly gross—was to use the ugly boil on Jean-François's neck as the signal. She was to identify him by the nasty blemish, still visible above his collar. In the months since he visited Gibraltar, it still had not healed.

Jean-François agreed and set out across Bayonne to Le Perroquet.

The problem was that Max had forgotten to tell Lily what signal she was looking for. She had simply done as Max told her—she went to the café and sat down on a bench outside, assuming that Jean-François had some means of recognizing her.

Lily had walked here from the train station, crossing the Pont Saint-Esprit and the smaller Pont Mayou, which span the rivers Nivelle and Adour just at their confluence. Even in winter and stripped of its foliage, the center of Bayonne had a monumental quality that belied the war and its occupation. As Lily approached the chic café right along the river, fashionably dressed young men and women were seated at café tables, sipping coffee, smoking and chatting. She thought it was far too elegant for a plain-dressed girl who was carrying a beaten-up little purse, and who was supposed to be sixteen years old. So she decided to keep walking and sat down instead on a bench beyond the café in the adjacent public gardens. She could observe the whole scene: girls flitted about, appearing to be waiting for someone, perhaps one of the German officers who ambled about and mingled in the crowds of French strollers on the brisk winter day. There were men laughing and drinking, and women—coquettish girls, really—playing up to the Wehrmacht officers and enlisted men who sauntered by.

Pretty soon, the situation was apparent: Max had sent her to the café, and she was waiting for a man she'd never seen before, who wasn't showing up. She felt more and more uncomfortable and out of place. And she was worried about traitors. Was Max a traitor? Would he turn her in to the Nazis? Whom could she trust?

Jean-François arrived at 11 A.M., on schedule. Le Perroquet was a popular meeting place for young people. He was wearing a plain jacket and white shirt and did not attract particular attention. At first, he looked around, focusing on young women, expecting Lily to catch his eye and realize it was him. When nothing happened, he grew impatient. More minutes passed, and when no girl approached him, he forced the matter, circulating from table to table, dipping his shoulder too obviously and revealing the scar on his neck. He did not succeed in ingratiating himself with anyone at the café, nor did he find Lily.

He left after a few more minutes, frustrated and worried that if he stayed longer, he'd either attract the attention of the Gestapo or be thrown out of the place for being insane.

Lily was there all the time, of course. Even on the park bench, she felt transparent to those at the café, a country girl in her drooping little-girl clothes. She saw a young man come along, stop at each table, tilting his head in an exaggerated gesture as he did so. Strange. Perhaps he was begging for money. After an hour or so, she went back to find Max Roger.

No problem, said Max. If he wasn't there, you can go up to the train station and meet him with Auntie Go. They'll be there at 6:00 P.M.

So she walked around Bayonne the rest of the afternoon and finally made her way to the train platform at the appointed time. Auntie Go was plainly shocked to see the waif-sized girl and said so.

What are you doing here? Auntie Go asked. *What are you doing in France? Why aren't you in Brussels?*

I don't know, I'm here, Lily replied, turning to Jean-François with surprise.

I saw you there at the café, Lily said.

The confusion settled, Lily discussed the situation in Brussels. In the two weeks after Bob Grimes left Brussels, Lily had provided passage for a dozen more men. It wasn't until she arrived in Bayonne that she found out about the Christmas Eve disaster on the Bidassoa River and the deaths of Burch and Jacques Cartier. She was saddened of course, but grateful and relieved that Bob Grimes had survived.

"Some of them you remember more than others," she said. "It's human nature. Bob was a good boy with a strong character."

Lily told them about the deteriorating security situation in Brussels. She'd fled under a cloud of imminent disaster. Soon after Bob left, it became clear that she was not able to operate as safely as she had before. The arrest of her friend Jane Macintosh was a disaster. First, Jane had the address of Mademoiselle Camusel's apartment. But Jane also had called attention to Lily's importance to the escape line. Nazi counterintelligence services were trying to hunt her down. And without Jane's perfect English, Lily was no longer able to verify that Allied airmen were native English speakers and not German plants. In addition, Hélène Camusel's arrest was too close for comfort. Since the arrest of her parents and her sister, Lily had managed to avoid danger by analyzing the odds, operating largely on information and instinct. Now she needed help.

She had discussed the security situation with her Comet colleagues in Brussels. Yvon Michiels was running the operation—Lily was his subordinate. He said he understood the danger.

You can leave Brussels, he said. *But you must write down a list of your contacts for us.*

I'm not writing anything, she answered without hesitation. *Nothing in writing. Why would anyone ask such a thing in the current climate?*

The last thing she wanted to do was leave a trail with contacts written down on a piece of paper that the Germans could find. The suggestion was ludicrous. It was her major complaint with the people she worked with. Lapses in common sense and lack of discretion had already cost too many lives. Perhaps she was young, which made her deferential by nature—or rather it told her that she should be polite to those who were supposed to be more experienced. But every day for her had been an exercise in caution and outwitting the Nazis. Why should she write something down? Young or old, boss or underling, she wouldn't do it.

Then we're not letting you go, Yvon said.

She didn't reply. It seemed to her incredibly naïve and insensitive to expect her to break security by jeopardizing herself and anyone whose name she wrote down. It was evident that traitors were afoot. She trusted no one.

Without waiting for the approval of her Comet superiors in Brussels, she asked for the advice of her father's old resistance comrade, René, who was still operating undercover and running agents throughout France.

The situation was immediately clear, the resistance chief said. Not even a close call.

Enough. You have to get out, René said. *We have a courier leaving in two days. You're going with her.*

Before leaving, she'd taken time to make sure trained and capable agents were in place. Jules Dricot would be escorting the fliers in Lily's place and Miroir and Henri Macard would focus on securing safe houses.

On January 10 she took the train south to Paris and made contact with Jérome—Jacques LeGrelle, the agent MI9 had sent from London to work with Comet. The next day she was in Bayonne, where she sought out Jean-François's bicycling partner, Max Roger.

Jean-François listened carefully. It was clear that the Nazis were applying pressure up and down the line. The accident at the river was bad luck, but there appeared to be some sort of coordination between Brussels and Paris. He said he would check up on the situation and, since he needed to go to Brussels anyway, he would meet the new operatives and visit Jacques Cartier's family there and break the news of his death. From Brussels he would go back down to Paris to meet with Jérome. When he returned south, they would coordinate the revised operation and plot out an assignment for Lily either in Paris or on the border.

Meanwhile, Lily waited at Auntie Go's house.

Jean-François took the express train that night to Brussels. His visit to Brussels was brief and the meeting with Jacques Cartier's family was sad, of course. Jean-François maintained his focus on the work before him. Jérome came up to Brussels with him for a final meeting with resistance members there to ensure the continuity of the line. It was Jérome's last visit for a while, because six months were up. Since he was a London-trained agent, MI9 expected him to rotate out across the Spanish border and down to Gibraltar. There were also new warnings about his safety in occupied territory. Jérome left for Paris on the afternoon of January 17.

Au revoir, Jean-François, Jérome said. *See you in Paris tomorrow.*

Jérome took the train to the Gare du Nord and went to the apartment on the rue de Longchamp. Waiting in the shadows were agents of the Gestapo, dispatched by the traitor Jean Masson, who was now back on the street.

Masson's return to active operations was a success. The safe house on rue de Longchamp was still operating. Now it was just a question of waiting to see who else would fall into Masson's trap.

Masson was waiting at the Gestapo headquarters at the rue des Saussaies when Jérome was led in.

Bonjour, Jérome. Where is Franco? Masson asked, referring once more to Jean-François's code name.

I don't know.

Masson smiled. *You will talk, my friend. You will talk.*

Jérome was desperate, not so much for himself, but for Jean-François, who was planning to follow him the next morning right into the same trap. There was no way to warn him.

Where is Franco? they asked.

He said nothing, praying that Jean-François would elude capture. Jérome could see the Gestapo had no information about the southern sector, and he did nothing to help them. But they knew all about the Paris operation and even mentioned Airey Neave.

They stripped him and beat him with a woven rattan whip until his back was raw and bleeding. His ankles and his knees were tied back to his haunches and his hands were manacled behind his back; then they placed him in front of a bathtub filled with water. Seventeen times they forced his head below water, each time until he felt he was drowning. Before losing consciousness, he was hurled backward and the water in his lungs poured down his body. Each time he thought he would be allowed to die. Each time there were beatings and he was tied to the wall. The beatings lasted until 8:00 A.M.; seven of his ribs were broken.

Before Jean-François could leave Brussels, he had one more arrangement to make. He'd been asked by friends to transport a young Belgian fellow named Renaud de Pret south so that he could cross the line and escape to England.

Renaud rode the handlebars on the only bike Jean-François could find for the nighttime ride across the Belgian-French border. The Lille-Paris train pulled into the Gare du Nord at about 8 A.M. on Tuesday, January 18, 1944. Jean-François and Renaud headed directly to the safe house in the sixteenth arrondissement. Close to the Trocadéro, they turned onto rue de Longchamp, walked into the apartment building and went right up to the sixth floor. Jean-François knocked on the door, expecting to see Jerome or his friend Rolande. But when the door opened, he stood nose to nose with a large man in a dark suit. Farther back in the room was another man. It wasn't clear who was more startled. Never before had Jean-François realized that it was possible to smell a Gestapo agent when you found one.

He had seconds to react and his first instinct was to bolt. He knew the building well and had an even chance of diving down the stairs, making it to a side door and out through the back alleys. However, just as quickly, he realized that doing so would be a virtual death sentence for his young companion. This he could not do. He stood his ground and decided that he would gamble on his wits and help the boy survive.

The Gestapo men did not move. The man in the background had his gun out.

Hands up!

As the Nazis searched Jean-François and the boy, putting them in handcuffs, one of the men pulled a photograph from his pocket. He looked at it and then at Jean-François and back again.

You are Franco, he said. The agent was quite satisfied, although he was confused by Jean-François's casual behavior. The young Belgian was relaxed and smiling.

Franco, there's nothing funny. You're in trouble, the agent said.

Jean-François looked at the Gestapo man and decided not to tell him what he was thinking about. He'd realized that the German was wearing the necktie that had been missing ever since the previous June, when Jean-François had come to Paris looking for Monsieur de Jongh at the rue Vaneau safe house.

Jean-François trudged down to the German field car, and the agents herded him and the boy into the backseat. Somehow, Jean-François got control of his nerves, emboldened by the knowledge that he needed to plan for their survival. This immediate transition from free partisan to prisoner presented a new series of challenges. Jean-François had a thousand thoughts, instinctively planning a survival strategy, according to what presented itself.

First was the boy.

Look, we're on avenue Victor-Hugo, he told him. *This leads right to the Arc de Triomphe and the Champs-Elysées. We'll cross right by the palace*, he said.

Jean-François's performance as a travel guide for the new visitor to Paris made the terror of the moment seem remote, actually. This was one of the more horrible ways to take a tour of the city—the route to the notorious headquarters of the Gestapo on the rue des Saussaies. But it had the desired effect. Jean-François had caught the attention of his captors.

Why, asked one of the Gestapo agents, *are you telling the kid about Paris?*

He's just a boy, Jean-François replied. *He's never been here before. I've never even met him before today. His only crime is that he wants to go to London.*

He repeated that story at Gestapo headquarters while the boy was being questioned briefly. Luckily the Germans never tortured him, because they figured he had no information for them. At least Jean-François's first objective was achieved.

Next, as he sat alone in a bare holding cell at the Gestapo headquarters, he needed a strategy that would help him withstand whatever torture they had in store for him. Perhaps he could develop a set of plausible lies that would keep them from killing him. He searched for the strength to withstand whatever came next.

After several hours, he was taken out of his cell and down the hallway to an office. A squat, sandy-haired man sat behind a desk, grinning smugly.

Franco, the man said, using Jean-François's nom de guerre. *I'm glad to meet you finally. I am Jean Masson.*

It was suddenly clear that this was the traitor who had decimated the Comet Line, who had captured Dédée's father and dozens of their friends in Belgium and northern France over the past year. He could hear from his accent that he was also a Belgian. Jean-François was sickened at the thought of this miserable turncoat having worked within the escape line and angrier that he would be unable to warn other Comet members.

Masson glared at Jean-François. *You have to admit I've done a good job.* He seemed to read Jean-François's thoughts. Masson felt that his hard work finally had triumphed. He had caught the leaders of the operation in Paris. How could it survive?

Jean-François was defiant, though, and would not allow Masson to see any reaction at all.

Perhaps, Jean-François said evenly, *but we also have done a good job.*

Masson was dismissive. He didn't need to be playing games with a prisoner. There was other work to do, besides chatting with the miserable sots who had been captured already. Confident and sneering, he got up to leave Jean-François alone in the room. Others would deal with him now. Another successful operation; this time, Masson had not even been working undercover. He'd used double agents and others to find the safe house, which led him to Jérome and Jean-François. It would be easier than ever to maintain his cover. None of the remaining Comet operatives on the street knew his name or would associate him with being a traitor. He would continue to pick them off one by one.

The first in a series of interrogators entered. Jean-François faced the unknown. How much torture could one take before one collapsed and told everything? He covered over his fear and managed to prevent himself from shaking. There were four days of isolation, filth and starvation. The interrogations proceeded under the threat of torture, which was a torture in itself. He'd heard of the electric shocks and the near drownings in the bathtub. One day, a bloodied man was led into the room. He recognized to his horror that it was Jérome, his face distorted with beatings, his wrists purple with the sores of the manacles he wore. Jérome had been tortured relentlessly all night by six men.

Now it was clear to Jean-François that Jérome could barely see. They shoved him quickly out of the room; Jean-François realized that his friend had not been broken. He could never judge a man who gave in to such torture, but he had boundless respect for a man who could resist.

Jean-François was handcuffed and manacled to the chair so he was unable to move. A week into his capture, nothing had changed. But then a new inquisitor appeared, possibly a chief inspector for the Gestapo, different from the rest. Perhaps now the torture would begin.

You are too young to be a leader of a resistance organization, the man said. *Who are your contacts?* the inspector asked.

The questions involved operations in southern France.

Only my chief knew the operations, he said. *For reasons of security, he never told me anything.*

But who is your chief?

Jacques Cartier.

How old is he?

He's fifty-two.

Where is he?

He's dead.

You're lying.

I tell you that he died on December 23.

But where?

On the French-Spanish border.

This is not true.

Call Hendaye. The German border police will tell you.

Finally, it was lunchtime at the rue des Saussaies, and a guard led Jean-François back to his cell.

At 2:00 P.M., the inspector summoned him. He had checked with the border police at Hendaye. Jean-François was telling the truth, and suddenly the Nazis no longer had much interest in Jean-François. After two weeks, he was sent to Fresnes prison, and then was transferred to St. Gilles, in Belgium, where Dédée had also been held. The sudden inspiration had worked. As with Dédée, the Gestapo refused to believe that people so young could defy them so successfully. Jean-François said a silent prayer of thanks for Jacques Cartier, realizing the sublime irony. *I was saved by the death of my friend.*

CHAPTER THIRTEEN

Lily's Defiance

Paris, France. March 1944.

About the same time that Creswell received word of Jean-François's arrest, he'd also gotten monumental news that would change the operations of the Comet Line. Airey Neave, at MI9 headquarters in London, sent a cable in early 1944 informing him that there would be more pressure than ever to rescue American and British pilots, because preparations for D-day, the Allied invasion of Europe, were about to begin.

There had to be contingency plans, Neave argued. There would be increased Allied bombings throughout the spring—and more men needing help. Unable to open a second escape line, Comet would not be able to handle the volume of airmen by itself. The bombings would target rail lines, which meant regular movement south across France to the Spanish border could be interrupted. It would become even more dangerous.

So while the escape line continued, MI9 wanted Jean-François and the others to know that there were other plans. Neave wanted to establish camps in rural areas where pilots could be guarded and hidden until they were liberated after the invasion began, assuming, as they did, that the invasion was successful.

Creswell had been planning to discuss the new preparations with Jean-François when he received word of his arrest. It was devastating, but as before, the war called for sacrifice in the names of those who had fallen.

Several weeks after the capture of Jean-François, Creswell called Auntie Go, Max and Lily—the longest-surviving members of the escape line—down to Madrid for a planning session.

All were determined to persevere in tribute to their colleagues. Immediately, MI9 sent in a new operative to take over the Paris section. He was a Belgian army commando officer, Jean de Blommaert, code-named Thomas Rutland. Airey Neave had overseen Thomas's training in England and then sent him into occupied territory. Thomas was a handsome, blond-haired fellow, well respected in London and in the field.

Max would continue to run the trains from Paris to Dax, and Lily would now work with him in Paris and from Dax to the border. Auntie Go and her husband, the Uncle, were still coordinating operations in the Basque country, and Kattalin was still able to provide use of her house.

Kattalin and Florentino were also stepping up the frequent deliveries of their underground post office for the Basque nationalist intelligence service, forwarding maps and coded messages from France down to British and American military intelligence in Spain. That operation could move independently from the arrival of airmen. Florentino was making frequent crossings of the mountains that spring.

As the number of airmen increased, they would establish camp perimeters and prepare for as many as 400 airmen in France and Holland. Neave called the plan Operation Marathon.

With new urgency, the Comet operatives returned to their posts in occupied territory. Plans continued throughout the month of February. Comet was moving pilots south and was starting to move agents north across the border as well. Creswell also was sending supplies, money and coded messages.

Lily crossed the Pyrenees for additional meetings with Creswell and on February 24 returned north from Spain with urgent news from MI9: London had reliable intelligence that Thomas was under surveillance by the Gestapo. There were no details on the source, but Neave said this had to be taken seriously. Implicitly, they were being told once again that double agents were at work among them. Neave ordered Thomas to return to London for consultation and planning until things cooled off. Lily arrived in Paris and conveyed the message to Thomas, who made immediate plans to return south with her the following day.

In the meantime, Lily set up a strategy session to speed up the escape procedures—transfers had been very slow since Jean-François's arrest. With Thomas leaving for London, Lily would be coordinating escapes in Paris, along with another operative, Martine Noel, a dentist who provided housing for pilots being transferred from Belgium. Martine had been alone for some time: the Gestapo had arrested her husband and sister. Lily was keeping her things at Martine's apartment, close to the French military academy.

On the evening of February 24, 1944, Lily met with the new team of helpers at a restaurant chosen by Martine. Strange, Lily thought, that meetings in Paris were held in restaurants. That would never happen in Belgium. But food was more abundant in Paris. The bistro was crowded and echoing with noise and laughter. Among the operatives joining them were several other helpers, including the Abbé Beauvais, a priest who gave sanctuary to pilots when they came to Paris. Seated directly in front of Lily was another fellow, somehow vaguely familiar. He was short and sandy-haired, with close-set eyes, strange and intense. He wore a garish purple coat along with a polka-dot tie that certainly made him stand out in the crowd.

Pierre, they called him, a Belgian from the border. Pierre Boulain.

Have we met before? Lily asked.

Pierre thought not.

I worked with Jean-François, Pierre said. *I helped get identity cards on the border into France. I can do that again.*

Lily had never heard the name Pierre Boulain before. Thomas said he'd offered to start bringing fliers in from Belgium again, for 2,500 francs each—he had his expenses.

Lily saw something about him she didn't like. Maybe she'd seen him before: blond hair, beady eyes. She knew what was bothering her.

Pierre, you know you're really lucky that Abbé Beauvais is the one introducing you to us.

The young man looked at her.

I don't know what you mean.

Because I don't know you myself.

And what does that mean?

Well, because you're wearing a polka-dot tie.

Martine and the others stopped talking and looked over to Lily and Pierre Boulain. Something was going on.

Hey, what's up with you? Martine said to her. *What kind of nonsense are you talking about?*

It was the polka-dot tie. A stupid thing, but she remembered something her father said before the Nazis arrested him. The next time you see someone with a tie like that, pay attention, he had said. It could be a signal.

A signal of what? She tried to put it out of her mind, even though she instinctively didn't like this young Belgian, with his strange smile. After all, the Abbé Beauvais had brought the young Belgian along, and Beauvais would know what he was doing. People had a right to wear ties without being accused of anything.

Pierre looked back at her. Perhaps they had met before. And perhaps at the time he was using his other false identity—Jean Masson.

261

But surely, Masson thought, Lily hadn't heard about undercover Gestapo operatives and how they signaled their identity to one another by wearing polka-dot ties. He was suspicious, though he responded mildly.

Whatever are you talking about? he asked.

Oh, nothing. I don't know. I'm just talking.

The chance encounter was the first breach in Jean Masson's anonymity. From that point on, Lily and Jean Masson, also known as Pierre Boulain, would remember each other. Masson knew what she was talking about. The polka-dot tie. He wouldn't have suspected that a little girl like Lily would know about the tie. Undercover agents were using it as a signal. She'd found him out and didn't even know it.

For the moment, though, nothing else was remarkable about the dinner. A fine meal, a light atmosphere befitting the sense that the Allies were taking the offensive. And then, the next day, Lily left for the south with Thomas and Charles LaFleur, an MI9 radioman who also was considered in imminent danger and had to leave the country. They would take a different path across the mountains, through Sare, about ten miles east of Biriatu.

The crossing was uneventful, even though LaFleur had a noticeable limp. Neave had sent him from MI9 headquarters on October 20 with orders to parachute into France in a Lysander glider to set up radio communications in the northern sector.

October 20 again. The date kept coming back to her. It was the same day that Bob Grimes, the American pilot, parachuted from his stricken B-17. And the same day that the Germans executed the eleven Comet members at the shooting range in Brussels.

LaFleur was a short, dark, tough-talking French-Canadian. The best idea, even with forged papers, was for LaFleur to keep his mouth shut in public: his accent would give him away. He told how he'd been successful for a time, moving from house to house in the vicinity of

Reims, exchanging signals with London. But the Germans were closing in, using mobile vans to monitor electronic signals.

One night in late November, he'd been transmitting as usual when he found the house he was in had been surrounded by German troops. He fired at the Germans, hitting several of them and maybe killing one. Then he dove from an upper window and ran off in the night, even though he'd hurt his leg in the fall.

It was time for LaFleur to get back to London. Even with his bad leg, they made it across the border. Lily conducted LaFleur and Thomas to the British consulate in San Sebastián. She rested briefly, said good-bye to her comrades and headed to the mountains for France. She was scheduled to return to Paris a few days later.

As spring 1944 arrived, change was in the air—but so was danger. The war had been in a status quo during the winter months, but now the air raids over mainland Europe increased. Bombardments were reaching farther south into France. There even had been raids along the French coast as far south as Bayonne. Meanwhile, with the losses in Italy and Patton's army moving north from Rome, the tide was now against Germany. Everyone knew an invasion of Europe could come at any time. With that knowledge came the danger that the Germans would fight more brutally where they could. The Germans could still apply pressure and do considerable damage against the resistance forces in France. Lily and the remaining members of the Comet Line knew they would be facing a growing threat.

Even though London was emphasizing rural camps for the growing number of airmen needing to hide from the Nazis, Lily and Auntie Go knew they could still use the mountain crossings to rescue some men. She planned to reorganize the escape line despite the dangers. "We still have Florentino," she told Auntie Go.

But train schedules were becoming intermittent. Allied pilots, flying with increasing impunity over France, had managed, as anticipated by MI9, to bomb the main rail lines. Trains were backed up, and Lily didn't manage to return to Paris for many days later than she said she would. She assumed her friend Martine the dentist would be worried.

When she finally arrived at the Gare du Nord, she rang up Martine's apartment on the rue des Champs-Fleury.

A woman answered the phone.

Oh, it's you, Micheline, the woman said. *Micheline, we've been waiting for you. Come on over.*

Lily was startled.

Who was the person on the other end of the phone? It wasn't Martine.

Is Martine there?

Not right now, but come over. She'll be back, Micheline.

Lily answered in a casual and noncommittal tone.

Okay, I'll be over.

She hung up the phone. "Micheline," the woman had said. Lily's real name—she hadn't been using it for almost a year. No one in Paris knew Lily's name. She was not the type of person to panic, but she was not to be taken for a fool either. The danger had reached a new level. She had no intention of returning to Martine's apartment.

Instead, she headed out to Martine's dental office in the suburbs, surveying the area and approaching cautiously.

Don't go in, said the concierge, stopping her at the door. *The Germans have been here. Everyone is under arrest.*

The concierge sent her to the home of a friend of Martine, who provided details; everyone at the restaurant that night was under arrest and had been taken to Fresnes prison on the outskirts of Paris. Someone had been watching them.

Lily knew she was in danger of capture at any moment. The Germans knew her name and where she'd been living. She needed a plan, but for her immediate safety, Lily took a train back to Bayonne to figure things out.

One possibility was to cross the border and talk to Creswell. He would have told her to head for England, that it was too dangerous to keep operating in France right now. Lily was not of the mind to do that. If there was a traitor picking off members of the Comet Line, she had to find out who it was. She contacted a trusted ally, code-named Diane, another operative on the line and a mutual friend of Martine. She was the lovely young woman who'd jumped into Art Horning's lap several months earlier, saving him from an identity check on the train to Paris.

Let's go to Fresnes, she told Diane. *I want to find out what happened. My friends will be able to tell me what happened.*

Lily hoped that she might be able to save the Comet Line and protect others from falling captive to the Nazis. Her reaction was the same as when her sister and parents were arrested in 1942: Go directly to the enemy's front door. Somehow, they would be unprepared for the direct approach. She was willing to greet the enemy in their own house. After that, she would improvise.

On March 13 they doubled back in Diane's car about thirteen hours north toward Paris. The Fresnes prison was just outside the city. Lily had no apologies or second thoughts about heading for the prison. She had to find out how Martine had been arrested; somewhere she would unearth a traitor. When they approached the vicinity of the prison, they drove once around the perimeter and stopped the car about 500 yards from the gate. Diane waited in the car, and Lily walked up the road and over a railroad bridge to the prison gate. The prison was a notorious place, a stone fortress built in 1898.

She asked to visit a prisoner; the authorities were dumbfounded. People just didn't walk up to the jail unannounced. Lily was taken into custody as soon as she got there and locked in a room with little to eat. The guards interrogated her several times that first day.

But I was just looking for a friend who is a prisoner here, she protested.

It must have been confusing for the prison warden. Where did this girl come from? No one had the audacity to come to Fresnes prison.

Lily remained calm and was able to lie well enough to confuse the guards. All the while she was buying time, trying to figure out how to contact Martine.

It soon became evident that the other prisoners were able to help her. There was an elaborate communication system. People could communicate at the sides of the walls and around corners using taps, echoes and shouts. The jail was built in a classic hub-and-spoke design, and the inmates were organized enough to track down Martine and bring her close to Lily's room so that they could talk to each other along the perimeter of the wall.

Martine! Martine! Lily called.

Martine could hardly believe she was hearing her friend's voice.

Who's calling me?

It's me, Martine, it's me! Tell me, who is the traitor? Who is the traitor?

Martine answered after a brief pause. It was almost expected.

C'est Pierre. Pierre Boulain!

That was all the communication they dared have before the guards came along on their rounds. But it was enough. Lily had been thinking about Pierre Boulain. The dandy clothes, the vacant eyes. She realized she'd seen him once before. His name was Jean Masson.

With the rush of people she'd encountered all these months, she couldn't remember Masson's face at their restaurant meeting. But now there were connections. She recalled a final meeting in Brussels in June 1943, two days before Dédée's father was arrested in Paris. Members of the Comet Line met at a safe house in Brussels. Masson was among them, responsible for operations between Brussels and Paris, with special expertise in border crossings. He had contacts and could get the border guards to provide false identification papers. Whenever Masson was around, the guards seemed to look the other way. Monsieur de Jongh had been impressed with Masson's uncanny ability to cut through bureaucracy.

The following day, Lily remembered moving two airmen on the tram for a rendezvous with Masson in Brussels at the memorial to those who died in World War I. They were riding tram fifteen, which makes a loop around the city. She spotted Masson standing in the plaza with an unknown man. In the background were two other men, and Lily had had the unshakable feeling at that instant that Masson and the others were Gestapo. Ever since Masson arrived, things operated too smoothly. Paperwork sometimes had been too quick, ID cards too easy to obtain, passage across the frontier practically handed over to them as if in gift wrapping by Nazi intelligence. Two days later Monsieur de Jongh was arrested in Paris. Lily went undercover and hadn't seen Masson after that. If only she had recognized him earlier.

Now that Martine had given her the name she wanted, she had to find a way to warn the other Comet members in Paris. Up to now, Masson had protected his identity because all those who knew him were always arrested. Lily was the only one capable of breaking his cover.

Lily slept two nights at the Fresnes prison, protesting her innocence all the while. She told the jailers—most of them were French—that she had no idea what Martine had done. The guards gave no indication of what would happen. But at about 3:00 P.M. on the third day, she was roused from her cell and taken to the prison warden.

The warden was also French. He tossed her French identification card on the table. Year of birth—1927, conveniently cutting six years off her age. And she looked even younger.

Seventeen years old. He would not accept the imprisonment of a seventeen-year-old girl. A family snapshot was sitting in a frame on his desk. Lily was left with the impression that the warden had a daughter about the same age.

Get out of here right now, he said. *The Gestapo is on the way.* Lily was allowed to walk out the front gate, the same way she'd entered. As she casually crossed the railroad bridge, just past the prison perimeter, a German staff car was approaching. The Gestapo officers drove by without a glance.

Diane and the car, of course, were long gone. Lily went out to search for her friends in Comet. Everyone was in danger until Jean Masson could be stopped. But after the prison, she had one advantage. She knew who he was.

CHAPTER FOURTEEN

Tracking Jean Masson

Occupied France. April 1944.

Neave and his colleagues at MI9 in London were concerned about how the Germans would react as the war news turned toward the Allies and as events led up to an expected invasion. Reprisals could take the form of summary execution of Comet operatives, along with deteriorating conditions for the airmen awaiting rescue via the Comet Line. In response, Neave and the others at MI9 headquarters were making progress on their new plan, Operation Marathon, to shelter far more pilots than could safely be moved across the border by Comet, especially with the German harassment and the increased pressure of Allied bombing, which was rendering travel in France irregular at best. Operation Marathon would create collection zones in France, at Châteaudun near Orléans and in the Forêt de Fréteval in Tours; and the other would be in the Belgian Ardennes. It was decided that despite the risk, Thomas Rutland, who'd been sent back to London a month earlier under threat of capture by the Nazis, should now return to France and run the French camps. For the Ardennes, MI9 chose

Bob Grimes's old friend Daniel Mouton, an increasingly important operative after his Christmas escape from Spanish custody. Mouton also was in London for the spring meetings.

Neave went down to Tempsford Airfield on April 9 to see Mouton and Thomas off before they were dropped back into France. He felt personally responsible every time he sent an agent into occupied France. And he was impressed with the bravery that his men showed as they risked their lives.

Thomas and Daniel parachuted into occupied territory that night, hid in the countryside and quickly made it back to Paris. Within a few days of their arrival, Lily tracked them down and told them about her adventures and the news that the traitor was now identified.

And who is the traitor?

Pierre Boulain. He's also known as Jean Masson.

Thomas and Daniel were incredulous. Pierre Boulain had come well recommended. Earlier in the year, he had worked successfully with Jean-François and Jérome and had played an instrumental role in transferring airmen to Paris. It was uncanny the way he could obtain foolproof identification and cross the border undetected. And now Boulain was to play a role in organizing one of the Operation Marathon escape camps. In fact, because of Pierre Boulain's ease of movement and efficiency, Mouton was about to give him 500,000 francs for advance work to establish the camp in Belgium.

It was dangerous and deadly to accuse someone of being a traitor. They wanted to know if Lily could provide more than just the brief word from Martine behind the walls of Fresnes prison.

No problem, she said. *What do you want to do?*

Mouton asked her first to confirm the identity of the man they were dealing with. Relations with Boulain were tight enough that they'd planned a meeting with him the next day.

We're meeting at the restaurant tomorrow morning.

Again, thought Lily, *they're taking me to a restaurant.*

Daniel, you know I don't like to go to restaurants by myself.

Okay, then. Look, tomorrow morning, don't go to the restaurant. Sit outside. We're meeting him by the statue of King Albert. He's delivering some airmen for us to move down the escape line.

That's better, said Lily; *I'll be nearby watching.*

The next morning, May 7, Lily walked along the Seine in the seventh arrondissement and crossed over the Pont de l'Alma, which commemorates France's first victory in the Crimean War. It's not far from the Place de la Concorde. It was springtime and the outdoor cafés were open; people were strolling about. She was on time, and she thought about how she hated to be late and hated when others were late. Still, her job was to stay out of sight. She bought a magazine, and sat down to read.

She saw Daniel arrive after a few minutes, and shortly thereafter a man accompanied by a woman. Lily sat at a distance, but she could see. In the light of day, she could see it was Jean Masson, the same Jean Masson she'd seen in Brussels a year earlier, the same man who called himself Pierre Boulain that night in the restaurant. There was no question, as she looked at him from behind her magazine, watching him sit down with Daniel.

Why hadn't she made the connection earlier? She couldn't explain it. Perhaps it was the light; or perhaps he had subtly changed his appearance—or perhaps it was a result of the attempt that they all made to avoid being conspicuous. But now she recognized him.

Daniel and Masson spoke briefly, and then Masson and the woman stood up, bade farewell and walked off along the Seine in the direction of the Place de la Concorde. Daniel waited a while before coming to see Lily.

It's him, Pierre Boulain, the traitor.

It's not possible, said Daniel. *I'm telling you, he's working with us.*

I swear to you, this is the man, Lily said.

Unspoken, they were dealing here with the life and death of a man. Daniel wanted to be sure.

Follow him some more, he said. *See what happens.*

I will.

So Lily crossed back over the Pont de l'Alma, walked around along the banks of the Seine toward the Place de la Concorde from the opposite side, the direction in which she'd seen Masson walk away. She rounded the square, walking toward the Palais Bourbon with the Chamber of Deputies at the far end.

Paris was immense and stately, even as it awaited liberation from the Nazis. To one side was the Pont Alexandre III, to the other the Obelisk. There, by the Chamber of Deputies, she spotted him again, walking with the woman. And at that moment, Masson looked up; their eyes met.

In an instant, each could read what the other was thinking. Their eye contact made it clear that Masson's game was up and that Lily knew who he was. Lily had trailed him and now here he was, walking where he should not be, as if he were king of the city. For the first time in the war, he was truly discovered and vulnerable.

He was neither passive nor slow in reacting. In the crowd, with all the people, he started moving toward her. Lily turned briskly, and as she reversed direction, Masson kept pace. Each of them was moving in tandem. She remembered she'd just passed by an entrance to the métro, and she aimed in that direction. When she looked back, he was following, ever faster. She also increased her pace, avoiding running, knowing that if she ran, the police might stop her and deliver her to Masson and the Gestapo. But Masson also measured his pace, hoping not to attract attention and blow his cover entirely.

When Lily reached the crystal and iron métro sign at the Concorde station, she bounded down the stairs and out of sight, skidding around the rounded corners of the tunnel, which wove in a series of serpentine levels down toward the platform. As she vaulted around each level and down into the subway, she knew Masson was still following her.

The rumbling of a train grew near. She looked for angles to make herself as low to the ground and hidden by the crowd as she could. The train entered the station and squeaked to a halt. Masson moved to the platform in her direction. She avoided even budging for fear of giving herself away, but when the doors of the train opened, she practically leapt through the legs of the man in front of her and sat low behind him, out of the view of the windows; the men and ladies in their hats made it difficult to see. She felt so thin but willed herself to be even tinier and indistinct so Masson would not see her.

Masson was short and did not see over the throng of people as he scanned the crowd for a sight of her. Perhaps she'd already headed out another passageway to the street.

As the car doors closed and the train pulled out of the station, Jean Masson was turning in circles, glimpsing faces in the windows and on the platform, but he was unable to see Lily as she peered low. The subway train disappeared into the dark tunnel.

Even Lily knew she had to get out of Paris. She took a train the next day to the border and stopped with Auntie Go in Bayonne.

You must leave, Auntie Go told her. *The Germans know you. You must leave. They will kill you if they catch you.*

Lily understood the danger, but she wanted to keep fighting. Nevertheless, she agreed to go to Madrid for a while with Creswell. At Auntie Go's urging, she didn't even wait for Florentino to show up and accompany her. On May 11, Lily headed down to the mountains on her own, crossed the Pyrenees and was in Spain.

The British consulate in San Sebastián supplied a car and drove her south to Madrid. Creswell was waiting for her. He'd lost Dédée and

Jean-François because they wouldn't listen to him, and he was absolutely determined to save Lily from capture by the Germans.

He was not alone. In London, British intelligence was unanimous in wanting Lily to stay out of France.

But they could not give her orders; persuasion was required. Creswell used all arguments at his disposal, telling her that for the present, at least, it would be impossible for her to operate in the open. Masson had recognized her; her cover was blown. Whether or not Masson was found, he told her, it was imperative to go to London immediately. Creswell told her the Gestapo would kill her if she returned to occupied territory.

MI9 gave her a commission as an officer in the British Army. They told her she was needed in London to help organize for intelligence operations once the invasion started. Reluctantly, Lily stayed in Madrid, hesitant to leave Spain, hoping for the situation to change.

Creswell felt like tying her up in a locked room rather than seeing her try to go back to France. He had in fact used subterfuge to keep Florentino out of harm's way that spring, getting him so drunk on cognac that he couldn't see to climb the mountains. Auntie Go came to fetch Florentino in San Sebastián, where he promised to stay on the wagon. He fell off the following day, somewhere between Sarobe and the river. Auntie Go told friends she saw him snorting from a *bota* along the way and that he took a histrionic leap into the river when they reached the border.

The incident in the métro station at the Place de la Concorde finally convinced Daniel Mouton and Thomas that Lily had the right man—Masson was a German agent. The Comet Line was in evident peril. Daniel took charge of the situation. He called in members of the French Résistance; they were trained and skilled in exterminating enemies. In truth, the Comet Line members didn't carry weapons, had never identified traitors before and were not a paramilitary operation. Yet every one of them knew the obvious truth: traitors had to be killed to protect everyone else.

Several days after Lily escaped, Free French partisans captured a double agent they believed to be Pierre Boulain. They took him to a room in the city, slapped him and beat him until he confessed—he was Pierre Boulain.

It was not so. They described the man they had captured, and he was not a short, blond-haired, beady-eyed fellow with a Belgian accent. Daniel knew that Masson was still at large.

On May 16 Daniel got a signal from Masson and they had another scheduled meeting at a restaurant on the Seine. Daniel, of course, was risking arrest, but he didn't think that would happen. He had leverage, because the man he knew as Pierre Boulain was greedy. Faced with the prospect of receiving money for working with the Comet Line, he would go through the motions as long as he could. He would want to pocket the money before any arrests were made. Nevertheless, members of the French Résistance were nearby when Daniel walked along the Seine and entered the restaurant. It was obvious that some of the people in the restaurant would also be Gestapo protecting their fellow agent.

Daniel and Masson had a brief meeting. They talked about the plan for gathering up airmen in Belgium and France until the Allies could rescue them. Jean Masson appeared taciturn and unenthusiastic. Of course, he knew that Lily and Daniel had worked together, but he couldn't tell if Lily had been able to contact Daniel after she escaped in the métro station.

Both men were operating with a margin of safety, since their own undercover agents surrounded them. Daniel also had reason to feel safe until he delivered the 500,000 francs for expenses in setting up the rescue camps in Belgium.

Daniel said the 500,000 francs was on its way. Another meeting would be planned.

When? Masson wanted to know.

Tomorrow, Daniel said. *I'll bring the money tomorrow.*

The money would of course never reach Belgium; Masson intended to pocket the money and have Daniel arrested. No one would have to know anything about the money.

Agents were planted all around them. Gestapo agents were there. And sitting separately was another man, nameless, with impeccable credentials and probably a good cover ID. He was an executioner from the Free French Forces. His mission was to get a good look at Jean Masson and then to track him down and kill him. There was no time to waste.

No one ever spoke the name of the executioner. He saw Masson, and the plot was set quickly.

When they left the restaurant, Daniel and Masson slipped off into the streets of Paris. The agents were inconspicuous.

The executioner moved as rapidly as was expected.

Masson was still living on the rue de Douai. When he left his apartment the next night, perhaps he was off to his favorite bistro for a nightcap and an evening of gossip.

A car parked on the street pulled out slowly and followed him at a distance in the shadows. The car approached Masson as he walked on the deserted street and the silence of the Paris night was broken by a gunshot. Masson fell dead on the sidewalk. The car sped off; the Gestapo was there in minutes, but no killer was identified.

On May 22, Daniel Mouton conferred with Thomas one last time to exchange information before each of them departed for their respective staging areas to receive Allied airmen.

Daniel reported on the French Resistance and the executioner who had been following Masson. The Gestapo had turned up the heat, searching for resistance fighters everywhere. It was an apparent confirmation that the resistance had in fact killed someone important. Daniel was convinced—the resistance had taken care of Jean Masson.

Le coup est fait mais ça chauffe. It has been done, but the heat is on.

But British intelligence, through its agents, had no confirmation that the man believed to be Masson that night was actually Masson.

CHAPTER FIFTEEN

A Matter of Time

Occupied France. D-Day.

By D-day, June 6, 1944, when the Allies stormed northern France at the start of the long-awaited invasion, Daniel Mouton and Thomas Rutland already had been out in the field for two weeks. Daniel and Thomas had left Paris separately after May 22 to set up their clandestine camps for Allied fliers in the Belgian Ardennes and French Châteaudun under Operation Marathon, which had been launched by Airey Neave and his colleagues at MI9. They had gathered more than 100 airmen in the Forêt Fréteval, near Cloyes, about 120 miles southeast of the Normandy landing, and another 100 men in the Ardennes, farther inland, near the French-Belgian border.

Supplies, including tents, food and medicines were air-dropped to the forest locations, and communications were also maintained with Auntie Go, who managed to keep the escape line open even after the Allies began heavy bombing campaigns before and during the invasion. Auntie Go and Kattalin even tried shipping a mobile radio to Thomas in Châteaudun, but it was lost en route, possibly blown up in a random U.S. bombing of a train.

Auntie Go, Kattalin and Florentino had continued moving people and equipment across the Pyrenees. Another forty airmen crossed into Spain in the first six months of 1944. They even sent five airmen over the mountains on the night of June 4, the eve of the Normandy invasion. The escapees were three Americans, Thomas H. Hubbard, Donald K. Willis and Jack D. Cornett; and two members of the British Royal Air Force, Leonard A. Barnes and Ronald T. Emery. And then, after the invasion in June, the flow of escaping airmen arriving to cross the Pyrenees slowed down. Most of the Allied fliers were being taken to the MI9 camps in France and Belgium. Rail transportation was increasingly spotty and dangerous.

Meanwhile, Michael Creswell, seeking to avoid more tragedies now that victory was imminent, tried several times to block Florentino from his dangerous crossings, especially when reports came in that large numbers of German patrols were out hunting for Allied agents as well as deserters from their own ranks. But Florentino was not easy to control, and he continued carrying contraband and secret messages back and forth from Spain.

Creswell and Neave conspired with more success to keep Lily away from the front lines. Transferred from Madrid to London via Gibraltar, Lily got a desk and a uniform and stacks of debriefings and other paperwork to handle. She was miserable. Every time Lily showed up at Room 900 of the War Office, she begged Neave to send her back.

I belong with my friends, she implored.

Neave was unyielding, because he feared that she would be captured.

It is too dangerous.

———

MI9 wanted no more deaths among members of the Comet Line. Dozens had been arrested and there was no way of knowing how many had survived. Neither Allied Intelligence nor the Red Cross had information about whether Lily's sister, Nadine, and her father, captured in Brussels two years earlier, were still alive. At least Lily could be kept safe.

You escaped by the skin of your teeth, Neave told Lily. *You're staying here.*

By the end of 1944, however, Neave had set up MI9 field operations in France, as the Allies liberated occupied territory and began marching toward Berlin. Lily followed after the liberation of Brussels and Paris. The orders were to find MI9 agents and remaining airmen. Neave had trouble receiving logistical help from American commanders but finally managed an armed escort to the Forêt de Fréteval. He documented 152 Allied airmen camped there, under the supervision of Thomas. Another 145 were bivouacked at the Belgian Ardennes camp set up by Daniel Mouton.

But Florentino still was carrying a stream of intelligence documents between Allied agents in Spain and operatives in France. As always, he timed his trips so that he traveled the most dangerous portions in the dark. The work was more difficult than ever. The Nazis had reinforced their efforts along the border, mostly in an attempt to arrest the escalating numbers of deserters from the Wehrmacht. At the end of June the patrols increased noticeably along the north bank of the river. The vigilance was so intense that Florentino's fellow smugglers couldn't even come over to Spain to warn him about the heightened peril.

Creswell, who had reports of the increased German activity, had been trying to slow Florentino down to protect him. When Florentino showed up, Creswell always plied him with cognac, hoping he'd be too drunk to cross the mountains; but Florentino laughed and stumbled off for the hills.

On June 26, three weeks after the Normandy invasion, Florentino had just crossed the Bidassoa River. On a clear night, he was carrying a pack of contraband, some clothing and intelligence reports that he would drop off with Auntie Go. At about 3:00 A.M., a German squad was conducting a patrol on a dirt road that ran near the smuggler's path just after the river on the French side. One of the Nazi soldiers heard a sound, and the squad stopped to listen.

Florentino heard the soldiers and crouched in the underbrush.

When the Germans turned on their searchlights, they saw in the shadows of the trees, the silhouette of a man, close to the ground casting a long shadow, several hundred yards away.

Halt! one of them shouted. *Hands up!*

Florentino had been pinned down more than once by guards on both sides of the river, and he was not about to give up. He used the terrain as cover and started running a zigzag course away from them.

The soldiers followed and shouted once more, tracking Florentino with the searchlight. They fired their rifles and machine guns.

Dodging the gunfire, Florentino kept running, but the Germans found a clear sight line and caught him with two rounds that shattered the lower part of his right leg; another round hit his thigh and a fourth, the shoulder blade.

He was still devising a plan as he fell hard to the ground. He needed to hide the intelligence material he was carrying for the resistance. Rolling into some bushes, he was out of sight for an instant. He quickly removed the documents from his backpack and hid them in the tall grass behind a boulder. With the gunfire still sporadic around him, he then realized that the Germans might spot the hiding place if it were close to where they found him. Seriously wounded and almost immobilized, he managed to use his arms to roll to a ledge and then about fifty feet down a slope so the Germans would detour away from the incriminating documents.

That was how the Nazis found him. What they saw was an old Basque, bloodied, with one leg shattered by machine-gun fire. They searched the backpack and found women's clothing, Auntie Go's outfit from her last crossing with him to Spain. He answered their questions with mostly unintelligible monosyllables, delivering a false name. The Germans were given to understand—and this only after extensive questioning and translation—that he was a poor Basque farmer who was coming to visit a niece who lived in France. They had no idea who he was or what he was doing. But there was a danger that Florentino would be seen as the Germans drove him the twenty miles on the highway from Hendaye to the hospital in Bayonne. Florentino was so well known in the area that someone might spot him and thereby tip his true identity to the Gestapo.

The Germans deposited him at the hospital in Bayonne with orders that he be kept there until he recovered from his injuries. Auntie Go received word of his capture shortly afterward.

The Comet members, remembering their abortive attempt to rescue Dédée more than a year earlier, sought a more methodical way to reach Florentino before the Nazis moved him away. Auntie Go crossed to San Sebastián and met Creswell, who agreed that this time something had to be done. As with Dédée eighteen months earlier, and as with Jean-François, his closest and bravest friends in the Comet Line were in danger and close by.

Creswell contacted MI9 in London, which considered mounting a British commando operation or hiring other smugglers to reach Florentino. But it sounded like a suicide mission with no guarantee that Florentino would not also be killed in the process. They considered contacting the French Résistance and providing resources for an escape. Again, the question centered on staging an operation that would protect Florentino's life.

The dilemma was part of the long-standing argument about British control of Comet. The local members thought that their own low-intensity operations could be more successful than elaborate schemes and preparations organized from London.

One thing was certain—Florentino would never reveal operational details. But if his importance were discovered, he would surely be tortured and killed.

Auntie Go went back to France. She and her husband, the Uncle, didn't have to think very long about what to do. They were not going to depend on a British escape plan. In a sense, they'd been positioning themselves the entire war for this moment. They'd been on the southern border for almost four years. Black marketeering was a great cover for working with the Germans, because once acknowledging their deals, the Germans didn't really care. Some of the Germans were making money doing the same thing. The Gestapo never discovered that they were working for the resistance.

The Uncle had maintained cover throughout the war as a civilian employee of the Feldkommandantur office of the German army. As a trusted interpreter, speaking German, Flemish and French, he had access to official passes and identification cards. He knew how the Gestapo operated and realized that rivalries and fear could be used to their advantage. He had access to operational details and movements, which usually kept Comet one step ahead of Nazi capture. Together, the Uncle and Auntie Go complemented each other's role well, all the time gathering and funneling information and supplies to their Comet friends. If the Germans saw strange people showing up at their door—well, that was the nature of working on the black market. Together they also gathered juicy black market information about local German officers. They were rumored to have blackmail material on anyone they might need to use.

With the arrest of Florentino, they decided to risk everything. The Normandy invasion had come and, sooner or later, the Nazis would flee back to Germany. They had to rescue Florentino immediately.

Shortly after Florentino's arrest, Auntie Go went to visit the director of the hospital, Monsieur Petriac. She told him that she needed his help. He was a frightened Frenchman who had never worked for the resistance. The Gestapo had given him personal responsibility for Florentino, leaving a document which declared that Florentino—under a false name—was to be held at the hospital until further notice. The Gestapo made it clear that Petriac had to comply on penalty of death. But Auntie Go convinced him that she could take care of the document. They would borrow it, and when the time came they would substitute a forgery that would protect him. He agreed to cooperate as long as his role could be hidden.

From that moment, hospital staff cooperated with Comet. The doctor attending Florentino delayed putting a cast on Florentino's damaged leg, a risky maneuver so they could buy time for the escape plan. But he warned that Florentino might be left permanently lame if they delayed too long.

Auntie Go went down to the room where Florentino was held. Despite the cooperation, she carried forged identification, thanks to her husband.

She found him in a room on the ground floor, lying in bed with his legs braced and bandaged. When no one else was around, she knelt close to him.

Don't worry, we're going to get you out of here.

Florentino stared at the ceiling as if in a trance. She knew he was listening. For several weeks more, Auntie Go visited frequently, bringing along a Basque friend so she'd be sure Florentino would understand her messages.

The group waited a few weeks for Florentino's superficial wounds to heal. On July 26 they realized they could no longer wait. The hospital staff warned Auntie Go that the Gestapo in Hendaye planned to take him away for more extensive interrogation. Auntie Go immediately returned to the hospital and approached Florentino once more.

The Basque friend knelt down to tell him the news in Euskera, his own language, so there would be no mistake.

Florentino, biha zure billa etorriko dira, arratsaldean. Florentino, be ready. We're coming to get you tomorrow.

He acknowledged her but said nothing.

Now it was up to the Uncle and their friends from the Résistance.

We have to rescue Florentino tomorrow, Auntie Go said.

And how do you plan to get him out?

Through the front door, of course. There's no other way.

At 12:50 P.M. the following day, July 27, 1944, a municipal government van pulled up to the hospital entrance. The van was equipped with a cot and sometimes had been used as a makeshift ambulance. Two gruff Gestapo officers swept into administration, their black coats breezing by nurses who wept and pleaded that the sick and injured prisoner be shown mercy.

But the lead Gestapo officer, flashing his credentials with disdain and speaking loudly in German, was uninterested.

This is an outrage, he said, posturing and prancing. *The section in Hendaye has responsibility for this prisoner. Bring him to us immediately.*

The hospital staff, quaking at the presence of Gestapo officers, begged that Florentino not be moved.

We are taking him with us. Los, Los! Schnell! the German shouted, and Florentino was helped to the waiting van. The escape took no more than a minute.

The Gestapo officers took a final measure of the quaking hospital attendants, shrugged in satisfaction and drove away. They left a perfect forgery of a German document with the hospital director, the trembling Monsieur Petriac, showing the prisoner had been dutifully removed and was now safely in Gestapo custody in Hendaye.

It was Comet's tour de force—adopting a fake Gestapo operation and playing the Nazis against their own orders.

The forgery was so convincing that when the Bayonne Gestapo

branch arrived and saw the paperwork, they initially believed that they were to blame for having committed a breach of decorum. They were disinclined to cross jurisdictional lines by even mentioning the subject to their colleagues to the south.

By the time the ruse was complete, Florentino was safe; and despite roadblocks and searches, the Nazis never found him.

Unable to hide their glee, the Uncle and his companions laughed and celebrated. But they drove an indirect escape path, at first taking the road south as if they really were headed for Hendaye. Finally, they doubled back on side roads and stopped at a safe house owned by their friend Charles Gaumont in Biarritz.

Auntie Go was waiting; there was a celebration. They poured Florentino his first glass of cognac in a month, and he downed it thirstily in a gulp. A doctor worked on Florentino's wounds, but the injuries were substantial and the delay in treating him was crippling. After Liberation, Florentino still needed six more months of recuperation in Biarritz. When he returned to Saint-Jean-de-Luz, he had a permanent limp, limiting his ability to move about his beloved mountains. Surgery and the damage from the machine-gun fire had left one leg an inch shorter than the other.

Brussels, Belgium.
July 27, 1944.

Coincidentally, on the same day that Comet engineered Florentino's escape, two of its leaders, Jean-François and his friend Jérome, stood before a German military tribunal in Brussels.

"It will be a glorious death," Jérome had said with resignation to Jean-François after the traitor Jean Masson arrested them in Paris.

Perhaps, thought Jean-François. *But there is a possibility we will not die.* Since his arrest in Paris on January 18, Jean-François was counting the days. He knew that the Germans imposed an overlay of legality on their actions against political prisoners. It would take an average of six months from arrest to execution by firing squad.

The key to staying alive, Jean-François told Jérome, was time. The Allies would soon liberate Europe; the trick was somehow to prolong the pseudolegal process of trial and sentencing. Jean-François even stole a watch and kept it hidden throughout his imprisonment, first in France and now in Belgium. He wanted to keep counting the days.

On the morning of July 27 Jean-François, Jérome and several other political prisoners stood before a Luftwaffe tribunal at the Palace Hotel in Brussels. The Germans had chosen an ornate setting for the trial, with three uniformed German officers presiding. The Germans continued to be scrupulous in parading the rule of law. Jean-François invoked his legal right to make a declaration.

A court-appointed defense lawyer asked the basis of Jean-François's defense.

I am an escaped prisoner of war, never recaptured, he said, seeking to provoke the Germans, since real defense was impossible. *As a result, I am protected by the Geneva Convention. All I have done is to continue fighting the enemy, only this time as part of the Résistance.*

After preliminaries, Jean-François sat at a defense table with his court-appointed attorney—as well as another defender, hired by his family, who said the case was hopeless.

"What is your nationality," asked the chief German military prosecutor, seeking to distinguish between French- and Flemish-speaking Belgians, "Flemish or Walloon?" The Germans thought they would attract support by identifying Europe as a collection of nationalities. But with the Allies already overrunning Nazi territory, the tactic seemed more hollow than ever.

"I am Belgian," Jean-François replied, not willing to participate in German sophistries.

Then followed a long list of charges of espionage and illegal activity on behalf of the Allies. Testimony from the prosecution centered on evidence found in Paris that Jean-François was producing false identification papers and had been seen moving Allied airmen.

Jean-François's defense attorney parroted what Jean-François had said before, "Belgian patriot, escaped prisoner, idealist," though probably out of fear, he avoided speaking with much conviction.

By the afternoon, the court said it would retire to consider a verdict.

A black-uniformed member of the Waffen-SS approached Jean-François. He recognized the rotund little man as one of his inquisitors in the first days of his arrest.

"Don't worry, my friend," he said. "You still have about fifteen days to live." He assured Jean-François that Field Marshal Göring would personally take up the appeal in the case.

Oh, thank you so much, Jean-François said effusively. *What an honor.*

It took ten minutes for the military court to return their guilty verdict.

The accused are condemned to death, declared one of the officers.

But Jean-François was neither surprised nor dismayed by the decision. In the course of the trial, he'd been given the chance to meet with family and friends and they'd given him the news: *The Allies have invaded: the Germans are in retreat.*

I don't think I will die, he told his family. *It is a question of time.*

One month later, execution had been delayed by a more-than-embarrassing logistical problem facing the local Nazi command. On August 24 Allied forces were overrunning Belgium and France. The Nazis and all of their prisoners would withdraw to Germany.

Jean-François hid his watch out of view under his sleeve as he and other prisoners were herded onto a train headed for Bayreuth. He stole a pencil so he could keep a diary, and he counted the days, never doubting for a moment that he would be set free.

On the French-Spanish Border.
August 24, 1944.

The Germans were in retreat all around occupied Europe. At the French-Spanish border, the British consulate had moved some of its personnel to Irún, within view of occupied France. Creswell was poised to be among the first British diplomats to cross the border once the Germans retreated.

On August 21, 1944, more than two months after D-day, the time had come. At the bridge between Irún and Hendaye, France, the German commandant in charge of the Wehrmacht French-Spanish border zone donned ceremonial dress and marched one last time to greet his Fascist colleagues in Spain. He shook the hand of the Spanish officer in charge and returned to France, where the Nazi flag was lowered. The Nazis were retreating to Germany. A member of the French Forces of the Interior raised his country's tricolor flag as the Germans departed.

The occupation over, the British and American delegations led by Free French officials in Spain and Ambassadors Hoare and Hayes traveled north within days and were met by boisterous, flag-waving crowds. Michael Creswell took up the temporary post of British consul in Hendaye, the first Allied diplomat to assume a post in France after Liberation.

The jubilant though anarchic mood in the French Basque country was not shared on the Spanish side of the border. The Spanish government closed the crossing at Irún, fearing that armed Spanish Republicans and Basques would foment opposition to their Fascist government.

Enterprising Basques intent upon unity and celebration more than revolution at that moment, would not be held back. The smugglers' roads over the Pyrenees remained open. And in the waning summer days, a French Basque jai alai team, having been challenged to a game by a team in Irún on the Spanish side of the Basque border, took the old route over the mountains and across the river. The game was played despite official restrictions.

Basques would have to wait thirty years to be able to speak their language freely and to teach their history and culture in the open. United States policy after the war tilted toward Franco's authoritarianism and turned away from his opponents, who were wrongly considered to be dominated by the Communist Party. The British journalist and historian Hugh Thomas estimated that, apart from 365,000 dead in the Spanish civil war, at least 100,000 people were executed in Franco's Spain from the end of the civil war to his death on November 20, 1975. It would be simplistic to describe civil strife in summary terms, but the suppression of Basque civil and cultural aspirations certainly was a precursor to the separatist movement in the Basque country, which has simmered on after the Spanish dictator's death at a cost of far too many lives.

One month after the German retreat from the Spanish border, Sir Samuel Hoare, who had been elevated to Lord Templewood in 1944, did finally acknowledge the work of the Basque and Belgian escape network, though he cited no one by name. In a secret memo to Sir Anthony Eden, the Foreign Secretary, he credited Michael Creswell's work through MI9 in saving more than 1,000 Allied airmen, most of whom were Americans who had been recovered on the Comet Line. He took a warranted swipe at the American lack of interest under the Hayes embassy in the escape operations. "Whilst British personnel predominated in the earlier months, the American proportion subsequently exceeded our own numbers. The growth of the American figure did not, however, diminish our own responsibilities. The lines through France were our affair and the want of American organization in Spain made it necessary for us to do most of the work that should have fallen upon our Allies."

He also recommended that "a careful and immediate examination should be made of this heroic chapter of self-sacrifice and that the men and women who have deserved so well of us [sic] and who are still alive should be individually rewarded. One of their leaders, a Belgian girl who constantly brought airmen through France into Spain, is now in the hands of the Gestapo in Germany. We should do our utmost when we enter Germany to obtain news of her and if she is still alive to ensure her repatriation and reward."

The Belgian girl was Dédée, but she was still missing behind Hitler's Nacht und Nebel campaign. She suffered the horror of Ravensbruck, where tens of thousands of people were killed and thousands more were submitted to ghastly medical experiments. By the time of the Allied invasion of Europe, the camp had grown from several thousand women prisoners to almost 80,000 men, women and children, many held in a series of satellite camps. Earlier in the war, prisoners were killed by shooting them in the back of the head. The Nazis built gas chambers there in early February 1945 and two months later, when Russian troops liberated Dédée and the other sick and dying prisoners of Ravensbruck, more than 2,200 more people had been put to death.

CHAPTER SIXTEEN

Justice Restored

Paris, France. Fall 1944.

Throughout the fall MI9 conducted searches for its agents around liberated Europe. Neave coordinated the effort on the ground, hitching rides with American and British occupation troops and commandeering platoons when he could to track down his people. He arrived in Châteaudun and greeted Thomas and his 152 Allied airmen. By the time Neave made it to Brussels, Daniel and 145 liberated airmen already were celebrating freedom at a party in the Hôtel Métropole, where Bob Grimes and Lily had clandestinely sipped lemonade in the fall of 1943, before they both left Belgium for safety in the south.

But the Nazis had executed hundreds of helpers on the Comet Line and other escape organizations. Many others were unaccounted for—the Nazis had moved many prisoners to Germany ahead of their retreating armies, Jean-François and Dédée among them. British intelligence searched for news about where they were and whether they were still alive.

While the last remnants of Nazi control collapsed, Lily was back in Paris, participating in the search for missing MI9 agents in the field, to liberate those who had been arrested and to find out the status of prisoners held in the containment camps. Life was different now. For one thing, she could abandon her nom de guerre, proudly and openly reclaiming her identity, Micheline Dumont. Attached to the Allied Command, she had cars and drivers and uniforms and good food at her disposal. The war was still on, but the Allies had crossed the border into Germany and were pummeling the Third Reich.

One of the most startling discoveries by MI9 was that they'd lost many more airmen than they had supposed. Lily's intelligence unit, working with Comet veterans and Allied military intelligence, reviewed the escape records and soon realized that the Gestapo and the Sicherheitsdienst had been able to stop more than 150 men and had shipped most of them off to POW camps. Several died in concentration camps. It was obvious to Neave and the others at MI9 that an informer was still at large and somehow connected to the line, but no one could determine who it was.

U.S. military intelligence had detected the operations of a man they described as "primary agent for the SD counter-evasion service." The agent was transporting unsuspecting Allied aircrews to a collection point at a hotel on rue Pigalle in Paris. He was, a military file said, "a German intelligence agent with a long and bloody record of penetrating resistance and evasion organizations."

Although the Nazi army was in retreat in the summer and fall of 1944, some members of the Gestapo and its aligned organizations had decided they would not give up the fight. Allied intelligence determined that one agent was very successful in harassing efforts to rescue Allied airmen, even though the German war effort was collapsing. This Nazi agent was delivering dozens of Americans to imprisonment amid deteriorating conditions. He was short and suspicious-looking, and he'd been seen in the company of several women. Intelligence got a tip that he could be found on the rue de Douai, not far from Pigalle, but the man matching his description had moved out several months earlier. The man was Jean Masson.

There had been confusion on the night that French Résistance tracked down and executed the man they reported was Jean Masson. It was someone else. Perhaps the dead man was Masson's colleague, Prosper Desitter, "the man with the missing finger." In theory, one could identify Desitter because of the missing digit. No one had done so, and the confusion was never resolved. Desitter never surfaced after the war; and Masson was very much alive.

With disdain for the arriving Allied forces, Masson continued to hunt down airmen on behalf of the Führer. Indeed, after his supposed liquidation, he enjoyed his most successful period, delivering scores of Allied airmen to the custody of the Sicherheitsdienst.

As Allied control was secured in Europe, military intelligence was on his trail. He had visited his grandmother in Tournai in July to borrow money. In August he was said to have fled to Nancy in advance of conquering American troops. And then he disappeared.

Allied military investigators along with the Free French police were gathering material on Masson. Camille Spiquel, who'd inadvertently introduced Masson to Monsieur de Jongh, was eager to help track him down. Camille escaped capture by the Gestapo despite Masson's efforts. After Liberation, she returned to France and conducted her own private investigation in hopes of tracking down the Nazi double agent. French authorities arrested Marie-Antoinette Orsini, Masson's old consort, who admitted working with him. She claimed that she was an unwitting accomplice, but she clearly realized that fliers she transported with Masson ended up in the hands of the Gestapo.

A bulletin was issued: "Masson is clearly a vicious German agent who needs to be followed with every possible effort to locate him and bring him to justice before French courts. It is essential to secure a photograph of Desoubrie so that it may be discovered that he was indeed the person known as Jean Masson."

Finally, intelligence officers received the photograph they needed.

And Lily, in Paris, received a phone call rather late one night from Allied headquarters. It was Lieutenant Harold Cherniss, an American officer she'd made friends with at the intelligence division.

We'd like you to come right down here; it's important.

I'm just turning in for the night. How about tomorrow?

The American insisted that the matter needed immediate attention.

What can it be? she asked. *There's a war on today, and no matter what we do, the same war will be waged tomorrow.*

Nevertheless, I'm sending a car for you.

When she arrived at the Allied intelligence command, her friend ushered her into an office. He placed some ID photos on a table. She looked up at Cherniss and then back at the ID cards, confused.

Two different likenesses, but the same man, she said. *It's Jean Masson.*

Jean Masson had survived, brazenly offering himself to work as an agent for the Allies. Upon Lily's confirmation of his identity, Masson was arrested and held in an Allied military jail.

PART FIVE

1945

CHAPTER SEVENTEEN

Liberation

Amberg, Germany. April 1945.

After the kangaroo court in Brussels, Jean-François was transported to a series of prisons in Germany—Bonn, Nurnberg, Bamberg, Bayreuth and finally Amberg. The day of his execution never came. He thought he was being saved for an eventual prisoner exchange. The companionship of fellow Comet members Jérome and Raymond Etterbeek made life passable. It also added to the theory that they had been grouped together so that sometime in the future they might become bargaining chips in a prisoner exchange with the Allies. The three men were crowded into cells meant for one and were fed watery gruel that became increasingly scarce as the Allies advanced on Germany. Jean-François slept on a musty, fetid cement floor in the summer of 1944, and endured the overwhelming cold and damp conditions that winter. Through it all, Jean-François motivated those around him. He was inspired to study the Gospels, celebrate holidays and imagine a life outside prison. A group of imprisoned Belgian Boy Scouts remembered that Jean-François distributed Bible passages for meditation when despair was greatest. Group activities offered great solace, for the only comfort and protection in German custody was human warmth.

Now it was spring. The days were longer, the cold was receding and Jean-François realized that something strange was happening. First, one of the German guards came along to ask Jérome for advice. Trying to be friendly, the guard offered a cigar in return and asked a humble question: What was the proper way to surrender when the Americans arrive?

Next, Jean-François noticed changes in the Allied bombing campaign. The Allies had ruled the air for months, but this week the sound of planes was incessant and there was gunfire in the distance. It was clear that it wouldn't be long: liberation was close at hand. But even so, it was hard to celebrate. Food had been so scarce that the prisoners had been overcome by the weariness of starvation. Jean-François was breathing with difficulty and was in pain. He and his friends spent most of the day resting in their bunks.

Then on Monday morning, April 23, 1945, Jean-François was conducting morning prayers for his cellmates and giving thanks for their survival all these months when he was interrupted by the approaching roar of tanks. The ground rumbled, the treads of the tanks clanked as they rolled to a halt.

The prisoners ran to the windows and saw German guards racing by in one direction. Then there was silence, broken by the occasional sound of gunfire. No one moved; no one in the prison spoke. They shuffled slowly out of their cells. No guards could be seen.

They heard voices and activity outside the walls. Suddenly, the main gate swung open. A single soldier stood before them, bearing a rifle and wearing a uniform that Jean-François did not recognize.

For an instant, no one knew how to react, and they stood in silence. After a beat, the camp erupted in prolonged cheer as the prisoners recovered from their shock. This was an American soldier. The war was over. The Americans had come.

Within days, MI9 sent a special plane for Jean-François. He flew to Brussels and was reunited with his family. A great celebration was organized at his parents' house, but he could hardly eat and before the party was over, Jean-François asked to be taken to bed. When he was liberated, Jean-François weighed ninety pounds and was suffering from tuberculosis.

Like Jean-François, Dédée saw a series of prisons: in Essen, Zwei-brucken and Westphalia; eventually she was sent to Ravensbruck in Germany. It was a women's camp about fifty miles from Berlin. By liberation, more than 70,000 inmates were there, subjected to medical experiments, shot, gassed and cremated. Upon liberation by Russian troops on April 30, 1945, Dédée was still under a Nazi death sentence. She also thought that her life was spared because the Germans intended to use her in possible prisoner exchanges. She'd seen enough death. She described herself as "no more than a number, lost in a multitude of other numbers, all of us anonymous." Unlike many others, she had survived.

Nadine, Lily's sister, was in German custody under appalling conditions for almost three years, from August 11, 1942—when she was arrested with her father and mother—until liberation on April 22, 1945. After her defiance of the Nazi interrogators in Brussels, she was transported to a series of German prisons in Essen, Cologne, Saar-brucken and Gros Steiglitz, before being sent to the Mauthausen concentration camp. Nadine was defiant and confronted her imprisonment with the same attitude she showed her Nazi guards when she laughed at them in Brussels and asked if they ate the fruits from the pear tree in their garden. Survival was in her nature. She set out telling herself that she would outlast this war, a conflict that the Nazis would eventually lose. Life was harsh, conditions brutal. At least she would not be executed, she told herself.

She focused on the successes of the Comet Line rather than the horrors and indignities of her imprisonment. She recalled hearing little children speaking German at a school just outside the prison wall at Saarbrucken. It was strange to hear innocent voices speaking the language used by the Nazis.

At Gros Steiglitz, she shared a four-foot-by-six-foot cell with two other women, a sixty-year-old and a girl her age. They received a small pot of water every day for all of their drinking and bathing. And at Essen, she recalled the night an Allied incendiary bombing run lit up the sky. The prison guards double-locked the jail cell bars for extra security and went to their underground shelter. Nadine felt a mixture of pleasure that the Allies were attacking with the realization that she would have no escape if the bombs hit the prison. She was held in a segregated area at Mauthausen for two months before liberation. Mauthausen was a concentration camp built near Linz, in Austria.

"I was there I suppose two months. I don't speak to you about the conditions. But it was awful. I don't like to talk about it. When we arrived . . . they put us in a place where there are showers. So we thought that they would put gas in the showers and kill us. No, but it was a real shower. We knew in Mauthausen about the gas.

"In Mauthausen, every day in the entrance, they shot twenty men, every day, in the neck. Mostly, they were Poles and Czechs. One thing I will say, one day we were upstairs, we went near the door. And we saw a man with his hands behind his back, against the wall. It was February. They threw water on him and it froze on his face and on his body and they let the man die like that. And we saw that. You can imagine. And we saw a train. We saw them take the arms and legs of naked prisoners on the train to take off the gold and teeth and anything they wanted before they burned the bodies. We saw that. And we are thinking, maybe my father, maybe my friend. I always think of survival. Nine out of ten women would have fainted when they saw that. But we knew that we would be killed very soon if we fell down."

Mauthausen was not classified as an extermination camp, but Jews from Austria, Holland, Italy and Hungary were transported there. An estimated 40,000 people died at Mauthausen.

"I will not focus too much on those things," Nadine said. "I don't like to remember and to talk about them."

The three old friends were reunited in Brussels shortly after victory in Europe, weak but unbowed. Dédée de Jongh, Nadine Dumont and Jean-François survived Nazi imprisonment through luck and force of will. Beaten down physically, they began collating the catastrophic rolls of those who died at Nazi hands. At least 155 Comet members died while working to save escaping airmen, among them Eugène Dumont, the father of Lily and Nadine, who apparently died at Gross-Rosen just before liberation in the spring of 1945. Nadine and Lily thought he was among prisoners burned alive in railroad cars by SS guards when Russian troops approached the concentration camp. Dédée's father, Frédéric, was executed by firing squad at the Mont Valérien range in Paris on March 28, 1944, along with several other allies. It was a bitter memory that would never be forgotten and would never heal. Like Eugène Dumont, Frédéric de Jongh received numerous posthumous honors. Elementary School Number 8 in Schaerbeek, Belgium, where he served as headmaster before his capture, was renamed in his honor. On the anniversary of Monsieur de Jongh's death, children at the school lay a wreath in his memory.

By the end of the war, Comet rescued at least 770 and possibly as many as 850 airmen, including those protected in the Belgian Ardennes and the French forests of Châteaudun and Fréteval under Operation Marathon.

Britain, France and the United States awarded a series of honors to the participants in the Comet Line. Among them were the Croix de Guerre, the George Medal and the Order of the British Empire. Dédée and her friends received full recognition at Buckingham Palace in an audience with King George VI. France and Belgium also bestowed tributes. The United States awarded the American Medal of Freedom to Dédée, Jean-François, Lily, Nadine, Florentino and many of their colleagues, both those who survived and those who did not. Consular officials in Belgium and France conveyed that honor locally. The honorees were never invited to the White House nor formally thanked by the president of the United States, even though the majority of the men they rescued were Americans.

Saint-Jean-de-Luz, France. September 14, 2002.

T he cemetery in the village of Ciboure is just down the road from
Saint-Jean-de-Luz, on a hill overlooking the Atlantic Ocean. On
a warm, late summer morning, Nadine Dumont stood there at attention among the monuments with several other veterans. Before her
was a gravestone that read: "Florentino Goikoetxea, March 14,
1898–July 27, 1980. In Memoriam." Not far away was the grave of his
old friend Kattalin Aguirre, who died in Ciboure on July 22, 1992.

I had been invited by a group of survivors and descendants of the
Comet members to participate in a walk across the Pyrenees. Florentino's grandniece and two grandnephews were there, along with two
of Kattalin's grandchildren, among about seventy people, marking the
sixty-first anniversary of Comet with a commemorative hike on the
trail to freedom in Spain.

Florentino, though crippled by his wounds, had spent the rest of his
days in the French Basque country, settling down and working for the
municipal government. His bad leg limited his climbs in the mountains,

but he could still be seen ambling slowly through the hills and valleys of the Basque country. When he died, his family set up a display of his many honors at the Caserío Altzueta in Hernani, where he was born. They include the Médaille Commémorative de la Guerre 1940–1945; Médaille de la Résistance Belge; Médaille de la Libération, France; British medal for courage; the U.S. Medal of Freedom; Croix de Guerre 1939–1945 avec Palme; Chevalier de l'Ordre de Leopold II avec Palme et attribution de la Croix de Guerre 1940 avec Palme, Belgium; Chevalier de la Légion d'honneur, France.

Nadine complained that she could no longer ride her bike nor climb through the mountains as she would have liked on such a beautiful, cloudless day on the path overlooking the Bay of Biscay. It was not so much a question of her age. She'd been riding bicycles for years. But those months in solitary confinement and close quarters under the Nazis had damaged her hips. She'd come down from Brussels to meet a group that would hike across the Pyrenees on the same smugglers' route, preserved as it was when Florentino evaded Hitler's Wehrmacht and Franco's Guardia Civil sixty years earlier.

Kattalin's grandson, Beñat Castet, was a guide for the marchers; we headed toward Urrugne, where streets have been named for Florentino and Kattalin and other members of the Comet Line. We stopped at the town hall in Urrugne, where the hymn to the resistance was played and an honor guard laid a wreath before a monument to the fallen. At one end of the square was the cathedral tower, the one with the Latin inscription *Vulnerant omnes, ultima necat—Every hour wounds, the last one kills.*

The path wends down farm roads, up past the farm known as Bidagain Berri, where Dédée and her friend Frantxia were captured on January

15, 1943. Frantxia died at Ravensbruck on April 12, 1945. One of the neighbors had a childhood memory of the Nazis marching into the community and leading away the adults. She cried as she remembered that night.

The marchers stopped for a commemoration and a toast at Frantxia's house, and then set off again.

From there, the trail dissolves into hilly forest, two hours past fields and precipitous climbs that are unchanged over the years. Many of the hikers had experience in the Pyrenees, and some were carrying modern accoutrements such as gravity-supplied water bottles and metal-tipped staffs.

Just as Bob Grimes recalled, the trek was confounding. When it appeared one was reaching the highest point, there was a jog in the road, and we faced the side of a mountain and another uphill climb. Kattalin's granddaughter, Marie-Thérèse, held back for a moment in the glaring sun to look at the scenery below. True to Jean-François's description, she could see the lighthouse at Fuenterrabía, on the Spanish side of the river and the French Basque coastline all the way to Bayonne.

The Basques joked when some of the participants complained about the pace. They've always climbed these mountains; it is in their blood. It was several more hours downhill to the river on steep, rutted roads, stands of pines and chestnuts providing thankful shade. We slid down the last embankment to the river and stripped off our hiking boots. "What about alpargatas?" one novice hiker asked. Not a good idea, someone said; modern rubber-soled waders give better footing. We crossed the Bidassoa gingerly. The water reached our waists and the current was strong. The Basque guides formed a chain with their arms in case anyone slipped, but everyone managed without much trouble. Nearby, kayakers marked off slalom runs, practicing grade 2 level rapids.

Nadine, who had motored ahead with other veterans to greet us, stood watching at the riverbank on the Spanish side. "Now imagine what it was like that night," she called out. "Crossing the mountains is hard enough, but imagine what it was like in the winter with much higher water in the rain and in the dark, with the Nazis chasing you."

The once-patrolled Spanish border is now a picnic area. On the shore was an open space that once had been the railroad right-of-way, but the broken-down, little train depot, which gives this site the name—San Miguel—was still there. Just beyond the depot was an embankment, and above that, cars raced along the Irún-Pamplona highway.

Although it was half hidden by the trees on the French side, a bit up from the river, we could just make out a cement cross, marking a death on the river on Christmas Eve, 1943, erected by the family of Antoine d'Ursel—Jacques Cartier. Its inscription read: *Comte Antoine d'Ursel, Alias Jacques Cartier décédé le 23 décembre 1943. Count Antoine d'Ursel, Alias Jacques Cartier, deceased, December 23, 1943.*

Juan Carlos Jiménez de Aberásturi Corta, scholar, historian and chronicler of the Comet Line, was an organizer of the event. He said he hoped to contact the family of James Burch, who died the same night, so that another monument could be placed in his memory.

Local television covered the crossing, and Aberásturi spoke in an interview about the bravery of the Comet Line participants. The Basque organizers served grilled sardines, cheese, bread, sidra and wine, and then everyone set off for home to rest for the next day's climb. The second day of the hike was up the mountains on the Spanish side to the Castillo Inglés, Bosbieta and Sarobe in the valley toward Oyarzun. Paco Iriarte-Recalde and family were waiting at Sarobe, smiling and generous as always when they greeted hikers from the hills. Paco had been the little boy who so admired Florentino, watching him come down from the mountains with escaping airmen. He pointed to the stone path where they descended from the mountains at dawn. "It hasn't changed, everything is just the way it was," he told visitors.

Epilogue

———

Lily—Madame Micheline Dumont-Ugeux—lived 400 miles east of the border, in Provence. She didn't attend the reunion march. To get to Provence from the Bidassoa River, we drove east along the Autoroute just above Saint-Jean-de-Luz. There were many reminders of the Comet Line and the period of Nazi occupation along the way. The highway passed close to Dax, where Jean-François and Max had a tacit deal to keep their bicycles safe at the railroad station; and continued off into the Hautes-Pyrénées, where escaping pilots traveling on their own or with guides had to deal with the majestic but dangerous snow-covered mountains.

Dozens of pilots escaped on other paths through the high mountains, some with smaller organized resistance groups, some on their own, notably Chuck Yeager, who later went on to show the right stuff in breaking the sound barrier in experimental rocket aircraft. Yeager's P-51 Mustang fighter was shot down on March 5, 1944, and he hiked through the snow-covered Pyrenees to safety, hoisting a wounded comrade along with him.

Lily lived in Saint-Siffret, a hamlet built on a hillside halfway between Nîmes and Avignon in Provence with her husband, Pierre Ugeux. He also was with British Intelligence when they met in 1944 in London. They soon married, both still in uniform. After the Allies chased the German army out of France, Pierre and Lily crossed back to the mainland and worked for the liberation of intelligence agents and prisoners of war. Pierre later became a director of the Belgian Power Authority, while at the same time pursuing his hobby of collecting and racing sports cars. The couple moved to Provence after retirement. Their daughter, son-in-law and grandchildren visited often.

In the summer of 2002 they were just back from a visit to Brussels.

Saint-Siffret was recovering from a flash flood. A high-water line was visible about three feet up the wall in the dining room. Faced with a flood that washed away other homes in these hills and throughout the valley below, Lily's reaction was just what one would expect. She was undaunted, considering the flood as a minor setback, nothing more. Life goes on.

"Fortunately, we have many friends here and they helped us clean up," said Lily, unblinking. It could have been worse.

She prepared a dinner of mutton and fresh vegetables and told about her days in Comet over a bottle of wine. Her descriptions were crisp and detailed—she easily repeated dialogue of conversations from more than half a century earlier.

Why did she do these things?

She had no ready answer, so she just shrugged and smiled. She said she agreed with her sister, Nadine, that both of them grew up with feisty temperaments. Their father raised them to be independent; he had fought against Germany in the Great War. It was natural for them to fight oppression. Sixty years after World War II, she was as certain, as tough-minded and as idealistic about her fight against the Nazis.

But the painful memory of her father's death in a concentration camp always clouded the conversation. After a while, when the talk moved from the Comet Line to questions about Jean Masson and those who were imprisoned and killed, she said she could not bear the painful memories.

"Too many people died. Let us not talk more about these things," she said.

Occasionally, usually on Christmas, she was in touch with Bob Grimes, who recalled enough French to write letters of his own. Bob and his wife, Mary Helen, visited Pierre and Lily in France in 1991.

There is a file about Lily's exploits in the National Archives in College Park, Maryland. Included is an item from U.S. military intelligence, reading in part: "Her gallantry stands as a bright light for her countrymen and her great material contribution to the Allied victory merits the profound admiration of the peoples of all the United Nations." More eloquently, a British document cited her efforts in recommending her for the United Kingdom's George Medal:

> Mlle. Dumont must have handled in the course of her long and astonishing career with this organization more than 250 evaders, and her name became a legend amongst the countless airmen who had been shepherded across Brussels by the famous Lily. In spite of the arrest of her family, in spite of the fact that she herself was imprisoned for two days in Fresnes Gaol, in spite of the fact that she was hunted by the Gestapo, Mlle. Dumont pursued those ideals of patriotism and duty with unflinching determination, fearing nothing and ready to sacrifice all, with the result that through her gallantry and devotion countless airmen were able to escape from the enemy. Her story is a saga in the annals of evasion and her example of the finest tributes to the heroism of the Belgian people.

Attached to the document as evidence was testimony about her heroism given in London in 1944 by Lieutenant Robert Z. Grimes. Bob Grimes, who had attended several previous reunions, sent along regards to Lily. "Tell her we think of her often." He and his wife decided to pass up the trip because of health problems.

Standing ramrod straight, Bob gardens and plays golf regularly. He said there were few days when he didn't think about his escape from the Nazis. There had been a period of many years, though, when he forced it out of his mind and avoided even telling his family about what had happened. He was obeying the oath of secrecy he signed after returning to Britain in January 1944. The army called it a matter of national security but never indicated when and if the secrecy provision ever expired.

In the 1980s, with growing interest in untold stories of World War II, he began corresponding with other veterans who had formed an organization, the Air Forces Escape and Evasion Society. He attended periodic meetings of the organization, including one in Tampa, Florida, in 2002.

About a year after leaving Europe, Bob got an eerie message, the result of a typical Army snafu—his old footlocker from Snetterton Heath, relayed by the quartermaster depot at Fort Leavenworth, Kansas, arrived at his front door in a big crate. A note was attached saying that the locker contained "all the belongings of the deceased Lt. Robert Z. Grimes." The mistake notwithstanding, the shipment brought back memories. But Bob noticed that the regulation gear in the locker was clean and new, nothing like what he remembered leaving behind unwashed under his bunk in England on the morning of October 20, 1943. Bob figured that the military got rid of his old clothes and sent new gear back home as a gesture, so bereaved survivors would have something to hold on to.

Bob remained in the military. He was a thirty-year Air Force man and served stints as a pilot in Germany during the Berlin Airlift, and as a staff officer in France and Vietnam. He finished his military career with the rank of colonel as Chief of the Logistics Operations Division in the Joint Chiefs of Staff in the Pentagon. After military retirement Bob was an associate superintendent of schools in Prince William County, Virginia, for ten years. Bob celebrated his eightieth birthday at home in Fairfax, Virginia, on November 24, 2002, with his wife and sweetheart from his B-17 training days, Mary Helen, their three grown daughters and grandchildren.

"One of my goals was to be able to cut my grass and play eighteen holes of golf when I was eighty, I'm happy to say I reached that point and now I will have to set some new objectives. When I was twenty years old and flying combat missions in Europe, I never even thought about this far in the future. I was happy to complete one day at a time. So I have been blessed to be here and I feel very lucky and very thankful."

He took out a box of memorabilia he had with him ever since the days he evaded capture by the Nazis. There were letters and clippings, and a Brussels lace doily made from part of his parachute by one of his Belgian helpers. There was also an aluminum shoehorn engraved with the date 10-20-1943, which had been fashioned from a piece of the fuselage of his B-17. The morning of October 20, 1943, was vivid in his memory. "I still wake up thinking about it all, about the mission. I'm flying the plane, trying to figure out if I could have done anything else to save the plane. It never goes away." He pulled out one other special memento: the 13-millimeter German machine-gun bullet fragment that Dr. Rouffart took out of his leg in Brussels in 1943. He'd carried it all the way through.

Over the years, Bob maintained contact with his surviving crew members and other veterans from the old Army Air Corps. He corresponded with Art Horning, who returned to Cleveland after the war and published a memoir of his experiences. Horning and his wife also took a tour of Belgium and France, meeting some of the people who gave him shelter and helped shepherd him to safety, including Diane—Amanda Stassart—and her husband. Lloyd Stanford returned to his job as a telephone company worker in Augusta, Georgia. Stanford died in 1994; Horning died in 2000.

Second Lieutenant Art Pickett, Bob's copilot, Staff Sergeant Jerry

Nawracaj, left side waist gunner, Staff Sergeant Fred McManus, the radio operator, and Staff Sergeant Carl Janser, the tail gunner, were killed in action when their B-17 came down on October 20, 1943. Their bodies are buried at the American Military Cemetery in Margraten, Netherlands. On October 20, 1993, Harchies, Belgium, renamed its town square La Place de Art Pickett, commemorating the fiftieth anniversary of Pickett's death. Pickett's name was added to a memorial to Belgians killed in action in World War I and World War II.

The navigator, Second Lieutenant Jim McElroy, the right waist gunner, Staff Sergeant Harold Sheets, and the ball turret gunner, Staff Sergeant Bob Metlen, all bailed out successfully and evaded capture on October 20, 1943. With the help of Jean-François, Florentino and other members of the Comet Line, they escaped to Spain and returned home.

The bombardier, Second Lieutenant Charles (Chuck) Carlson, also bailed out successfully. He evaded capture and crossed from Belgium into France, where he was sheltered by a family until the end of the war.

The flight engineer, Tech Sergeant Ted Kellers, parachuted safely but was captured by a German patrol near the French-Spanish border. He was sent to a prisoner-of-war camp in Poland, where he stayed for a year and a half.

In 2003, Bob Grimes and his surviving crew members, Bob Metlen in Ontario, Oregon, and Ted Kellers in Akron, Ohio, commemorated the sixtieth anniversary of their final bombing run. They maintained contact in person, by mail and by phone. Bob Grimes commissioned a plaque placed in the memorial gardens of the Mighty Eighth Air Force Heritage Museum, near Savannah, Georgia.

The family of Jim Burch was shattered by the young lieutenant's disappearance, and never heard what they considered definitive information about the circumstances of his death. There were letters from friends he had made during his sojourn in Holland and Belgium, and a visit from a relative of Jacques Cartier. Lloyd Stanford followed up on his promise to visit the copilot's family. But Jim's wife, Olga, and his mother never adjusted to Burch's sudden disappearance. Despite searches and rumors in the French Basque country, the graves of Burch and Jacques Cartier were never found.

Dédée was unable to travel in 2002; she was at home in Brussels. At eighty-six, she was in frail health and thought that she was suffering increasingly noticeable neurological aftereffects of her time in the German concentration camps. Right after the war, still recovering from disease and malnutrition, Dédée received a stream of letters from Allied airmen who wanted to marry her. She never accepted and never married. After the war, she took training in tropical diseases and then served for many years as a nurse missionary in a lepers' colony in Ethiopia. She also did nursing and charity work when she returned to Belgium. In 2002 she was still receiving weekly visits from her friend Nadine.

Michael Creswell had a long diplomatic career after the war. After temporary duty in Hendaye, he went to Athens in 1945, was counselor of the British embassies in Tehran and Singapore, and was minister at the Cairo embassy, before postings as British ambassador to Finland, Yugoslavia and Argentina. He died in 1986 at the age of seventy-seven.

Ambassadors Hoare and Hayes returned to their respective homes in retirement after the war. Both wrote memoirs about their wartime experiences. Hoare, who died at seventy-nine in 1959, wrote several books, the zaniest of which focused on his passion for bird-watching, even as Europe burned. Hayes was content in his illusion that Franco was a better option for Spain, because he thought communism was knocking at the gates. He was wrong. He died in 1964 at the age of eighty-two.

———

Airey Neave served on the tribunal of the Nuremberg trials after the war. He wrote several books about his experiences as a prisoner, about his role at MI9 in the escape organization and about Nuremberg. Retiring from the military, though not necessarily from intelligence work, he became a member of Britain's Conservative Party and served as a member of Parliament and in a number of government posts. He was an early supporter and mentor of Margaret Thatcher, and shared responsibility for helping her become prime minister. Neave's final years are the subject of intrigue and controversy. As Thatcher's secretary for Northern Ireland, he had many detractors. But there were hints that he was conducting secret negotiations toward compromise in the British battle with the Irish Republican Army. He was killed on March 30, 1979, by a bomb planted in his car as he left the parking lot at the House of Commons. The motive and killers were never determined. He was sixty-three.

Jean-François spent a year after the war at a sanatorium recovering from tuberculosis. Always deeply religious, he spent his months of captivity studying the Gospel and was a comfort and an inspiration to other prisoners during his time there, where he focused on his Bible studies. Many imprisoned with him said that when they were close to cracking under the strain of captivity, he would circulate a passage from the scripture for a group meditation. All were soothed by Jean-François's presence.

After that, he entered a seminary to become a Roman Catholic priest of the order known as Little Brothers of Jesus.

Still recovering from his confinement, not long after the war, he was summoned to testify at a French military trial in Lille. For the first time since his arrest in January 1944, Jean-François stood face-to-face with a Belgian man named Jacques Desoubrie, better known to his victims in Belgium and Paris as Jean Masson. Jean-François made two appearances in the court, standing before the tribunal as Masson listened. He testified without embellishment, describing the events that led to the death and imprisonment of more than 100 of his comrades.

Lies, Masson replied to all of the events and circumstances Jean-François recounted. *I have never before met this man.*

Jean-François turned to Masson, speaking without rancor.

I am sorry to say that I know you. You are a traitor.

Masson was convicted and condemned to death for having participated in the capture and assassination of members of the resistance and for sending Allied military to their death in violation of the Geneva Convention. While Masson awaited the execution of his sentence, Jean-François sent him a letter with some spending money and asked if he needed anything. Jean-François had heard that Masson was on a hunger strike, demanding to see his children. Jean-François offered to visit them, to give them money as well. He told Masson to use the money he sent to buy food or cigarettes for himself at the prison canteen.

Jean-François was remembering his own time in prison, after being moved from Paris to Brussels. Held in leg irons and manacles, he was given nothing to eat for five days until a German guard came in, motioning him to be quiet. "He brought me food and opened the handcuffs while I ate. Then he put the handcuffs back on and left. It was an act of charity. I didn't even know who he was. It was a dangerous thing to do. Only God and I saw him do it." Jean-François thought that any man, even Masson, deserved charity.

Masson answered Jean-François. "He thanked me, but he was very bitter, a truly miserable person," Jean-François said. "He asked me not to write to him anymore."

Jean-François also wrote a letter to President Charles de Gaulle, seeking commutation of Masson's death sentence. He said that charity was a better weapon than vengeance. "I believe in redemption," he said.

"I never wanted to do anything that would make me seem like the

Nazis," he said. "I didn't think we should sink to their level. That was the essence of our fight."

Appeals and requests for clemency were rejected. Masson was executed by firing squad under the terms of the Allied War Crimes Tribunal. Jean-François considered Masson a bad seed, a lost, miserable soul worthy of charity. "They told me that when he died, the last thing he said was 'Heil Hitler.' In a way, I'm happy to hear that. It means that twisted though it was, he died for his beliefs. It's better than dying because of the greed for money and power."

Other surviving members of the Comet Line respected Jean-François's religious fervor and remained close to him. But some said that Jean-François went too far in his dealings with Masson. The other members of Comet made a deferential but fervent objection to such a request being made by one of the leaders of the organization, which had been so battered by the actions of that one man.

Jean-François became a Roman Catholic priest and spent twenty years as a missionary to Amazon Indians in Venezuela. After that, he fell in love with an Italian woman and he left the priesthood, married and had two daughters. He maintained contact with his Comet Line friends by telephone weekly.

On a warm day in May 2002, I sat with Jean-François in his modest apartment in a middle-class neighborhood in the north of Rome, off the Piazza Vascovia. He was an unassuming man in his eighties. He served coffee and biscuits and showed me some of the mementos he has saved from the Comet years. "It was really only one of my lives. After that, I went to the seminary and became a priest. And then I left the priesthood, with the calling to have a family. It has been a long journey."

Jean-François said his wife and daughters were always calling him a hero. He said he was a bit uncomfortable with the idea. "It was the natural thing, it was my job, the thing I should have done. They call me that, but I don't know."

Retired now, he read the news, listened avidly to Vatican Radio and occasionally contributed articles to religious periodicals. He also served as an editor at the International Maritain Institute, named after the nineteenth-century French Roman Catholic philosopher, Jacques Maritain.

He thought about the war days often, musing about the young man that he was and the exploits that now seemed both reckless and idealistic. "Well, it was Dédée's belief that we be independent. I respected that and followed it after she was captured. We wanted to belong to no government. We wanted to show that we could act with our own initiative and skill, not employed by the Allies. It was a beautiful time, a perfect life. One had the feeling of utter freedom in the midst of the war. It was the proper fight. I have the feeling of being content with my life, having accomplished everything I could have hoped to do."

The butter was simmering in a pan on the gas stove as Jean-François spoke. His eyes were watering a bit; it was probably the chopped onions. He sliced potatoes into cubes, took out the eggs from the refrigerator, sprinkled on some salt and pepper, and then poured the ingredients into the sizzling pan. A familiar aroma wafted through his small apartment. "It's an omelet that I love, just the way they used to make it for us when we crossed the mountains to Sarobe."

Sources

This is a nonfiction narrative based on personal interviews, published and unpublished memoirs and histories, as well as archival material from the National Archives, College Park, Maryland; Cambridge University Library, Cambridge, England; and the Public Records Office, Kew, Surrey, England. Dialogue in italics is described by at least one source. Quotation marks indicate directly reported dialogue.

Spellings of names and places are generally based on the most common usage. The coordination of character names was complicated. Some people described in the book had multiple aliases and *noms de guerre*. For simplicity, I've identified characters by names that combine common usage and minimize confusion. Jean-François Nothomb, for example, was known at the time by his code name Franco. I've avoided that nickname because of potential confusion with Francisco Franco, the Spanish dictator. I've also anglicized some names—Tante Go became Auntie Go, and l'Oncle became the Uncle—for ease of reading in English with such a large cast of characters. Some of the people mentioned were only known by their assumed names; others were known by multiple names. Jean-François told me he considered the character of his youth, Franco, to be a special personality. He signed his correspondence in the course of my research with him, "your friend, Franco."

Notes

Chapter One

Interviews with Jean-François Nothomb, Stanley Hope and Nadine Dumont

3 Urrugne is in the hills above the Bay of Biscay, in the French province of Landes.

3 Based on Juan Carlos Jiménez de Abérasturi Corta, *Red Comète*; Rémy, *Réseau Comète*; Airey Neave, *Saturday at MI9*; correspondence with Stanley Hope, May 2003. There are discrepancies in the number of people present and other details.

6 Village by the sea: Ciboure, France, adjacent to Saint-Jean-de-Luz.

6 Saboteurs: Some of the detailed description comes from a visit to the house in Urrugne, talks with the neighbors who remember the Nazi raid, and correspondence in May 2003 with Stanley Hope.

7 Where is: Jiménez de Abérasturi Corta, *Red Comète*, 100; and Airey Neave, *Saturday at MI9*, 158–59. There are discrepancies in the number of those captured in the versions.

8 By the time: Neave, *Saturday at MI9*, 127–34.

9 "But you": Neave, *Little Cyclone*, 14.

11 Auntie Go: In French, Tante GoGo, a nickname derived from her dog,

GoGo. Tante GoGo and l'Oncle lived in the village of Anglet, just outside Bayonne.

12   The British: Neave, *Saturday at MI9*, 129.

17   "His long": H. J. Spiller, *Ticket to Freedom*, 124.

18   Once Florentino: Jiménez de Abérasturi Corta, *Red Comète*, 42; and
        interviews with Venancio, Vicente and Luciano Arbide Garayar.

18   Are you ready: General Albert Crahay, *Vingt héros de chez-nous, 1940–
        1964*.

20   Deeply regret: Neave, *Saturday at MI9*, 157.

21   By luck: Bar Gachy was owned by René and Faustine Gachy. Rémy,
        Reseau Comète, 18–19.

21   Attention: Jiménez de Abérasturi Corta, *Red Comète* 103.

22   Les enfants: Rémy, *Réseau Comète*, 36.

22   The cometitean: Unpublished memoirs of Jean-François Nothomb.

26   Radio operator: His name was Sergeant Henri Ducat.

26   Neave drove: Neave, *Saturday at MI9*, 163.

Chapter Two

**Interviews with Jean-François Nothomb, Nadine Dumont, Micheline
Dumont-Ugeux, and Venancio, Vicente and Luciano Arbide Garayar**

29   Creswell: Martin Gilbert, *Winston S. Churchill*, vol. 5, *Prophet of Truth:
        1922–1939* (London: Heinemann; Boston: Houghton Mifflin, 1976), 631.

30   Hayes thought: Hayes thought that Spain was freely allowing Dédée and
        Jean-François and Florentino to bring in Allied airmen. "It knew about our
        'chains,' [escape organizations], and actually abetted the latter by entrust-
        ing the refugees to us." Carlton J. H. Hayes, *Wartime Mission to Spain*.

31   In late February: From the unpublished memoirs of Jean-François
        Nothomb.

38   Jean Notol: Interview with Jean-François Nothomb, May 2002. Jean-
        François said he chose this name so that if someone—say, a double agent—
        called out to him with his real name on the street, the sound of this false
        name was close enough so that he'd have an excuse for having responded.

40   She withstood: Crahay, *Vingt héros de chez-nous, 1940–1964*.

43   The Spanish government: Bulletin issued by the civil government of
        Guipúzcoa, March 30, 1943. Rentería Municipal Archive, Section E,

series II, Book 13, file 20 (reproduced in Jiménez de Abérasturi Corta, *Red Comète*).

43   Red refugees: Archive of the Ministry of Foreign Affairs (Madrid), R-Leg. 2224, file 23, cited in Jiménez de Abérasturi, Corta *Red Comète*, 88.

43   Hoare protested: Templewood Papers, University Library Cambridge. XIII.5.9. The Treatment by the Spanish Government of Escaped Prisoners of War.

46   Be ready: Airey Neave, *Saturday at MI9*, 168.

49   The night: Neave *Saturday at MI9*, 175; interview with Jean-François Nothomb.

Chapter Three

Interviews with Robert Grimes

63   Luftwaffe Junkers: *www.milartgl.com/karlGeyR*.

67   This gal: Letter from Art Pickett to Vic Zeller, October 17, 1943.

Chapter Four

Interviews with Jean-François Nothomb and Robert Grimes

89   The railway: National Archives, College Park, Maryland, Record Group 226, 190.108.211.

92   One of the airmen: Francis X. Harkins, "Down Memory Lane: Return to Belgium and France," *www.390th.org/warstories/Memory%20Lane.htm*

95   Sarobe: Interview with Francisco Itiarte-Recalde, February 2002.

Chapter Five

Interviews with Robert Grimes and Micheline Dumont-Ugeux

103   The news: This is the text of the report, quoted in Rémy: *"The Belgian citizens, Eric de Menten de Horne, Jean Ingels, Emile Delbruyère, Albert Marchal, Henri Rasquin, Ghislain Neybergh, Gaston Bidoul, Robert Robert-Jones, Georges Maréchal, also two Frenchmen, Edouard Verpraet and Antoine Renaud, were condemned to death by a war tribunal for their activities on behalf of the enemy.*

"The judgment has been carried out by firing squad. Some of the condemned were acting as members of an organization set up with this intent. The others had no connection with the organization but had prevented the occupying forces from arresting enemy airmen who had been shot down, by providing them with civilian clothing, sheltering them and helping them by other means to escape. In this notice it is necessary to draw attention once again to the fact that the military tribunals will enforce without pity the most severe penalties the law provides for any future cases of aiding the armed forces of the enemy. Consequently, anyone who gives help of any sort of way to enemy airmen, anyone who fails to report members of the enemy armed forces to the nearest German headquarters, must realize the consequences of his action and may not count on any indulgence on the part of the tribunals."

104   Four men: Besides Pickett, the three other crewmen killed in action on October 20, 1943, were: Frederick W. McManus, the radio operator; Jerry Nawracaj, the right waist gunner; and George C. Jansen, the tail gunner.

104   His tags: Unpublished letter written by Mrs. Lefebre.

107   Kellers was: Kellers later was captured in southern France by the Germans and spent the rest of the war in a POW camp.

115   Anne Brusselmans: Quoted in Yvonne Daky-Brusselman's *Belgium Rendez-Vous 127 Revisited*, 57.

123   Not long after: Interviews with Robert Grimes and Micheline Dumont-Ugeux; Rémy, *Réseau Comète*, 520.

Chapter Six

Interviews with Rafael Beldarrain, Francisco Ferrer, Marisa Ferrer, Jean-François Nothomb, Alberto Elósegui and Merche Lacort

131:    The Germans had: See Paul Preston's classic work *Franco: A Biography* for a comprehensive study of Franco and his shifting alliances during World War II.

133:    On the day: *Diario Vasco*, October 22, 1943.

134:    This was the scene: Despite the Nazi presence, there are dramatic tales about Jewish escapees to Spain via San Sebastian. The Portuguese consul in Hendaye risked his life to help hundreds of Jews with visas to enter Spain from France. There were many other escapes across the broad expanse of the Pyrenees.

Chapter Seven

Interview with Jean-François Nothomb

140   The Rock: Description of the Gibraltar meeting also comes from Airey Neave's *Saturday at MI9*, 166–80, and from the unpublished memoirs of Jean-François Nothomb.

146   "I am asked": Airey Neave, *Little Cyclone*, 165. Neave was present at the meeting.

150   Jean-François: Interview with Jean-François Nothomb, May 2002.

Chapter Eight

Interviews with Jean-François Nothomb and Robert Grimes

158   Horning was: Horning's account is from his self-published memoir, *In the Footsteps of a Flying Boot.*

166   Watt left: George Watt, *The Comet Connection*, 107.

167   This bicycle: From the unpublished memoirs of Jean-François Nothomb.

171   There was very little: "*German authorities in France have asked Vichy to furnish special control service to control railroad travel on through trains when travel is forbidden on these . . . travelers must have an authorization identical with that issued previously for the occupied and unoccupied zones. Travelers not owning this authorization will not be able to travel on any but local trains and for no more than 100 kilometers.*" National Archives, College Park, Maryland, Record Group 226, entry 161, box 1, folder 64.

Chapter Nine

Interviews with Jean-François Nothomb, Nadine Dumont and Micheline Dumont-Ugeux

173   The Nazis: Details of Masson's life are from the National Archives files. Belgian Helpers, Brandy Line. National Archives, College Park, Maryland, Record Group 338, file 290.55.37, box 7. Also Record Group 338, file 290.55.21.2, box.3.

174   Airmen described: National Archives, College Park, Maryland, Record Group 338, entry 290.55.37, box 1. Escape, Brandy Line.

175 Nominal superior: Some sources spell Desitter's name as De Zitter.

176 M. Rabat: Jacques Delarue, *The Gestapo*, 235–36.

176 There were cells: Ibid.

177 Lily's sister: Interview with Nadine Dumont, in Tampa, Florida, May 2002.

177 Monsieur Adeline: National Archives, College Park, Maryland, Record Group 338, entry 290.55.37, box 1.

177 Pierre Brossolette: Delarue, *The Gestapo*, 236.

179 Knochen: Ibid., 204–7.

181 EVEN OS: National Archives, College Park, Maryland, Record Group 338, File 290.55.21.2, box 3. MIS-X files, undated.

184 Aguirre: Aguirre's agents first made contact with the same British officials in Bilbao who had established lines with Dédée. Among the Basque agents and associated members—whose principal operatives included the brothers Julio and Flavio Ajurriaguerra, Pepe Michelina and Emile Meyran of the French Résistance—had established listening posts with tentacles throughout occupied France.

184 Clandestine intelligence: National Archives, College Park, Maryland, Record Group 226, entry 108, boxes 211–234.

185 The latest: National Archives, College Park, Maryland, Record Group 226, entry 108, box 237.

187 Arthur "Pat" Dyer: Dyer, interviewed by historian Juan Carlos Jiménez de Aberásturi Corta, died in Bilbao in October 2002.

188 Hotel Euskalduna: Jiménez de Aberásturi, p. 72.

189 A case of the flu: Florentino's bout with the flu is a matter of record, as was the epidemic. The U.S. consulate produced a report in December 1943 detailing the extent of the outbreak but citing few deaths especially in comparison to the major worldwide influenza outbreak, dubbed the Spanish flu, in 1918.

Chapter Ten

Interviews with Robert Grimes, Jean-François Nothomb, Micheline Dumont-Ugeux and Nadine Dumont

194 Martin and Manuel: There is a discrepancy with the names of the two substitute Basque guides. In *Red Comète*, Juan Carlos Jiménez de Aberásturi

Corta identifies them as Martín Errazquin and Miguel Artola, code-named Manuel (13/n). But Jean-François Nothomb recalls them as Martin and Ramon.

195 Horning was: Art Horning, *In the Footsteps of a Flying Boot*, 44–48.

196 "In all": Ibid., 81–82.

196 Stanford and Burch: Stanford's account is from the National Archives, College Park, Maryland, Record Group 338, entry 290.55.19, box 10.

197 "I saw": Stanford refers to a Messerschmitt Bf110, a twin-engine fighter.

221 "There was": Jiménez de Aberásturi Corta, *Red Comète*, citing the Registres de l'état civil, Biriatu.

222 "We don't": Sixty years later there were still arguments about the burial site. Some locals contend that Burch and Cartier were buried in a cemetery in Saint-Jean-de-Luz. But historian Aberásturi said that no burial site has been found.

Chapter Eleven

Interview with Robert Grimes, Stanford account, National Archives

234 Irún was: Interview with José Albízu, February 2002.

240 Bob later: Even worse, the gasoline came from U.S. refineries. At the time, the United States was using fuel supplies as a negotiating tool to force Franco to limit his dealings with the Third Reich. January 1944, the United States suspended oil shipments to Spain.

240 "We know": Horning, *In the Footsteps of a Flying Boot*, 135.

241 Spain together: Testimony, Undersecretary of State Stuart E. Eizenstat, House Banking Committee on the U.S. Government Supplementary Report on Nazi Assets, Washington, June 4, 1998.

241 The Allied: Preston, *Franco: A Biography*, 511.

Chapter Twelve

Interviews with Micheline Dumont-Ugeux and Jean-François Nothomb

251 Jean-François: The unpublished memoirs of Jean-François Nothomb.

252 Jérome was: National Archives, College Park, Maryland, MIS-X, Record Group 338, entry 290.55.357, box 1.

Chapter Thirteen

Interviews with Micheline Dumont-Ugeux and Jean-François Nothomb

Chapter Fourteen

Interviews with Micheline Dumont-Ugeux and Jean-François Nothomb

269   Operation Marathon: Neave, *Saturday at MI9*, 249–60.

270   Neave went: Ibid., 252. "The calm and poise with which de Blommaert set off on this second mission after his narrow escape from treachery a month before, won my deepest admiration," he said. "Somehow I felt certain that he would survive and that we should meet again."

Chapter Fifteen

Interviews with Micheline Dumont-Ugeux and Jean-François Nothomb

281   On June 26: This version is based mostly on the work of historian Juan Carlos Jimenez de Abérasturi Corta, who has rendered a careful chronicle of Florentino's rescue comparing various conflicting versions of the story, including local writings, the work of Rémy and interviews.

284   The group: There are various versions of this episode, including Neave, *Little Cyclone*, 183–85, and National Archives, College Park, Maryland, Record Group 338, entry 290. 55.33.7, box 1. There are some minor discrepancies in various versions and no living sources were available to confirm the details.

285   The Basque: Abérasturi, *Red Comète*, 146. Additional material from National Archives, College Park, Maryland, MIS-X, Comet Line, Record Group 338, entry 290. 55.33.7, box 1.

286   Coincidentally: Unpublished memoirs of Jean-François Nothomb.

289   On August 21, 1944: *The Complacent Dictator*, 277–80; and Carlton J. H. Hayes, *Wartime Mission in Spain*, 256.

290   One month: Templewood Papers, University Library, Cambridge, England. XIII-24 (60).

291   He also: Ibid.

Chapter Sixteen

Interview with Micheline Dumont-Ugeux

292   But the Nazis: Neave, *Saturday at MI9*, 261–71.

293   U.S. Military: National Archives, College Park, Maryland, MIS-X, Record Group file 338, 290.55.35.7, box 1.

294   A bulletin: National Archives, College Park, Maryland, Record Group file 338, 290.55.21, box 1.

Chapter Seventeen

Interviews with Jean-François Nothomb and Nadine Dumont; unpublished memoirs of Jean-François Nothomb

Epilogue

Interviews with Jean-François Nothomb, Micheline Dumont-Ugeux, Nadine Dumont and Robert Grimes

315   Airey Neave: This biography of Airey Neave takes a look at his varied career: Paul Routledge, *The Elusive Life and Violent Death of Airey Neave* (London: Fourth Estate, 2002).

Bibliography

Aguirre y Lecube, José Antonio de. *De Guernica a Nueva York pasando por Berlin*. Buenos Aires: Editorial vasca Ekin, 1944.

Breitman, Richard. *Official Secrets*. New York: Hill and Wang, 1998.

Brown, Anthony Cave. *The Last Hero: Wild Bill Donovan*. New York: Vintage, 1984.

Buchanan, Tom. *Britain and the Spanish Civil War*. Cambridge: Cambridge University Press, 1997.

Caine, Philip D. *Aircraft Down*. Washington, D.C.: Brassey's, 1997.

Carroll, Peter N. *The Odyssey of the Abraham Lincoln Brigade*. Stanford, Calif.: Stanford University Press, 1994.

Crahay, General Albert. *Vingt héros de chez nous, 1940–1964*. Brussels: JM Collet, 1983.

Daley-Brusselmans, Yvonne. *Belgium Rendez-Vous 127 Revisited: Anne Brusselmans, M.B.E. Resistance, World War II*. Manhattan, Kans.: Sunflower University Press, 2001.

Dear, Ian. *Sabotage and Subversion: The SOE and OSS at War*. London: Cassell, 1996.

Delarue, Jacques. *The Gestapo*. Translated by Mervyn Savill. New York: Paragon House, 1986.

Downes, Donald C. *The Scarlet Thread*. New York: The British Book Centre, 1953.

Floyd, Maita. *Stolen Years*. Phoenix, Ariz.: Eskualdun Publishers, 1996.

Bibliography

Foot, M. R. D. *SOE: The Special Operations Executive, 1940–1946*. London: Pimlico, 1999.

Foot, M. R. D., and J. M. Langley. *MI9: Escape and Evasion, 1939–1945*. Boston: Little, Brown and Co., 1980.

Griffith, Aline, Countess of Romanones. *The Spy Wore Red*. New York: Random House, 1987.

Hayes, Carlton J. H. *Wartime Mission in Spain*. New York: The Macmillan Company, 1945.

Hemingway, Ernest. *By-Line: Ernest Hemingway; Selected Articles and Dispatches of Four Decades*. Edited by William White. New York: Charles Scribner's Sons, 1967.

Horning, Art. *In the Footsteps of a Flying Boot*. New York: Carlton Press, 1994.

Hyde, H. Montgomery. *Secret Intelligence Agent*. New York: St. Martin's Press, 1982.

Jackson, Gabriel, ed. *The Spanish Civil War*. Chicago: Quadrangle, 1972.

Jiménez de Aberásturi Corta, Juan Carlos. *De la derrota a la esperanza: políticas vascas durante la Segunda Guerra Mundial (1937–1947)*. Doctoral thesis, Instituto Vasco de Administracion Publica, 1999.

———. *Vascos en la segunda guerra mundial: La Red "Comète" en el País Vasco (1941–1944)*. San Sebastián: Txertoa, 1996.

———. *De la Guerra Civil a la Guerra Fría, 1939–1947*. San Sebastián: Editorial Txertoa, n.d.

———. *En passant la Bidassoa: le Réseau "Comète" au pays basque (1941–1944)*. Anglet: Ville d'Anglet, 1994.

Kahn, David. *Hitler's Spies: German Military Intelligence in World War II*. New York: DaCapo Press, 2000.

Kurlansky, Mark. *The Basque History of the World*. New York: Walker and Company, 1999.

Manderstam, Major L. H., and Roy Heron. *From the Red Army to SOE*. London: William Kimber and Company, 1985.

McIntosh, Elizabeth P. *Sisterhood of Spies*. New York: Dell Publishing, 1999.

Moon, Tom. *This Grim and Savage Game*. Cambridge: DaCapo Press, 2000.

Navas, Emilio. *Irún en el siglo XX: Monografía*. 3 vols. San Sebastián: Sociedad Guipuzcoana de Ediciones y Publicaciones, 1981.

Neave, Airey. *The Escape Room*. Garden City, N.Y.: Doubleday and Company, 1970.

———. *Saturday at MI9*. London: Hodder and Stoughton, 1969.

———. *Little Cyclone*. London: Hodder and Stoughton, 1954.

Nothomb, Jean-François. Unpublished memoirs.

Ottis, Sherri Greene. *Silent Heroes*. Lexington, Ky.: The University Press of Kentucky, 2001.

Paine, Lauran. *German Military Intelligence in World War II: The Abwehr*. New York: Stein and Day, 1984.

Persico, Joseph E. *Piercing the Reich*. New York: The Viking Press, 1979.

Preston, Paul. *Franco: A Biography*. New York: Basic Books, 1994.

Rémy. *Le Réseau Comète: La Ligne de Démarcation*. 3 vols. Paris: Librairie académique Perrin, 1996.

Spiller, H. J. *Ticket to Freedom*. London: William Kimber and Company, 1988.

Templewood, Samuel John Guerney Hoare, 1st Viscount. *Complacent Dictator*. New York: Alfred A. Knopf, 1946.

———. *Nine Troubled Years*. London: Collins, 1954.

———. *The Unbroken Thread*. New York: Alfred A. Knopf, 1950.

Watt, George. *The Comet Connection*. New York: Warner Books, 1992.

Yeager, Chuck, and Lee Janos. *Yeager: An Autobiography*. New York: Bantam Books, 1985.

Author's Note

This book could not have been written without the participation of my wife and partner, Musha Salinas Eisner. Beyond the emotional and moral support she provides, she was my cointerviewer, interpreter, editor and adviser. We also hiked through the Pyrenees together on a beautiful day in September 2002.

My wife's relatives have lived there for all of its recorded history. Our children have looked up their ancestors on parochial records in San Sebastián that go back at least 500 years. The constancy of the Basques mocks temporal political conceits and appeals to a child of the New World like me, remote from such history even though my grandparents were also European. The Basques have plied these hills and sailed the Bay of Biscay since well before the Roman Empire. When one lives among the Basques, history and tradition become part of the discourse.

What started as a series of vacation trips became a near obsession once I started following the considerable trail of provocative lore about the border region, particularly tales of what happened there during the Spanish civil war and World War II.

Many people fled the Basque country. San Sebastián and Bilbao, the two largest Spanish Basque cities, were left with a fraction of their populations. Musha's mother and aunt, Amparo María and María Teresa Leturia Erquicia, were teenagers during the civil war. They and their parents, Eusebio Leturia Sorozábal and Amparo Erquicia Urezberoeta, fled their San Sebastián home with dinner on the table when Francisco Franco's forces overran San Sebastián in 1936. Musha's grandfather, Eusebio, was a social democrat and was among the members of the Izquierda Republicana Party who were marked on Franco's death rolls. Her father, Agricol Salinas Artagoitia, a doctor who had fought as an officer in the Republican Air Force, was imprisoned by the Italians when Franco seized power. Agricol eluded the Italian army and probable execution; he feigned appendicitis, escaped from a hospital and fled to the mountains.

No one could be as lucky as I am not only to have a wonderful mate participating in the book, but also to have so many family members providing their support. Thanks to my daughters, Isabel and Marina, for their love, support, patience and advice; to my mother, Lorraine Eisner, for proofreading the text and providing excellent suggestions; thanks to Amparo María and María Teresa Leturia Erquicia, who helped introduce me to the Basque country and read multiple versions of the manuscript, offering crucial suggestions and thoughtful comments.

I was also fortunate to have my extended family and friends helping in Spain: María Pilar Iturria de Mendizabal, who provided logistical help, and the late Rafael Beldarrain, who pointed me toward this story in the first place. My love to them and their families, who welcomed me as a relative and friend. Also my thanks for the friendship and support of Merche Lacort and Agustín Lacort, and Francisco Ferrer and Marisa Ferrer.

I'm especially indebted to the historian Juan Carlos Jiménez de Aberásturi Corta, the eminent Basque historian, for his friendship and help. His scholarship and writings on the Comet Line and on Basque history in the twentieth century are authoritative and deserve to be more widely known. Thanks to him for his time and for inviting me on the reenactment trip across Florentino's old smugglers' trail in September 2002. Thanks to Beñat Castet and his sister Marie-Thérèse, grandchildren of Kattalin Aguirre, for serving as guides during the crossing.

Thanks also to: Paco Iriarte and his family at Sarobe for their hospitality and a wonderful meal; Alberto Elósegui; Adolfo Eibar; Venancio, Vicente and Luciano Arbide Garayar; and José Albizu and his wife.

It was an honor to meet Jean-François Nothomb, and thanks to him for welcoming me in Rome; I was also honored and grateful for the hospitality of Micheline Dumont-Ugeux, Lily, and her husband, Pierre Ugeux, in Provence; and thanks to her sister, Nadine Dumont, for a warm conversation about her experiences, and also to Raymond Etterbeek for his friendship in Tampa.

In the United States, many thanks to the members of the Armed Forces Escape and Evasion Society for accepting me among them during their meeting in Tampa, including Ron Pearce, Clayton David and especially Yvonne Daley-Brusselmans. I'm indebted to and inspired by my self-effacing friend Colonel Robert Grimes and his wife, Mary Helen; thanks for their time and hospitality. Thanks also to my friends Peter Perl, Neal Levy, Miguel Pagliere and Beth Brophy for reading the manuscript. Special thanks to my friend George Englund for also reading the manuscript and providing constant support and heartfelt counsel as required. Thanks to my longtime friend Mireille Luc-Keith for taking the time to refine the manuscript and check my French; to Kenton Keith for his support and friendship; to Les Payne for two decades of mentoring and leading by example; and to Mario and Miriam Salegui.

Thanks to my agent, Flip Brophy, for her support and friendship all along the way, and to Henry Ferris at William Morrow, whose enthusiasm and sensitive editing were always appreciated.

This book is also dedicated to the memories of the members of the Comet Line, who dared to stand up and fight, and to the young people they saved. I hope I've done them the justice that their unassuming natures and simple courage merit.